God, Science,
and Religious Diversity

God, Science, and Religious Diversity

A Defense of Theism

Robert T. Lehe

CASCADE *Books* · Eugene, Oregon

GOD, SCIENCE, AND RELIGIOUS DIVERSITY
A Defense of Theism

Copyright © 2018 Robert T. Lehe. All rights reserved. Except for brief quotations in critical publications or reviews, no part of this book may be reproduced in any manner without prior written permission from the publisher. Write: Permissions, Wipf and Stock Publishers, 199 W. 8th Ave., Suite 3, Eugene, OR 97401.

Cascade Books
An Imprint of Wipf and Stock Publishers
199 W. 8th Ave., Suite 3
Eugene, OR 97401

www.wipfandstock.com

PAPERBACK ISBN: 978-1-5326-1958-8
HARDCOVER ISBN: 978-1-4982-4595-1
EBOOK ISBN: 978-1-4982-4594-4

Cataloguing-in-Publication data:

Names: Lehe, Robert T.

Title: God, science, and religious diversity : a defense of theism / Robert T. Lehe.

Description: Eugene, OR: Cascade Books, 2018 | Includes bibliographical references and index.

Identifiers: ISBN 978-1-5326-1958-8 (paperback) | ISBN 978-1-4982-4595-1 (hardcover) | ISBN 978-1-4982-4594-4 (ebook)

Subjects: LCSH: Apologetics. | Religion and science. | Religious pluralism.

Classification: BT1103 .L40 2018 (paperback) | BT1103 (ebook)

Manufactured in the U.S.A. 08/02/19

For Marcia

Contents

Preface | ix

Introduction | 1
1 Challenges to a Theistic Worldview | 8
2 Religion and Science | 22
3 Science and Naturalism | 41
4 God and Big Bang Cosmology | 67
5 Eternal Inflation and the Multiverse | 86
6 Cosmic Fine-Tuning | 103
7 The Challenge of Religious Diversity | 121
8 Byrne's Version of Religious Pluralism | 137
9 Buddhism, Theism, and Science | 157
Conclusion | 176

Bibliography | 179
Index | 185

Preface

I have been interested in the relation between religion and science since high school and in the problem of religious diversity since a college summer break I spent in Nagano, Japan, which included frequent visits to the great Zenkoji Temple. This book originates from several years of teaching a science and religion course at North Central College. The course was designed to satisfy a college requirement of an upper-level seminar that deals with intercultural issues, and so it includes an investigation of how different religions respond to modern science. The impulse to write this book came in part from a need for a textbook for the course that deals with some of the issues I wanted to examine, in a way that was both scientifically accurate and accessible to undergraduates and others interested in the relation between religion and science.

Two of the biggest obstacles to religious faith in the twenty-first century are the belief that religion is incompatible with science, and the problem of religious diversity with the apparently intractable disagreements between different religions about the nature of ultimate reality. Both issues arise from the contrast between the impressive success of science in giving us knowledge, and the apparent lack of rational means of justifying claims about any reality that is beyond the reach of science. Furthermore, the success of science extends even to the study of religion, and recent investigations seem to suggest that religion is a complex of phenomena that can be explained scientifically by anthropology and evolutionary psychology. This book addresses both of these challenges to faith and explores the relation between them. I argue that science and religion are not only compatible, but that some major, recent scientific discoveries support a theistic worldview. The diversity of religions is widely believed to undermine the credibility of religious belief because of the perpetual and intractable disagreements between different religions. I argue that one rational way to resolve disagreements between the claims of diverse religions is to assess their consistency with contemporary science. On this count I find theism superior to Buddhism, a major nontheistic religion, which has a rich tradition of rigorous engagement with science.

The Big Bang theory supports the proposition that the universe began to exist in the finite past. Recent valiant efforts by scientists to avoid the inference that the universe had a beginning or to find a satisfactory scientific explanation of the beginning of the universe have not succeeded in providing a more reasonable explanation than the Christian doctrine of creation *ex nihilo*. Recent discoveries that reveal an amazing degree of fine-tuning of the fundamental parameters of nature provide evidence that increases plausibility of belief that the universe was designed by a supremely intelligent creator. These scientific discoveries suggest that theism is better supported by contemporary scientific cosmology than the nontheistic metaphysical framework of Buddhism, with its commitment to an eternal, cyclical universe and the impossibility of a transcendent creator. The fact that theism is more harmonious with recent developments in scientific cosmology than nontheistic religions suggests that science can help us find ways of dealing with some of the disagreements between different religions.

This project could not have been completed without the help of friends and colleagues, to whom I owe huge debts of gratitude. Olin Joynton, Daniel Kolb, James Peters, and Marcia Lehe read early drafts of the manuscript and provided valuable feedback and suggestions for improvement. North Central College colleagues Paul Bloom, of the Physics Department, read and helped with the science chapters, and Brian Hoffert, of the East Asian Studies Program, provided feedback and suggestions on the Buddhism chapter. Physicist Jean Robert Lehe read a draft of the manuscript and provided much useful feedback about the scientific content. Former student and longtime friend Jonathan Matuzak proofread the manuscript and made numerous typo corrections and stylistic suggestions that improved the readability of the book. Former student Katelynn Moxon helped with proofreading. Thanks to North Central College for summer research grants to support the development of the science and religion course and the research for the book. Thanks to the journal *Religious Studies* for permission to republish my 2014 article, "A Critique of Peter Byrne's Religious Pluralism," which constitutes a major part of chapter 8. Above all, special thanks to my wife, Marcia Lehe, without whose support and encouragement completion of the book would never have been possible, and whose editing, proofreading, and stylistic and substantive suggestions greatly improved the quality of the final product. Of course, I assume responsibility for whatever deficiencies remain.

Introduction

Two of the most serious challenges to Christian belief in contemporary Western societies are the thought that religion is incompatible with modern science and the belief that the diversity of religions undermines the credibility of their truth claims. The purpose of this book is to defend the plausibility of belief in the existence of the God of the Bible against these two challenges. Against the first, I argue that modern science is not only compatible with the existence of God, but that it favors theism over metaphysical naturalism, the view that only the natural world exists and that all phenomena are governed entirely by the laws of physics. For many people who are open to the idea that there is more in the world than what is discoverable and describable by modern science, acceptance of Christian theism is impeded by the second challenge—the thought that the diversity of religions and lack of criteria for resolving disagreements between them undermines the credibility of any one religion over the others, and that consequently, it is no longer feasible for an intelligent, well-educated person to believe in the existence of the God of the Bible. These two reasons to be skeptical of the religions of the Bible are interconnected. The growth of scientific naturalism has made it difficult for many people to take seriously the supernatural aspects of biblical religion and has undermined the credibility of appeals to miracles and the resurrection of Jesus as supports for belief in the God of the Bible. As cultural phenomena, religions seem explainable by the methods of anthropological and psychological research, and so from the point of view of the social sciences, the truth claims of no one religion seem any more credible than those of any other. All religions seem to be constructs of particular cultures and more or less equally valid interpretations of the world and the place of humanity in the world. For a growing number of people it is no longer plausible to think of any one religion as offering the ultimate truth about the universe and the human condition. This book examines these challenges to theistic belief posed by modern science and the problem of religious diversity and defends the plausibility of belief in God in response to these challenges. I defend Christian theism as a worldview against critiques based on naturalism and religious pluralism.

The book has two main theses. The first is that modern scientific cosmology is not only compatible with religious interpretations of reality but that it adds to the credibility of Christian theism. The second thesis is that consideration of how effectively different religious traditions harmonize their beliefs with modern science turns out to be helpful in the attempt to adjudicate conflicting truth claims between diverse religions. Since Buddhism is a religious tradition with an especially rich intellectual heritage, which has grappled with modern science and the relation between science and religion, I examine and compare the responses of both Buddhism and Christian theism to modern scientific cosmology. I argue that Christian theism is more harmonious with modern scientific cosmology than the nontheistic Buddhist metaphysical framework, and that this fact increases the plausibility of the Christian theistic worldview over a Buddhist worldview.

In response to the widespread belief that religion is incompatible with science and the belief that religious diversity renders belief in the superior truth of any one religion untenable, I defend the following claims:

1. Science does not support a purely naturalistic worldview, and given the results of modern science, Christian theism is more defensible than naturalism.

2. Modern scientific cosmology is not only compatible with religious interpretations of reality, but supports the plausibility of Christian theism.

3. The diversity of religions does not support religious pluralism, the view that all religions are equally true and that conflicting truth claims of diverse religions cannot be rationally adjudicated.

4. Assessment of how effectively different religious traditions harmonize their beliefs with modern science helps us to adjudicate between conflicting truth claims between diverse religions. Christian theism fares better than the nontheistic Buddhist metaphysical framework in harmonizing with modern scientific cosmology, and this fact increases the plausibility of a Christian theistic worldview over a Buddhist worldview.

Chapter 1 outlines a Christian theistic worldview and the challenges to it from metaphysical naturalism and religious pluralism. A theistic worldview is one which sees the entire world as ontologically dependent on God as its creator. Theism provides, among other things, a coherent set of foundational beliefs about the ultimate source of all that exists, which can serve as the basis for a comprehensive worldview. According to Christianity, God is the omnipotent, omniscient, and supremely good creator of everything that exists other than himself, and the whole creation is ordered for the sake of the fulfillment of his purposes, which are ultimately good. A worldview based on this conception of God offers a comprehensive view of reality that sees everything in light of God's ultimate purposes. Because the Christian God is by nature rational, the world that God has created is intelligible and thus subject to rational investigation by the methods of natural science. The Christian sees no inherent conflict between science and religion. Since God is transcendent, his agency is not construed as one among the various causal factors that determine the course of events in the world. His agency consists primarily of his creating a world subject to causal laws. Thus miraculous intervention may be expected to be rare, and for the most part the course of events in the world as conceived by the Christian theist will proceed as expected by the natural scientist.

A major challenge to theistic belief is metaphysical naturalism, which is widely believed to be required by natural science. The naturalistic worldview denies the existence of God and holds that the physical universe is all that exists, that it is knowable through the methods of the natural sciences, and that modern science renders religious belief rationally untenable. Space and time, matter and energy (as conceived by a completed physical theory) are all that exist, and everything is ultimately explainable in terms of the laws of nature.

The second major challenge to theistic belief considered here is the fact of religious diversity and the supposed lack of rational grounds for adjudicating between conflicting truth claims of different religions, which seems to undermine the credibility of the claim that any one religion reveals ultimate truth. Religious pluralists respond to the problem of religious diversity by finding truth in all religions. Pluralists deny metaphysical naturalism. They affirm that there is religious truth and a sacred reality, but deny that any one religion is truer than others. Pluralists affirm the existence of a sacred, transcendent reality that is the concern of religion and affirm the value and importance of religion, but because they also deny that any one religion is truer than others, they deny that we can know that the sacred, transcendent reality is the God of the Bible. So although religious pluralism affirms religious truth and the reality of the sacred, it denies the unique, distinctive truthfulness of biblical religion. Although many Christians are sympathetic with religious pluralism, most orthodox believers regard it as a threat to distinctive truth claims of Christian theism.

I argue in chapter 2 against the myth of the ancient war between science and religion. Religion is not an archaic form of pseudoscience motivated by an attempt to explain natural phenomena before people figured out how to do real science. Centuries before the modern scientific revolution the Christian theologian Augustine acknowledged that interpretation of Scripture must harmonize with knowledge gained from other sources such as natural science. Most of the pioneers of modern science were not only religious believers but were motivated to pursue their scientific investigations by their faith in an intelligent creator whose creation was rationally ordered and intelligible to human reason. The Christian theist can be confident that crucial doctrines of faith are not contradicted by science.

Contrary to what is assumed by many contemporary scientists, I argue in chapter 3 that the methodology of the natural sciences does not entail metaphysical naturalism, the view that the material world is all that exists. Belief in the existence of a transcendent God does not require an irrational rejection of scientific truth. A theistic worldview is actually preferable to naturalism, even from the point of view of natural science, insofar as theism helps explain the intelligibility of nature. The object of scientific investigation is the natural world, and thus science cannot, within the bounds of natural science, rationally affirm or deny the existence of what exists beyond nature, such as a transcendent creator. The denial of the existence of God goes beyond the range of scientific discourse. In thinking of the created order as the product of a rational creator, the theistic worldview helps explain the possibility of nature being amenable to scientific investigation. On the other hand, if the cognitive faculties of human beings are entirely the product of undirected biological evolution, driven by random variation and natural selection, as naturalism holds, then it is much more difficult to account for the truth-conduciveness of the operations of our cognitive faculties. Naturalism, it turns out, has difficulty explaining the possibility of scientific knowledge.

Modern scientific cosmology, which deals with the nature of the universe, seems to be a fruitful place to begin an examination of how different religions can harmonize their worldviews with modern science. In chapter 4 I discuss a major development in twentieth-century cosmology with metaphysical and potentially religious implications—the Big Bang theory. The Big Bang theory supports the proposition that the universe began to exist in the finite past. That the universe began to exist is consistent with the biblical doctrine of creation by the transcendent, omnipotent God. Although the fact that the universe began to exist does not prove that the universe was created by God, it does support a premise for a credible philosophical (not scientific) argument for the existence of God. Philosophical arguments can be marshalled to support the claim that the Big Bang must have been caused and that the cause of the Big Bang must have been a being beyond nature—beyond space and time, matter and energy. It is hard to find a better candidate for such a being than the God of the Bible. I do not claim that the existence of God is proven with certainty by arguments that utilize the Big Bang theory, but such arguments do support the plausibility of theism.

In chapter 5 I examine some recent attempts to avoid the inference from the Big Bang theory to the claim that the universe began to exist in the finite past. I argue that even if the Big Bang that occurred 13.8 billion years ago was not the beginning of the universe, whatever existed before the Big Bang had to have had a beginning. I also argue against efforts to deny that the beginning of the universe must have been caused. A universe that comes into existence uncaused seems less plausible than a created universe.

A second major discovery in contemporary cosmology, discussed in chapter 6, is the fine-tuning of the universe. There are several characteristics of the universe that have recently been discovered to be required in order for the existence of life to be possible anywhere in the universe. These characteristics include, among several others, the fundamental constants of nature, such as Planck's constant, the gravitational constant, and the cosmological constant. These constants, which are not determined by the fundamental laws of physics, determine such basic parameters as the strength and range of the fundamental forces of nature, the mass of the fundamental particles, the mass density of the universe, the rate of expansion of the universe, and several others. The values of such parameters have been measured, and it turns out that they are very finely tuned, in the sense that they must be almost precisely what they are, within very close tolerances, in order for the universe to permit the possibility of life. If any of these factors were even slightly different, life could not exist anywhere in the universe. The probability of the universe having just the right characteristics to make the existence of life possible is vanishingly small. This has suggested to a number of thinkers that it is more plausible to attribute this fine-tuning of the universe to an intelligent designer and creator than to mere chance.

Some scientists have argued that the hypothesis that there are many universes obviates the need for a God to explain fine-tuning. The basic idea is that no matter how improbable it is that our universe is fine-tuned for life, if there are a vast number of universes, with randomly varying fundamental constants and laws, the odds are pretty good that some of them will have just the right characteristics to make life possible, and this universe just happens by chance to be one of those life-permitting universes. This universe just happens by sheer dumb luck to have hit the cosmic jackpot. It is not surprising that we find ourselves in a fine-tuned universe, because after all, if this universe weren't fine-tuned, we wouldn't be here to discover that it was and to be amazed by it. I argue that the many worlds or multiverse hypothesis might indeed be true, but even if it is, it does not undermine the fine-tuning design argument. Even a multiverse is more likely to have been designed than to have by chance the capacity to produce a vast range of possible universes with randomly varied fundamental laws and constants. So the Big Bang theory and the multiverse theory are not incompatible with theism. Modern science is not only compatible with belief in the existence of God, it supports theism.

In chapters 7 and 8 I deal with religious diversity as a challenge to theistic belief. I discuss several versions of religious pluralism and argue, contrary to pluralism, that the fact of religious diversity does not undermine the possibility of rational assessment of religious truth claims and the adjudication of competing claims of diverse religions. I argue that John Hick's version of religious pluralism is problematic because it undermines religious realism—the idea that religion can offer objectively true statements about God. Chapter 8 deals with Peter Byrne's version of religious pluralism, which interestingly defends both religious realism and pluralism. The religious realism affirms the real existence of a transcendent, sacred reality, which can in principle be referred to and known. The religious pluralism denies that conflicting truth claims among different religions can be rationally adjudicated. I argue that this combination of realism about religious truth and agnosticism about specific doctrinal claims of religion cannot be maintained. Contrary to the religious pluralism, I argue that we are not without rational means of adjudicating between conflicting truth claims of diverse religious worldviews. There are rational criteria by which conflicting religious truth claims can be fruitfully assessed. I suggest that one important way that we can adjudicate between some of the basic specific doctrinal claims of different religions is to assess how well they comport with current scientific knowledge.

In Chapter 9 I consider how the response of different religions to modern science provides a way of adjudicating between conflicting truth claims between those religions. I consider how Buddhism fares in harmonizing its beliefs with modern cosmology, in particular the Big Bang theory and cosmic fine-tuning. Buddhism is an impressive example of a great non-theistic religion, and Buddhist scholars have conspicuously argued for the superiority of Buddhism on the basis of the claim that it is more compatible with modern science than is Christianity. Contrary to this claim, I argue that the Big Bang theory favors a created universe rather than the eternal cyclical universe of Buddhism. Theism also provides a better explanation of fine-tuning than the Buddhist theory of dependent origination and the interdependence of consciousness and matter.

The existence of the God of the biblical religions can be rationally defended as a more plausible basis for a coherent, comprehensive worldview than either metaphysical naturalism, which flatly rejects all religious truth, or Buddhism, which offers a nontheistic conception of religious reality that is less fruitful in accounting for the beginning and fine-tuning of the universe.

1
Challenges to a Theistic Worldview

For the past thousand years Western culture has been based to a large extent on a monotheistic worldview. Christianity has been the religious tradition that has been most dominant, but the other two great monotheistic religions—Judaism and Islam—have contributed significantly to the development of theistic worldviews. The dominance of theism as a cornerstone of Western culture has come under threat in the last two centuries. The sources of the cultural forces that challenge theism are numerous and complex. This chapter will summarize a Christian theistic worldview and address two major sources of challenges to theism. One major source is the rise of modern science and the metaphysical naturalism that is often associated with, and thought by many to be entailed by science. Another major challenge to the cultural dominance of theism is the growing appreciation of the implications of religious diversity, which for many people undermines the credibility of theistic religions as the only or most viable religious options. Although modern science originated in the West, there is in some quarters the sense that Eastern religions are more compatible with modern science than Christianity. I will address both the question of the compatibility of science and religion and the challenge that religious diversity poses for Christian theism. I will argue that Christianity is compatible with modern science, and contrary to religious pluralists, that Christian theism is defensible in the face of the diversity of religions in the world as a plausible religious option. I will argue that Christian theism is better than other religions at harmonizing its core doctrines with the findings of science, and that its superiority over other religions in this regard is a powerful reason favoring the plausibility of Christian theism.

WHAT IS A WORLDVIEW?

Nearly everyone has a worldview that addresses issues of ultimate concern, no matter how carefully worked out or coherent it may or may not be. Why does the universe exist? Does my life have a purpose? Is there a God? How should I live my life? As Aristotle pointed out, all human behavior is goal-directed, and persons pursue what they at least implicitly assume is their ultimate good. A worldview articulates, among other things, assumptions about the nature of the world, the ultimate *telos* of human existence (or lack thereof), and the basic values by which one should live. To the extent that one is rationally reflective, one has some sense of how one's ideas about these things hang together.

Worldviews are philosophical frameworks that organize one's beliefs about ultimate questions of existence, meaning, and value. A worldview is a network of beliefs in response to these questions. Typically the fundamental beliefs in one's worldview are assumed without being justified on the basis of other beliefs. Beliefs that are foundational to one's worldview are usually assumed without being supported by other beliefs, but they may provide part of the basis for the justification of other beliefs that make up one's worldview. Insofar as basic beliefs are assumed without thoroughgoing rational justification, worldviews are to some extent matters of faith, which gain plausibility by their capacity to help one organize one's beliefs about issues of ultimate concern and coherently make sense of one's life. To the extent that a worldview enables persons to make sense of various aspects of their experience, it gains credibility and plausibility. For persons who have religious beliefs, their worldview is largely based on their religious beliefs, which may be thought of as beliefs concerning a dimension of reality that is transcendent, regarded as sacred (of supreme value and the source or ground of all value and perfection), and that pertains to the ultimate *telos* of all human endeavor.

Religion has been said to be the most complex cultural phenomenon that exists. Scholars of religion have defined and analyzed religion in various ways, and many think there is no essence of religion that can be defined by stating necessary and sufficient conditions that would cover everything that can be regarded as a religion. It is not my purpose to try to offer an adequate definition of religion. However, there are various components that are widely regarded as characteristic of most of the great world religions. Of particular importance is the presence of a doxastic component. Virtually all religions teach a body of doctrines that make various descriptive and normative truth claims about the world, human beings, and usually an ultimate reality that in some sense transcends the physical. Religions typically offer a diagnosis of the human condition that involves a characterization of some fundamental problem with, or flaw in human beings and their situation in the world. Although the universe is amazingly ordered, human existence is fraught with difficulties that involve suffering, frustration, disappointment, and finally death. Religions typically involve teachings that include analysis of a fundamental problem confronting human beings, and this usually is conceived as involving the relation between human beings and ultimate reality. Perhaps the fundamental feature of human experience that accounts for the origin and ubiquity of religion is the prevalence of human suffering and the fact that a large portion of suffering is the result of morally bad human behavior.

This leads to a second general feature of most religions, a characterization of the means of rectifying or ameliorating the fundamental problem of the human situation. This is the salvific component of religion, which describes the solution to the basic human predicament. Different religions have different terms for this aspect of religion, but I will use the admittedly Christian term *salvation* to refer to all of them. The salvific component is usually associated with moral teachings that instruct adherents of specific religions in how to be a good person and attain salvation. Closely associated with the ethical norms of religions are teachings concerning various other practices, such as rites, rituals, and celebrations that assist devotees in attaining salvation and becoming integrated into the religious community. This brings us to a fourth element of religion, the communal aspect, whereby individuals are united into a community of persons of common belief and practice. I am primarily concerned with the doxastic aspect of religion, as this is the aspect most relevant to one's worldview, where religion most obviously comes into potential conflict with science and naturalism, and where different religions come into conflict with each other. Since a main focus of this book is the relation between religion and science, the aspect of worldviews that is most relevant is their accounts of the nature of ultimate reality and the relation of humanity to that reality.

A CHRISTIAN WORLDVIEW

A worldview attempts to provide plausible answers to fundamental questions about the meaning of human existence and the nature of the world. How such questions are framed will depend to some degree on the kind of worldview one accepts. The following are some questions that Christians typically think that a worldview should address:

1. Why does the world exist? Is there an ultimate purpose of the existence of the world and of human beings, and if there is, what is it?
2. What is the fundamental problem that confronts human beings and what is the solution to the fundamental problem?

According to a Christian worldview, the answer to the question why anything at all exists is that God is a being who exists necessarily and is the creator of everything else that exists. The most fundamental tenet of theism affirms the existence of the creator God. God is the supreme, infinite, transcendent being, who is absolutely other than the universe or any part of the universe. God is omnipotent (all-powerful), supremely rational, omniscient (all-knowing), and perfectly good. God is a necessary being, not in the sense that God's existence is logically necessary (the statement, "God does not exist" is not logically self-contradictory), but in the sense that there is no beginning or end of God's existence and that it is metaphysically impossible for God not to exist. God's existence is absolutely independent of all other existing things. God would still exist even if the universe did not exist, but the universe cannot exist without being created and sustained in its existence by God.

That God created the universe answers the question why the universe exists. Christians believe that God had a very good purpose in creating the world and that his purpose includes creating a society of persons who will finally enjoy everlasting, perfect happiness in communion with each other and with God. This belief answers the question why human beings were created. The question of the fundamental problem confronting humanity, which is the source of the suffering that characterizes much of human life, is answered by the doctrine that human beings are alienated from God by sin. Sin is rebellion against God and transgression against God's law. Sin is possible because human beings have free will, which is essential to their being persons, and they use their freedom to rebel against God. The solution to the fundamental problem confronting humanity is reconciliation with God, which Christians believe has been made possible by the vocation of Jesus Christ, who is believed to be both the fully human and the fully divine Son of God. Although God is transcendent and other than the created order, Christianity teaches that God became incarnate in Jesus and lived in the human world as a human person in order to be the redeeming mediator between God and humanity.

An important implication of the doctrine of the incarnation is that it entails a high measure of value and significance of the created universe. Many opponents of Christianity criticize it for being other worldly and for denigrating the significance and value of this life and this world. Some people reject Christianity because it seems to require that they forsake the goods of this life, the only ones they know for sure are available to them, and devote themselves entirely to the pursuit of the goods of the next life, which for all they know are illusory. This reasoning is based on a faulty conception of the teaching of Christianity. The doctrines of creation and the incarnation entail that this world is good and that God himself participates in the affairs of this world. The kind of life that Christianity advocates entails full involvement with the goods of this life as part of the preparation for the next.

A Christian worldview provides a holistic philosophical framework that unifies religious ideas with descriptive claims about the nature of reality that can be woven into a plausible, coherent, unified account of the ultimate source of existence, life, consciousness, intelligence, values, law, and morality. It provides an account of the meaning of human existence that a broad range of persons, of widely divergent aptitudes and temperaments, in a wide range of diverse cultures, find compelling. A full discussion of the details of a Christian worldview is beyond the scope of this book, but we will address the question whether belief in the existence of the God of Christian theism is compatible with modern science.

NATURALISM

A major challenge to a Christian worldview is metaphysical naturalism, which many regard as an implication of commitment to natural science. Naturalism is difficult to define precisely, and there are various versions of it in the philosophical literature. The basic idea of naturalism is that the physical universe is all there is and that everything that happens is governed by laws discoverable by the natural sciences, especially physics. The universe is a closed system. There is no reality beyond or transcendent to the universe, and all events in the universe have physical causes that operate entirely in accordance with laws that are in principle discoverable by physics. This entails that there is no God or supernatural being of any sort and that even if there were a God, it would not affect anything in the natural order. Although science is an ongoing endeavor and may never reach the final goal of complete knowledge of the universe, the ideal science, *if* it were ever reached, would give us a complete account of reality.

In the discussion that follows I will use the term *naturalism* to refer to the metaphysical view that entails the following theses:

1. Materialism: the physical world is all that exists, and it is entirely made of matter and energy, or whatever a final physics says is constitutive of matter and energy.
2. Causal closure: all things and events have physical causes and all causes are physical.
3. All phenomena are governed by laws of nature, discoverable by natural science.

The success and prestige of natural science is one of the strongest reasons that many people have for believing that naturalism is true. It is thought by naturalists that science allows no room for reasonable belief that any entities not discoverable by science exist. This entails that there can be no transcendent reality and no true religious beliefs that entail the existence of entities or processes that lie outside the bounds of the physical universe as described by natural science. If science is the only reliable or rational method of attaining knowledge of objective truth about the world, and if science permits only explanations that refer to natural objects and natural laws, thereby disallowing any reference to the supernatural, then no beliefs about anything that is beyond science can be rationally justified. The view that natural science is the only source of genuine objective knowledge is scientism. The view that science must eschew explanations that refer to anything supernatural is methodological naturalism.

Methodological naturalism is a view about how natural science should be conducted, not a metaphysical view about what really exists, but the combination of scientism and methodological naturalism supports metaphysical naturalism. Chapter 3 will discuss whether science requires methodological naturalism and whether methodological naturalism entails metaphysical naturalism. Naturalists think that science is the paradigmatic form of rational inquiry and the only source of genuine knowledge because it relies on observation and empirical tests rather than appealing to supernatural processes to explain natural phenomena. It is claimed that religious believers are not only mistaken in their beliefs about supernatural things, but also that they are irrational and guilty of offending against reason by accepting beliefs for which there is no empirical evidence. Naturalism is a major source of the intense hostility to religion found among the scientifically oriented "new atheists," such as Sam Harris, Daniel Dennett, Richard Dawkins, and Christopher Hitchens, who regard religion as not only false and foolish, but dangerous, morally bad, and the source of much of the suffering in the world.[1]

1. Dawkins, *The God Delusion*; Dennett, *Breaking the Spell*; Harris, *The End of Faith*; Hitchens, *God Is Not Great*.

The most extreme version of naturalism is sometimes called "strict naturalism."[2] According to strict naturalism, physics is the supreme science, and any other candidate for legitimate science must be ultimately reducible to physics. If sociology is a science, in theory at least, it must be reducible to physics, with a few stops along the way—at psychology, neurophysiology, and chemistry. The objects in society that sociology studies are complex arrangements of human beings, each of which is a complex physical object with a brain that can be studied by neuroscience. The brain is made of neurons, which are made of atoms that chemistry studies, and the atoms are made of various subatomic particles studied by the physicist. In the final analysis, everything that exists is made up of the components that physics investigates. In principle, all the sciences are reducible to physics. The less fundamental sciences operate at higher levels that provide convenient ways of dealing with certain kinds of objects, but the ultimate explanations of everything is to be gotten from mathematical physics, which tells us how the fundamental constituents of the world move and interact. Everything is made of matter in motion, and physics seeks the truth about what matter is like and the laws that determine how it moves.

How does naturalism answer the questions that we would like a worldview to answer? Why does the universe exist, why is there something rather than nothing? Lawrence Krauss tries to answer this question in his recent book, *A Universe from Nothing: Why There is Something Rather Than Nothing*.[3] As Krauss acknowledges, the nothing from which the universe comes is not the absolute non-being of Parmenides (a philosophical concept in which the physicist Krauss has little interest). The only *nothing* that makes sense scientifically is empty space or the quantum vacuum or whatever physical *something* space came from. Krauss tries to explain how the universe as we know it was produced by processes, describable by modern physics, which involve random quantum fluctuations in the quantum vacuum. Empty space, it turns out, actually contains an abundance of energy with a rather complex physical structure governed by physical laws. Where the quantum vacuum, the energy that it contains, and the laws that govern its behavior came from, Krauss does not explain. Perhaps future physics will have more to say about the physical sources of the quantum vacuum and the Big Bang that produced the universe. It is obvious that this kind of scientific explanation of the cause of the existence of the universe will not issue a final answer to the question why anything at all exists. Science does not give final answers to ultimate philosophical questions. Some naturalists

2. See Goetz and Taliaferro, *Naturalism*, ch.1.
3. Krauss, *A Universe from Nothing*.

simply accept the existence of the universe as a "brute fact," which has no ultimate explanation.

The question, why human beings exist, is answered by naturalism, not by stating a purpose for their existence, but by explaining how particles of matter on earth became arranged into living organisms, some of which developed brains capable of the kind of intelligence we find in ourselves. Richard Dawkins regards it as one of the finest human accomplishments that we are now able to explain the existence of intelligent life as the product of an evolutionary process that is reducible to particles of matter moving according to the laws of nature. The short answer to the question why we exist is evolution.

Naturalism's grand narrative of existence goes something like this. Once upon a time, or maybe before time, or perhaps when the universe was less than 10^{-43} seconds old and about 13.8 billion years younger than it is now, all the matter and energy of the entire universe was concentrated into an extremely hot, perhaps infinitely dense particle of spacetime of perhaps zero or near zero volume. Then, for reasons not yet fully understood, the universe began to expand, in what is now somewhat whimsically referred to as the "Big Bang." This term, however, is a bit of a misnomer, since it suggests an explosion, and most explosions we know about are rather more chaotic than the conditions that actually existed in the early universe. It turns out that the situation in the early universe was a highly ordered affair. Given the second law of thermodynamics, according to which the entropy, or level of disorder, of the universe increases over time, the condition of the universe in the first moments of its existence must have been the most ordered in the entire history of its existence. From the beginning of the universe until today and until its final demise, the universe gradually becomes less ordered. Eventually its expansion will reach the point where entropy overwhelms the possibility of sufficient usable energy and order to sustain life or any kind of intelligible activity.

Fortunately for us, the universe was ordered well enough in the beginning that it is taking a long time for it to become too disordered for us to exist. In the meantime, the expansion of the universe has created stars, galaxies, planets, living organisms, ecosystems, and intelligent life forms, including human beings. None of this required an all-powerful, intelligent creator. The universe exists and continues to unfold by processes governed by a combination of chance and necessity, according to the laws of nature. By the interplay of the laws of nature and dumb luck, atoms from dying stars have found their way to a small rocky planet in a spiral arm of the Milky Way galaxy and have become arranged into plants, animals, and human beings with brains complex enough to be able to figure out how all this happened.

So how does naturalism answer the question of what is the ultimate purpose of the existence of the world? The question implies that there *is* an ultimate purpose of the existence of the world, and of course if naturalism is true, there isn't one. The world has no ultimate purpose, because there is no God who created it for a purpose or intends any purpose for it. The very idea of a purpose for the existence of the universe is a relic of religion, which may be discarded in an age of science. Although to believe that there is some cosmic purpose of everything may be comforting to some, for naturalists such as Dawkins it is actually a mark of intellectual maturity to be willing to accept a rational view of reality and recognize that the universe exists as a brute fact for no ultimate reason or purpose whatsoever. There is no ultimate purpose for the existence of human life on earth. Our existence is the result of chance combinations of atoms on a planet that is itself also the result of chance combinations of atoms. Those who are smart enough and have enough courage are willing to recognize and accept the cosmic meaninglessness of our existence and create for themselves meaningful, valuable, and purposeful lives.

For naturalism there is no fundamental religious problem confronting human beings. The problems confronting human beings, according to naturalism, are to a large extent due to ignorance, irrationality, and immoral behavior, all of which are sometimes exacerbated by religion. Since there is no God to help us with our problems, we must use our own resources and intelligence to do what we can to improve our situation for the brief time that we have on this planet. How should we live in order to solve our problems? Only by living intelligently, rationally, responsibly, and ethically can we flourish as human beings. We don't need and we don't have a cosmic supervisor to help us. We are on our own, but we can and should cooperate with each other, and doing so enables us to greatly improve our prospects for good lives on planet earth. Of course there is no prospect for a life beyond our mortal coil on planet earth.

The growth of modern science is one of the most impressive of all human accomplishments. To the extent that modern science seems to support a naturalistic worldview, it seems to undermine the credibility of theism. I have said that worldviews are based on foundational beliefs that are articles of faith. This is certainly true of the theistic worldview. However, if science entails metaphysical naturalism, then obviously that would support the superiority of the naturalistic worldview over any religious worldview. We must consider carefully the question whether natural science does entail metaphysical naturalism as a worldview. Science attempts to explain all natural phenomena in terms of matter and energy governed by the laws of physics. Does this mean that only matter and energy exist?

Even though the acceptance of a worldview is to some degree a matter of faith, there are rational criteria by which the plausibility of worldviews may be assessed. One criterion is coherence. A worldview is a set of beliefs, and for them to be conjointly true they must be logically consistent. They must also be consistent with what we know from various sources of knowledge, including science and ordinary experience. Another criterion by which worldviews can be assessed is explanatory power. A worldview is supposed to provide a comprehensive belief system and framework that helps make sense of reality. Naturalism scores very high in this respect, enjoying a spectacular degree of success in explaining a wide range of natural phenomena. Where naturalism is less successful is in explaining the aspects of our experience with which religion is concerned—the spiritual, personal, moral, and generally normative dimension of human experience. Theism does not provide the same kinds of explanation of such matters as personhood, mind, values, and spirituality, as naturalism does for empirical phenomena, but it does provide an intellectual framework for thinking about those aspects of experience that do not readily fit into the naturalistic framework. The conceptual framework and belief system of a worldview should cohere with our deeply considered beliefs about moral values, aesthetic values, our sense of what it means to be human, and our sense of our place in the "grand scheme of things." A worldview should help us make sense of the broadest possible range of aspects of our experience.

One advantage enjoyed by the theistic worldview is that the existence of a supremely powerful, supremely intelligent, transcendent creator of the universe provides partial explanation of the origin of the universe, the orderliness of the universe, the existence of life, the existence of mind and consciousness, and the existence and importance of values, especially moral values in human life. As Peter Byrne[4] argues, the ubiquity of religion in human history, across virtually all cultures, testifies to the plausibility of the existence of a religious reality, whether conceived theistically or in terms of some impersonal transcendent, sacred reality. Religion provides not only a coherent framework for thinking about the world and ourselves, it also helps us make sense of the moral and spiritual dimension of our existence. Religiously informed worldviews help us to unify a wide range of aspects of human existence.

On the other hand, naturalism compels us to reject several aspects of our experience as illusory. According to naturalism, human beings are ultimately just bundles of atoms governed entirely by the laws of physics. As Francis Crick put it, "You, your joys and your sorrows, your memories

4. Byrne, *Prolegomena to Religious Pluralism*, 124–25.

and your ambitions, your sense of personal identity and free will, are in fact no more than the behavior of a vast assembly of nerve cells.... You are nothing but a pack of neurons."[5] We are ultimately not spiritual beings but wholly material beings, whose existence is entirely the product of accidental collisions of atoms. Our lives are devoid of ultimate meaning beyond what we forge for ourselves. According to naturalist philosopher Michael Ruse, "morality is an illusion—or at least our sense that morality is objective is an illusion...."[6] So rather than helping us make sense of ourselves as spiritual and moral beings, naturalism compels us to regard our spirituality as an illusion. The phenomenon of religion in human history is explained away by the theory of evolution in terms of learned behaviors that offer some adaptive advantage to human organisms. Characteristics of persons that are regarded by religious believers as giving human beings some special status among living things—qualities such as the capacity to love, moral virtue, heroism, nobility, and dignity—are really just the product of complex movements of atoms, and qualitatively no different from any animal behavior that improves the chances of surviving long enough to reproduce. A religious believer will find this naturalistic account of human existence not only depressing, but also to be an unjustified rejection of obvious truths about realities we experience every day of our lives.

I will argue in chapter 2 that theistic belief is compatible with science and that a theistic worldview is more plausible than naturalism, not only because it accounts for aspects of human experience that naturalism cannot, but also because it does better than naturalism in accounting for the possibility of science.

RELIGIOUS DIVERSITY AND RELIGIOUS PLURALISM

The plausibility of Christianity has also been challenged by increased awareness of religious diversity. For many people who are not completely persuaded by the naturalist's arguments that religion is completely false, and whose worldviews are still informed by an appreciation of the positive contributions to human life made by religion, it is rather the great diversity of religions, which parallels the diversity of cultures, that challenges Christianity's claim to be the default religious option in the West. Christians and non-Christians are keenly aware of the existence of a wide variety of religious traditions. Many Christians personally know devout and morally upright Muslims, Buddhists, and Hindus living in their neighborhoods. It is

5. Crick, *The Astonishing Hypothesis*, 3.
6. Ruse, "The Naturalist Challenge to Religion," 431–32.

considerably more difficult to brand non-Christians as lost "heathen" after getting to know in the workplace and the local neighborhood adherents of a variety of other faith traditions, who are at least as devout, sincere, and morally decent as the members of one's own church. When Christians encounter good people from other religious traditions, they may be provoked to rethink their own religious beliefs and to question the relation of their own religion to the myriad of others in the world around them. Of course there is a diversity of opinion in all areas of human concern, but since religion is largely a matter of faith, it is especially difficult to resolve religious disagreements. The impressiveness of several great religious traditions, the persistence of religious disagreements, and the apparent lack of neutral and objective criteria for assessing their claims and resolving the disagreements between them, may seem to support the naturalist's claim that all religious claims are false.

There are at least two responses that one might have to the problem of religious diversity. For many, the fact of religious diversity and the apparent lack of criteria for adjudicating religious disagreement are powerful reasons supporting religious skepticism. There are deep differences between the doctrinal claims, the diagnoses of the human condition, and the prescriptions for the remedy for the human predicament among the great religions, which leave many people doubtful that any religious claim can be objectively true. Many people see the diversity of religions, with their intractable disagreements, as a serious threat to the credibility of the truth claims of any one specific religion.

Another possible response is to try to find some common ground between different religions, and perhaps find a way of harmonizing their truth claims. In spite of the great differences between religions, they share in common the recognition of the reality of the sacred, as well as the need for persons to attain ethical transformation and restoration of a proper relation to the sacred. Religious pluralism is the view that many religions are more or less equally true, equally valid responses to the sacred, and equally successful in fostering salvation and the moral transformation of persons. Religious pluralism is motivated by respect for all religious traditions and a desire to affirm and appreciate the contributions of all to a common human quest for spiritual understanding and transformation.

Religions offer diverse descriptions and accounts of ultimate reality and salvation, but John Hick, one of the most influential religious pluralists, sees common themes in all the great religions and regards them all as equally valid responses to the fundamental issues of human existence.[7]

7. Hick, *An Interpretation of Religion*.

While the disagreements between religions are seemingly irreconcilable, the pluralist regards the differences as less important than the fundamental ideas that unite all religions in a common human spiritual quest. Hick sees the same fundamental idea of salvation in all great religions—the idea of overcoming self-centeredness and attaining reality-centeredness.

In spite of the similarity between religions insofar as they share the idea of a need for human beings to attain some sort of salvation and ethical transformation, there are also intractable and irreconcilable differences. Religions may agree at the most general level, just as physicians agree that health is good. However, they disagree on many of the details, just as practitioners of modern medicine and practitioners of traditional, prescientific forms of medicine disagree on how to treat cancer. God is in the details, and the details matter. Some critics of pluralism, especially Christian critics, see pluralism as incompatible with genuine Christian faith, which requires commitment to the truth of one's own beliefs, which are incompatible with many of the teachings of other religions. Many Christians see pluralism as incompatible with the truth of essential Christian doctrines.

So both responses to religious diversity—religious skepticism and pluralism—are problematic for Christian belief. Religious diversity in the eyes of many Christians remains a challenge to Christian belief.

In the last two centuries Christians have had to grapple with encounters with other religions and to respond to the challenges posed by natural science. Interestingly, one of the ways that religions have competed with each other involves their claims concerning their ability to respond to the implications of modern science. In responding to the challenges posed by developments in science, different religions searched for ways that science resonates with their religious beliefs. In some cases, adherents of a religion have argued for the superiority of their religion by arguing that their beliefs are more compatible with science than the beliefs of other religions. In particular, since the nineteenth century Buddhist thinkers have argued for the superiority of Buddhism to Christianity by claiming that Buddhism is in greater harmony with modern science. Christians have argued that developments in modern science, especially those in cosmology, are congenial to Christian theism. Christian philosophers have argued that the Big Bang theory, which seems to support the idea that the existence of the universe had a beginning, is consistent with and supportive of the Christian doctrine of creation. Some Christians have argued that the Big Bang theory is closer to a Christian cosmology than to cosmologies that teach that the universe is eternal and cyclical. I will argue in support of this claim in chapter 5.

In the next chapter I will argue that science does not support metaphysical naturalism, that science is compatible with theism, and that a theistic worldview is a better framework than naturalism for making sense of how the processes in nature could produce beings that are endowed with consciousness, the ability to exercise reason, and moral agency.

2
Religion and Science

The causes of the decline of Christian belief are various, but no doubt the growth of modern science and the widespread perception that science stands in conflict with religion are major contributors. It is well documented not only that most of the pioneers of the modern scientific revolution were Christians motivated by religious passion in their scientific work, but also that to a large extent it was their assumption that the cosmos was created by a wise and rational God that convinced them that the world was rationally intelligible and could be investigated by human reason. The success of the scientific enterprise and the assumption that this success depends upon the emancipation of science from religious assumptions has led to a growing conviction that as science progresses, religion must recede. Although conceived in an atmosphere of religious conviction, it is widely believed by its practitioners and cheerleaders that science reaches its full maturation in the context of a thoroughly naturalistic worldview.

Naturalists see the quest for naturalistic explanations of phenomena and the rejection of supernatural explanations as among the most important advances that humanity has achieved in the modern period. It is widely believed that it is the liberation from religion that has made possible the success that science has achieved. Science has made possible a genuine understanding of the world and the development of technologies that have greatly enhanced the quality of human life. It is believed by many naturalists that the residual tendency of some to cling to supernatural causes to fill in the remaining but gradually diminishing gaps in our scientific understanding of the world is contrary to the scientific spirit and an unfortunate hindrance to the progress of science. A critical issue is whether natural science requires or supports metaphysical naturalism as a worldview.

THE ANCIENT WAR BETWEEN SCIENCE AND RELIGION

According to a widely accepted belief, there has been a long-standing war between religion and science, and science has won. Religion seems to conflict with science in a number of different ways. According to naturalists, one major difference between science and religion is that science has a method of reaching agreement and enjoys considerable success in finding rationally justified explanations of natural phenomena and knowledge about the world, while religion suffers from endless disagreements and a lack of any method of resolving them. Science is successful in acquiring knowledge, and religion is not. Religion claims knowledge of the supernatural but lacks a reliable method of attaining the claimed knowledge. Science, on the other hand, is successful because it has a reliable method of testing its claims. The success of the scientific method is due to its rigorous insistence that only what can be subjected to empirical tests is worthy of acceptance.

The alleged war between science and religion in the West is largely a myth. To the extent that there is a perceived conflict today, that perception is by no means ancient. As a number of scholars have pointed out, most of the architects of the scientific revolution were Christians, many of them priests, and they were primarily motivated in their scientific endeavors by faith in a rational creator. This faith gave them confidence that the cosmos was rationally ordered and intelligible to human reason. It was believed that science is possible because both the rational order of the cosmos and the human mind capable of understanding that order were the product of the rational creator who intended humans to strive to understand the created order as a way of understanding the handiwork of God. Natural science developed in the West not only because the Christian worldview implied that science was possible, but also because scientific research was institutionally supported by the church. It has been noted that it was only in the theistically oriented West that modern science developed and grew. This is due not only to the fact that it was Christian thinkers, often theologians who were the pioneers in the development of science, but also that it was Christian culture that supported the institutions that allowed scientific research to flourish. As Peter Harrison points out, the main example of a supposed battle between science and religion in the period of the scientific revolution—the Galileo case—was not actually a religion versus science controversy.[1] The church was not in principle opposed to the heliocentric solar system on theological grounds, but opposed Galileo's publication of his defense of the heliocentric view because, not merely the theological consensus, but the

---

1. See Harrison, *Territories of Science and Religion*.

scientific consensus of the day favored the earth-centered view, and Galileo was not yet able to prove the Copernican view. Even the opposition to Darwin among Christians was based on scientific, not theological, reasons. There were in the period immediately following the publication of *On the Origin of Species* some scientists who opposed Darwin's theory and some Christians who supported it. One of the earliest American supporters of evolutionary theory, botanist Asa Gray, was a devout Christian who found no conflict between evolution and his faith.[2]

DOES SCIENCE CONTRADICT SPECIFIC CLAIMS MADE BY CHRISTIAN THEISM?

The modern scientific revolution took place in a culture where the dominant religion was Christianity, so many in the West who now see conflict between science and religion are particularly concerned with instances where science seems to contradict doctrinal teachings of Christianity. It is sometimes argued that there are specific claims about the world made by Christianity that are contradicted by science. There are numerous passages in the Bible that seem to some thinkers to involve claims that are incompatible with a scientific view of reality. Examples include the claim that the universe was created in six days, that each species of life was directly created by God, that the earth was once covered by a worldwide flood that destroyed the human population except for eight members of Noah's family, that the Red Sea was once parted so that Israelites could cross on dry land, that the sun stopped until Israel defeated its enemy, that Jesus performed the many miracles reported in the New Testament, and most impressive of all, that Jesus was resurrected after his crucifixion.

However, most thoughtful Christians are quite willing to avoid any interpretation of religious dogma that is flatly contradicted by well-established scientific findings. Since the medieval period Christian, Jewish, and Islamic theologians have taught that historical or scientific claims found in scriptural texts that are contradicted by good science must be interpreted in ways that allow the apparent contradictions to be resolved. It is widely recognized that the Scriptures of the major world religions were written in times when prescientific cosmologies were assumed, but theologians distinguish between antiquated, prescientific claims about the cosmos and the essential core doctrines of religion, and they do not see the former as undermining the credibility of the latter. They distinguish between essential

---

2. See *Biologos*, "How Have Christians Responded to Darwin's *Origin of the Species*?"

core doctrines and stories that should be interpreted figuratively and appreciated for their moral and spiritual significance rather than their scientific accuracy.

Augustine's commentary on Genesis recognized that the creation story is open to diverse interpretations and that it is appropriate for the adopted mode of interpretation to be guided by the need to ensure consistency with what is known on the basis of scientific investigation. Augustine writes,

> In matters that are so obscure and far beyond our vision, we find in Holy Scripture passages which can be interpreted in very different ways without prejudice to the faith we have received. In such cases, we should not rush in headlong and so firmly take our stand on one side that, if further progress in the search for truth justly undermines our position, we fall with it. We should not battle for our own interpretation but for the teaching of Holy Scripture. We should not wish to conform the meaning of Holy Scripture to our interpretation, but our interpretation to the meaning of Holy Scripture.[3]

Since Augustine believed that time was created by God and thus part of the created order, creation of the universe could not be an event in time. The Creator, apart from creation, must be timeless, and the creation of the universe must be instantaneous and not an event in time that takes time. Once the created order exists, it may proceed according to the laws of nature, which are created and given to nature by God. God's governance of the universe need not require frequent divine intervention.

In the sixteenth century, as the scientific revolution was beginning, an exegetical approach based on the idea of *accommodation* was developed. According to Alister E. McGrath,

> This approach argues that revelation takes place in culturally and anthropologically conditioned manners and forms, with the result that it needs to be appropriately interpreted.... This approach argues that the opening chapters of Genesis use language and imagery appropriate to the cultural conditions of its original audience; it is not to be taken "literally," but is to be interpreted to a contemporary readership by extracting the key ideas which have been expressed in forms and terms which are specifically adapted or "accommodated" to the original audience.[4]

---

3. Quoted in McGrath, *Science and Religion*, 10.
4. McGrath, *Science and Religion*, 9.

This approach was advocated by Reformer John Calvin, who "gave a religious motivation to the scientific investigation of nature." Science reveals nature "before our eyes as a most beautiful book in which all created things, whether great or small, are as letters showing the invisible things of God to us."[5] Calvin was aware that biblical literalism can be an obstacle to interpretations of Scripture that are compatible with recognition of divine truth revealed through the study of God's creation. Calvin recognized that divine revelation must be accommodated to its audience. God the teacher adjusts the means of communicating truth to the aptitude of the audience. Thus Scripture must be accessible to persons living at very different stages in the development of culture and different levels of understanding of nature.

Jewish, Christian, and Muslim theologians have grappled with issues concerning the nature of religious language and the relation between religious truth and literal propositional language about historical events and facts about the physical world. The greatest theologians have vigorously upheld the authority of rational discourse about the natural order and recognized that religious truth must cohere with scientific truth. "All truth is God's truth" as Augustine said, and all truth must cohere in one unified, logically consistent whole, as Thomas Aquinas said.

A fundamental claim made by Christian theism is that the world was created by God. What do we mean by "God," and in what sense did God create the world? David Bentley Hart points out that virtually all the great religious traditions have some notion of an ultimate, transcendent, sacred reality that is the ground and source of all that exists and the source of all that is good and beautiful.[6] Some religious pluralists such as John Hick avoid using the term *God* to refer to the ultimate religious reality because not all religions think of the ultimate, transcendent, sacred reality as a personal being to whom human beings can enter into something like a personal relationship. Hick uses the term "The Real" and distinguishes between personal and impersonal conceptions of The Real.[7] Many Christian theists are cautious about overly anthropomorphized conceptions of the transcendent reality and emphasize that whatever we mean by calling God a person, it is far beyond the sense in which we ascribe personhood to finite human beings. Philosophical reflection on the concept of "person" was enriched by Christian theologians grappling with the doctrine of the Trinity. According to Hans Urs von Balthasar, "The word person receives its special dignity

---

5. McGrath, *Science and Religion*, 10.
6. Hart, *The Experience of God*, 32.
7. Hick, *An Interpretation of Religion*, ch.16.

in history when it is illuminated by the unique theological meaning."[8] The concept of person was used to make sense of the distinction between God the Father, Son, and Holy Spirit as somehow distinguishable persons within one supremely united Godhead—one God in three persons. Even though this idea is paradoxical and mysterious, the Christian thinkers who worked out the idea of the Trinity from biblical sources did not think that the doctrine of God's being three persons compromised the unity and simplicity of God, nor did they deny the ultimate coherence of the doctrine. Ascribing personhood to God was not seen as diminishing God or anthropomorphizing him. Again, human personhood is far removed from and inferior to the personhood of God. We should not minimize the importance of the distinction between Christian conceptions of God and conceptions of the ultimate reality that Hick characterizes as "*impersonae* of the Real,"[9] but we should also appreciate that the sense in which many great Christian theologians think of God as personal is far beyond human personhood. Theistic traditions and traditions such as Hinduism and Taoism agree that the ultimate religious reality is other than any finite entity or person in the universe. The conceptions of the Tao and Brahman are closer to that of the God of theism than is that conception of God to the conception of finite personal gods of polytheistic religion or any conception of God as a particular being that is an entity alongside other entities within the universe. We will deal with issues concerning the distinction between personal and impersonal conceptions of the sacred in chapter 7.

What most great religions hold in common is the affirmation that the universe is dependent for its existence on a transcendent, sacred reality. Christian theism holds that the God of monotheism created the universe *ex nihilo*, which means that before (whether "before" is understood temporally or ontologically) God created the universe, there was no pre-existing substance, independent of God's creativity, from which the universe was fashioned. There was no chaos, void, prime matter, empty space, quantum vacuum, dark energy, or unstable "nothing," which is really something. This would seem to imply that the universe had a beginning, before which it did not exist. There is disagreement with this among some medieval Muslim thinkers, who, impressed by Aristotle's argument that time cannot have a beginning, interpret the creation story metaphorically.[10] They not only deny that creation means a six-day process, but also that creation means bring-

---

8. See Balthasar, "On the Concept of Person," 18.
9. Hick, *An Interpretation of Religion*, 279.
10. Avicenna argued for the eternity of the world on the basis of the goodness of creation and the eternal goodness of God. See McGinnis, "The Eternity of the World."

ing the world into being out of nothing in the finite past. On this view the universe did not begin to exist, but its existence is nevertheless still utterly dependent on God. Interestingly, some Islamic thinkers were willing to go further than most Christians beyond the literal reading of scriptural texts in order to avoid perceived conflicts with contemporary science. Theists generally agree that nothing can exist independently of God, however, whether or not the universe is thought to have had a beginning. Those theists who believe that the universe began to exist in the finite past also hold that the universe is dependent on God for its continued existence after its beginning.[11] They deny that the universe, once created, is capable of continued existence on its own, apart from God's sustaining its existence at every moment of its existence. This is clearly a metaphysical claim that cannot be supported or refuted by natural science. Science investigates this natural order, but whether the natural order as a whole is dependent for its existence upon a transcendent ground is beyond the purview of natural science, and therefore, science cannot prove that God does or does not exist.

Del Ratzsche formulates the essential core propositions of Christianity with the following five propositions, which he argues are not contradicted by currently held scientific theories:

1. A supernatural person—God—created the universe.
2. God cares about humans.
3. God ultimately controls cosmic and human history.
4. God can intervene in earthly events.
5. There is objective meaning/significance to human life, both now and after death.[12]

The first proposition is not contradicted by natural science, because science does not address or presume answers to questions regarding the transcendent. It is sometimes argued that although science does not contradict the proposition that God exists, the lack of scientific evidence for the existence of God puts theism at odds with science. Does a lack of scientific evidence for the existence of God count as evidence for the nonexistence of God?

There is no evidence for the existence of finite gods such as Zeus or Isis, who were thought of as beings within the natural order. In these cases, the lack of evidence constitutes good reason to be skeptical of the existence of such deities. However, the God of the great monotheistic religions, Judaism,

11. McCabe, "God and Creation," 408–15.
12. Ratzsche, "The Demise of Religion," 73.

Christianity, and Islam, is purported to be a transcendent being who exists in an order of reality that is utterly beyond the natural world that science investigates. Here a lack of evidence for existence is not so convincingly argued to constitute evidence against existence. In the case of Zeus it is plausible to argue that if he were a real being in the natural world, there would be empirical evidence for his existence. However, it is not obvious that if the God of Christianity really exists, there would be evidence for it that is accessible to natural science. Given the transcendence of God, it is possible that the world created by God was given an orderliness, law-likeness, and capacity to self-create that gives the order of nature the appearance of complete self-sufficiency. God does not appear on the scene within nature as if he were a part of the created order. This may make nature appear to be all there is—a closed system independent of anything beyond itself—to one inclined to skepticism about the existence of a transcendent order of reality.

Within the context of Christianity, there are beliefs about God and his purposes that are consistent with the idea that God might create a world that is to a large extent empirically indistinguishable from what an atheistic physicist would expect it to be like. It is possible for a theist to agree with Richard Dawkins that "the universe that we observe has precisely the properties we should expect if there is, at bottom, no design, no purpose, no evil, no good, nothing but pitiless indifference,"[13] and at the same time believe that such a universe is consistent with the universe actually being good and having the design and purpose that God intends. For some Christians, the world permits Dawkins's interpretation because of human sin, which both corrupts the world and blinds us to some of the good that does exist in the world. From a Christian perspective it is plausible that the creativity of God is such that he can endow nature with principles and potentialities that permit the world to unfold in ways that require nothing that would appear to be obvious acts of divine intervention. God's creation can appear to the atheist as Dawkins sees it and at the same time appear to Augustine and Calvin to be the handiwork of an omnipotent and all-good God. Natural science cannot decide which of the two alternatives is true. John Hick argues that it is essential to religion that the cosmos be "religiously ambiguous," which is to say that it must be possible to interpret it either religiously or naturalistically.[14] Hick regards the religious ambiguity of the world to be necessary in order to preserve the freedom of finite persons to interpret reality religiously or not, and holds that this freedom is essential to the possibility of being authentically religious. For Christianity, being religious entails loving God,

---

13. Dawkins, *River Out of Eden*, 133.
14. Hick, *Interpretation of Religion*, 73–128.

which is possible only for persons with free will, and according to Hick, the religious ambiguity of the universe is required in order for humans to have this freedom.

IS RELIGION PRIMITIVE SCIENCE?

Even if science does not support propositions that are blatantly inconsistent with core Christian doctrines, some defenders of the incompatibility of science and religion hold that the plausibility of religion is inevitably undermined by the advance of science. A common understanding of the alleged conflict between science and religion holds that religion is essentially a primitive, prescientific mode of understanding the world. Before we had science, natural phenomena that we could not understand rationally were "explained" by the agency of gods. With the advance of science there is progressively less for religion and gods to explain. Devotees of religion attempt to justify the retention of their outmoded beliefs by invoking God to explain what science has not yet succeeded in explaining. Religion conflicts with science insofar as it resists the progress of science in order to retain at least something for religion to explain. On this view, as science progresses, religion is no longer needed or relevant, and it is irrational to resist the progress of science in order to safeguard religion. Several major scientific developments seem to have progressively diminished the credibility of religion. The Copernican Revolution and subsequent cosmological discoveries showed that the earth is not the center of the universe, but is rather a mere pale blue dot in the outskirts of a vast cosmos containing "billions and billions" of stars and planets, many of them probably more impressive than earth. The Copernican principle was expanded into a general "principle of mediocrity," according to which there is nothing special about earth and our place in the universe. We are nothing special.

Newton was a devout Christian, so he did not see the alleged atheistic implications of his physical theory, but gradually the implications of the mechanical philosophy were understood. The mechanical philosophy conceives the universe as a mechanism governed entirely by physical laws. Although Newton himself thought that God was needed to create the machine and keep it working properly, Laplace recognized a century later that God was a hypothesis he did not need. The mechanical philosophy was developed in the context of Christian belief that God was the creator and sustainer of the machine. This belief led to deism, which regards the universe as created by God, but which once created, operates by natural laws without the need for divine intervention. The God of deism is not involved in, nor does it sustain the workings of nature or history. From deism it was a short step to atheism. The God of deism was not needed by science and was of no use to religion. A half century later Darwin made it even easier for scientists to do without the God hypothesis, thereby finishing the task of making it possible for atheists to find intellectual satisfaction by explaining even life in terms of purely material processes governed by physical laws. Once science became so advanced that it could apparently explain life, religion seemed irrelevant. For Richard Dawkins religion is detrimental to human progress because it stifles scientific inquiry. Religion gives pseudo-explanations that it pretends are final answers that bring an end to inquiry. For Dawkins "faith is the great cop-out, the excuse to evade the need to think and evaluate evidence. Faith is belief in spite of, even perhaps because of, the lack of evidence."[15]

Daniel Dennett admits that science is not logically incompatible with religion, but he makes the point that there are a lot of ideas that are not strictly contradicted by science but which science renders wholly implausible. Science is logically compatible with the view that the universe was created by Superman, but no one familiar with modern science can take "Supermanism"[16] seriously as an explanation of natural phenomena. Even though science and religion are logically compatible, Dennett thinks that theism is wildly implausible and the possibility of its being true not worthy of serious consideration. Darwinism renders implausible "one of the oldest ideas we have: the idea that it takes a fancy smart thing to make a lesser thing." Dennett calls this the "trickle-down theory of creation. You'll never see a spear making a spear-maker. You'll never see a horse shoe making a blacksmith. You'll never see a pot making a potter."[17] The idea that a designer is needed to account for the complexity of life used to seem plausible. Now Darwinism has shown how more complex organisms evolve from less complex by purely natural processes, without the need for a creator or designer.

It seems that we don't need God to explain the amazing things we find in the world. Once we have the scientific explanation, even if it does not logically contradict theistic belief, it removes the rationale for accepting it. The appeal to God in order to explain life did not really explain it anyway. To say that something happened because "God did it" is to leave it a mystery rather than to explain it. The success that science has enjoyed in explaining previously unexplained phenomena gives us confidence that science will continue to make progress in closing the gaps in our scientific understanding. It is rational to believe that gaps in our scientific understanding will be

15. Dawkins, Untitled Lecture at Edinburgh Science Festival, 1992.
16. Dennett and Plantinga, *Science and Religion*, 28–29.
17. Dennett, Interview in *Der Spiegel*.

closed by science, if they are to be closed at all. As Dawkins proclaims, to respond to an unanswered scientific question with "therefore God must have done it" is precisely to abandon science in favor of a nonrational response, probably motivated by wishful thinking and the need for comfort.

It is not as though scientists are confident that scientific answers to all questions will be forthcoming. Lawrence Krauss[18] is happy to admit that science may always be confronted with unanswered questions and lack of complete and adequate theoretical explanations. It is part of the wonder of the human condition that we keep striving to expand the frontier of science in the face of the possibility that it may be an endless task. Science assumes that nature is fully rational, but also acknowledges that human understanding is finite and that we may not ultimately be able to figure everything out. The fact that nature may ultimately be to some degree beyond human comprehension does not justify giving up the quest for scientific understanding and resorting to the easy answers of religion. The scientific spirit is inspired by the magnificence of nature and the commitment to the quest for rational understanding to the extent that human reason is capable of it. The appeal to God to provide pseudo-explanations of what science does not yet understand is a betrayal of the scientific enterprise.

Krauss has a kind of moral fervor in his appreciation of the magnificence of the scientific enterprise. He speaks of the quest for rational understanding as the noblest activity of which human beings are capable. He repeatedly demeans the mentality of religious believers for their willingness to accept easy answers without evidence. Much better is the commitment to reason and the demand for rational grounds of one's beliefs. It is even better still if this insistence on being rational is accompanied by a willing recognition that this magnificent universe in which we live is utterly devoid of human meaning and purpose. How great is the universe and how great are scientists who dare to inquire about it and not demand that it have some meaning for us! Naturalists like Dennett, Krauss, and Dawkins have an enthusiasm for the scientific point of view and its assumed moral and aesthetic superiority over the religious mentality, which they seem to regard as childish and contemptibly irrational.

However, Dennett's characterization of the god that he regards as silly to believe exists is not the God of Christian theism. The Christian God is a transcendent being who is the ground of the existence of the universe, and who allows the universe to unfold to a large extent according to natural laws. It is not a designer-craftsman within the natural order who manipulates nature like a magician in order to accomplish ends that nature could

---

18. Krauss, *A Universe from Nothing*, 182.

not have reached by strict adherence to the laws of nature. Such a god would be a finite being within the natural order, not the transcendent ground of the being of the whole natural order. The transcendent God of theism may provide a philosophical explanation of the existence of the universe, but thoughtful theists do not generally use God to explain particular phenomena for which scientific explanations are not yet available. That "God-of-the-gaps" approach is rejected by naturalists and most sophisticated theists.

Naturalists like Dawkins, Dennett, and Krauss are wrong in thinking that the point of religion is to offer pseudoscientific explanations of natural phenomena, although they are correct in saying that religion does make factual claims about the world, and to that extent has something in common with science. Theism is part of a worldview that offers a way to make sense of the whole of reality and the place of human beings in the grand scheme of things. Religion is concerned with understanding the human condition and how human beings may attain the ultimate solution to the fundamental problem of human existence. Factual claims about the cosmos are made by religious believers primarily because of their relevance to the soteriological concerns of religion—the quest for salvation. For Christians a theoretical description of the cosmos is less important than the religious, ethical, and existential aspects of the religious life. Christian theism claims that the world is God's creation and that God has a purpose and plan for his creation. It claims that the world has certain features that reflect God's purpose. Christian theism is not about providing scientific explanations of specific phenomena or structures, or filling in gaps in our scientific understanding with supernatural explanations. Theism as a worldview provides a general framework for thinking about the nature and order of the universe, the meaning of human existence, the place of humanity within the overall order of the universe, the diagnosis of the fundamental problem of the human condition, and the solution to that problem. Science has other concerns, and as far as the theist is concerned, the scientific theories do not intrude into the domain of theological truth.

The theist believes that nature is rational and law-governed. The naturalist and theist can agree that nature is intelligible, whether or not human beings will ever fully understand it. As science progresses we learn more and more about how amazing the order of nature is. Krauss, Dawkins, and Dennett write eloquently of the magnificence of the order of nature, and they seem to think that theism devalues the magnificence of nature. Krauss clearly regards the idea that nature requires a divine tinkerer to maintain its orderly operations to be the product of intellectual laziness and an affront to the grandeur of nature. Many theistic thinkers would agree. The issue here is whether the whole of nature is dependent upon a transcendent ground, and whether it is naturalism or theism that provides the better philosophical perspective from which to recognize, understand, and appreciate the magnificent order of nature. Theists do not think that the wonder of nature is undermined by conceiving of it as the handiwork of a creator. The theist sees the same beauty and awesomeness of nature as the scientist, and if sufficiently educated in science, can appreciate the mathematical order of nature as well. The theist also sees nature as pointing to a reality that is even greater and more splendid than nature—the creator of nature. So the theist has an additional reason to appreciate the magnificence of nature, and this additional reason augments rather than diminishes the appreciation of nature and the significance of scientific understanding.

Dawkins insists that the appeal to God is a science stopper. To explain a phenomenon by saying "God did it" is to offer no explanation at all, and its main effect is to end the search for an explanation, which is deadly for science. It is indeed not a good explanation of why your car battery is dead to say that it was God's will because he did not want you to go to that party, and no one should seriously offer that as an explanation. However, if the question is raised why the universe exists, someone might say, "because God created it." As an explanation for the existence of the universe, the claim that God created it is admittedly not a scientific explanation, but that does not mean that it is a bad explanation, unless one assumes that only scientific explanations are legitimate. Scientific explanations involve appeals to natural laws or causes, which are necessarily parts of nature itself. So explanations in terms of causes within nature cannot be sufficient to answer the ultimate question of why the whole of nature exists in the first place—Leibniz's question why anything at all exists rather than nothing. The reference to God as the explanation of the existence of the universe, albeit not a scientific explanation, has one major advantage over scientific explanations. It refers to an absolutely transcendent being, so it has a chance of providing an ultimate explanation for why the universe exists. To be sure, a theistic explanation of the existence of the universe does not describe the details involved in God's creating the universe. The proposition that God created the universe does not explain how he did it, but it does give a final answer to the question why the universe exists. Dawkins does not like explanations that put an end to inquiry, but in the case of the search for ultimate explanations, that is what one wants—a final answer that does not lead to further questions. Continuing the inquiry because we do not yet have the final answer is a good thing, and therefore we should do it. That does not mean that it is undesirable to arrive at a final answer that does not just push the question to another level, raising further unanswered questions. If we could know that the universe exists because it was created by a being that necessarily exists, any inquiry-ending tendencies that such an explanation might have would not be a bad thing. It is only bad to end inquiry before a final answer is reached, not after.

Even if science provides the only good explanations of natural phenomena, it would not mean that religious beliefs are necessarily irrational. If one accepts the legitimacy of science, one need not claim that beliefs that are not justified by scientific evidence cannot be rationally justified in some other way. Science is a way of investigating nature. Perhaps it is the only way of rationally investigating nature, but science, with its self-imposed restriction to the investigation of nature, is silent on the question whether anything beyond nature is real. Even if the affirmation of the existence of supernatural entities is beyond the purview of science, it does not require one to be antiscience to believe that they exist. Many scientists do believe that God exists. Belief in God need not be a matter of blind faith or an offense against reason. One might have philosophical arguments to support belief. One might believe on the basis of religious experience. Belief in God might, for some persons, be properly basic, as Alvin Plantinga has argued.[19] One might, in the context of religious life and practice in a religious community, find oneself with religious beliefs that are as credible as one's belief that love is good and cruelty is bad. Faith flows as naturally from one's total experience in the world and one's social group as does one's overall sense of what is valuable and significant in one's life. It may be a central part of one's orientation in the social and moral world in which one finds oneself. Even if religious belief is groundless in the sense of being basic and not based on more fundamental beliefs, it may still be rational in the sense of being the basis of many other beliefs that are rendered collectively more coherent and significant by their theistic underpinning.

The existence of a being that totally transcends nature cannot be proved by empirical science, but neither can science disprove it. What about a transcendent God who acts in the world? Religious belief in the occurrence of miracles may seem incompatible with a scientific view of the world. Some scientifically minded thinkers are hostile to the idea of an intervening God who sometimes disrupts the natural order of things and bypasses the laws of nature. The notion of a God who acts in the world is not contrary to science for a theist who holds that nature is continually sustained by God, for on such a view there need not be a sharp distinction between that which happens in accordance with the laws of nature and that which is the result of divine agency. Many theists would not use the term *intervene*, because it implies disruption or interference with nature, whereas the theist would

19. Plantinga, "The Reformed Objection to Natural Theology," 187–98.

think more in terms of God acting in the world as an agent to graciously assist humans in their endeavors. All natural processes are ultimately dependent on God, as are the laws of nature, so God is ultimately the cause of all existence and events. Christian thinkers, such as Herbert McCabe,[20] are very clear that creation means that God is the ultimate cause of everything in nature, so what appears from one point of view to be events happening in accord with the laws of nature can be understood at the same time, when viewed from a theological perspective, to be ordained by God. A theist can hold that creation by a perfect God means that everything in nature may conform to natural law, which perfectly expresses the will of the creator. So theism need not affirm the existence of a God who violates laws of nature, but neither does it affirm an order of nature that must conform to physical laws that operate independently of the will of the creator.

So in the view of some theologians divine agency need not involve suspension or violation of the laws of nature. Thomas Aquinas distinguished two levels of divine causality—primary and secondary.[21] God creating the universe is an example of God's acting as the primary cause of the existence of the universe. Christian theologians typically believe that the universe as a whole and everything and every event in the universe depends on God to sustain them in existence. Most of the events in the physical universe involve God's acting through secondary causes, which are the causes investigated by the natural sciences. Some Christians believe that God's creation of the universe involves his bestowing on the universe the potentialities required to realize his purposes through secondary causation, without the need for frequent subsequent intervention. Such a view is compatible with the notion that there are no gaps in the natural order, and that in principle all events in the material world are explainable in terms of natural causes, without the need for God acting by direct, supernatural, primary causation. It follows from divine omnipotence that God can and may sometimes act directly in the world in ways not explainable through natural causes. This would involve God acting as the primary cause of certain events, such as the creation of the first humans and acts that are crucial for human redemption. This amounts to divine action in the world, but not all Christians would hold that it entails violations of the laws of nature, any more than human agency entails violations of the laws of nature.

John Polkinghorne, the quantum physicist who became an Anglican theologian, sees divine action as involving a kind of top-down causality that

---

20. McCabe, "God and Creation."
21. Aquinas, *Summa Theologica*, Question 22, "On Providence."

is consistent with contemporary quantum theory.[22] Libertarian free will for humans is believed to be consistent with science by many scientists, who hold that freely performed human actions may cause events in the physical world that would not have occurred without human beings willingly choosing to act. If God is an agent, he would be no less capable of changing the course of events in the physical world than a human agent, who can act to change the course of events without violating any physical laws. So the claim that violations of the laws of nature do not occur is not incompatible with the existence of a transcendent God who acts in the world. Indeed, some theists insist that conformity to law is a hallmark of a universe created by a rational God and see theism as consistent with naturalism's disdain for deviations from law. On the other hand, science cannot prove that exceptions to the usual natural order of things are impossible, so has no grounds for claiming that a religious believer's acceptance of the possibility of occasional miraculous divine actions is incompatible with a scientific outlook.

Theism is flexible in accommodating itself to the conclusions of science. Theism affirms the existence of a transcendent being that is outside the bounds of what is investigated by the natural sciences. When science succeeds in explaining a phenomenon by finding a satisfactory causal explanation, this is consistent with the belief that nature depends on God, who works through secondary causes. Where science lacks an adequate causal explanation of a phenomenon, theists, especially if they are not also scientific experts, should not invoke God to fill the gap in the science. The God of theism is not a God of the gaps. Phenomena that currently lack adequate scientific explanation are not necessarily instances of divine intervention. God is the primary cause of all existence and change, most of which have secondary causes within the order of nature that are investigated by science. The God hypothesis explains why the universe exists, not particular phenomena within the universe that are thought to lack secondary causes discoverable by science.

Theism is compatible with the belief that it is in principle possible for science to reach a final theory that would eliminate all the gaps in our scientific explanations of phenomena in the world. This would not be, if it happens, an embarrassment to theists. On the other hand, until science reaches the ultimate goal of a complete final theory, which many of its prominent practitioners frankly admit may be beyond human attainment, it remains an open question whether science can in principle explain everything in nature. Whether or not we ever reach a final physical theory that explains everything in nature, such a theory will not answer the fundamental

---

22. Polkinghorne, *Science and Theology*, 88.

question of why nature exists or whether anything happens in the world for a purpose. Any possible scientific theory will assume the existence of nature, and unless nature itself exists necessarily, the answer to the question why nature exists will either have to be that it is an unexplainable brute fact, or it will have to appeal to something beyond nature, which by definition will be transcendent or supernatural. If the theory stays within the parameters of natural science, it will be incapable of explaining why nature exists. If it attains a vantage point that would give it a chance to address the ultimate question of why nature exists, it will no longer be natural science.

Science is compatible with the belief that the universe was created by and continually dependent on God. No purely scientific theory says or entails that the universe was not created by God. The transcendence of God entails that God is not a finite entity that exists in the order of nature as one of the entities that make up the totality of nature. Science studies nature, and while theists believe that the order of nature is dependent on God, God is not one of the entities that exists within the order of nature, which could be discovered by science. Whether nature as a whole is dependent on God is not an issue that can be settled by looking at nature itself. It may be that science sometimes offers clues of the existence of its transcendent cause, but perhaps the recognition of these clues depends on the perspective of the person who is looking, or not looking for them, or depends on whether one is open to the possibility of there being a transcendent creator. The study of nature does not disprove the existence of anything beyond nature. The lack of a scientific explanation of some natural phenomena does not support theism, and the existence of scientific explanations of previously unexplained natural phenomena does not support atheism. Theistic belief may be to some extent motivated by an effort to explain what science cannot in principle explain without going beyond its purview (such as personhood, free will, and objective moral truth), but it need not be motivated by the need to explain what science can in principle but does not yet explain, and it is not undermined when science finds an explanation for what was previously not understood. Religion is not a prescientific effort to explain nature, and its failure to do so is not grounds for rejecting religion. Science is about nature, not what transcends nature, and its silence about the transcendent should not be taken as evidence against the reality of the transcendent. There will be no temptation to think otherwise, unless one assumes that whereof science is silent, one must (in order to be rational and intellectually respectable) be dubious. This, of course, is the assumption of scientism, that whatever cannot be justified by the application of the scientific method cannot be legitimately accepted as knowledge. This arbitrary assumption is not only not justified, but is (as has been pointed out many times since the days of Plato) incoherent and self-refuting. The proposition that only what can be justified by the scientific method counts as knowledge is not itself a proposition that can be justified by the scientific method. That is to say, by the criterion that scientism lays down for what counts as knowledge, scientism itself fails to qualify.

Sean Carroll, a major figure in scientific cosmology, thinks that science makes materialism more rational to accept than theism. Carroll is not guilty of scientism and does not think that science can prove that God does not exist, but he does think that science provides us with the best way to describe and understand the natural world, that it is very unlikely that belief in God will contribute to our understanding of the world, and that when we understand the world scientifically there is nothing left for theism to contribute. What scientific cosmology gives us are models by which to describe the patterns and laws of nature. He asserts that "most scientists... suspect that the search for ultimate explanations eventually terminates in some final theory of the world, along with the phrase 'and that's just how it is.'"[23] When the theist says we need an answer to the question why the universe exists, Carroll's answer is "no we don't."[24] The felt need to ask this question, Carroll says, is a relic of Aristotelian metaphysics, which science no longer needs. Scientists might talk of causes of particular phenomena in the natural world, but what they are really talking about are patterns and sequences of events. The notion of causality is out of place when talking about the whole universe. We got into the habit of asking about causes when we were hunting for food and mates, but talk of causes does not apply to the universe as a whole. The universe just is, and that's it.

The theist's interest in defending the proposition that God is the creator of the cosmos is not primarily due to an interest in answering the question why the universe exists. It is much more to do with the fact that the doctrine of creation is fundamental to Christian theology and plays a role in establishing God's credentials as the absolute sovereign over all that is. Christian theology is not a competitor to astrophysics in the effort to come up with the best description of the patterns and laws by which the processes of the universe operate. When Carroll says that once science has finished its work there is no longer much point in believing that God exists, he is overlooking the principal reasons that people believe in God, which are primarily religious rather than theoretical. Most religious believers see little point in looking to science for evidence of God's existence or insight into how to attain salvation, but there are religious as well as metaphysical reasons

---

23. Carroll, "Does the Universe Need God?," 193.
24. Carroll, "Does the Universe Need God?," 193.

for being concerned with the question why the universe exists. If Carroll is satisfied with a theoretical account that describes the patterns and laws of nature and feels no need to answer the question why the universe exists, that is his prerogative, but others may want an answer. Christians who already believe that God created the world may be interested in the philosophical question why anything at all exists, not because they regard that question, as Leibniz did, as the most fundamental philosophical question, but because reflecting on that question is a way of wondering at the greatness of the God they worship. God is the ground of being as well as the source of all that is good, beautiful, and pertaining to ultimate human attainment. That a way of doing science can replace the "archaic" notion of causality does not diminish the value of the concept for religious and philosophical inquiry and reflection.

In spite of the fact that religion makes claims about the universe, it is not concerned with offering detailed explanations of natural phenomena. Religion is not primitive science, although fundamental descriptive claims of religion may provide elements of a worldview, which can provide a framework for making sense of important features of our experience of the world.

3
Science and Naturalism

Metaphysical naturalism is the view that only nature exists. The material world is all there is; there are no supernatural entities, such as spirits, angels, or God. As a metaphysical view, it is presumably not entailed by science. However, since most scientists hold that the scientific method must exclude any appeal to supernatural causes from scientific explanation, they typically regard methodological naturalism as essential to good science, and many are inclined to think that methodological naturalism leads naturally to metaphysical naturalism. A critical issue for theists who also respect science is whether good scientific practice demands a commitment to metaphysical naturalism.

METHODOLOGICAL NATURALISM

Methodological naturalism, as its name implies, is not a view about the nature of reality, but rather about the proper method for conducting scientific research. Methodological naturalism is a postulate of the scientific method, an assumption about how science should be conducted and what counts as legitimate science. To appeal to supernatural causes, such as gods, angels, or demons to explain the phenomena that we observe with our natural faculties is to abandon the scientific enterprise defined in terms of methodological naturalism. Some would argue that if science rules out an appeal to supernatural causes then we are not justified in believing that supernatural entities exist. This may seem to entail that religious belief is not rationally justifiable.

Methodological naturalism rests on a decision to adopt a certain method in carrying out the investigation of nature—a decision to allow only naturalistic explanations. Since only empirical evidence is allowed, and only natural causes are allowed to play a role in explaining phenomena, science so defined deliberately limits the scope of scientific investigation to the realm of nature. The rationality of accepting methodological naturalism rests on the fruitfulness of insisting that scientific explanations must not refer to non-natural causes or entities that cannot plausibly be regarded as constituents of the physical world. According to most scientists, the appeal to supernatural processes to explain natural phenomena is anathema to the scientific enterprise. This attitude is accepted by many religious believers who also respect science. Does the insistence that science seek only naturalistic explanations entail that no supernatural causes exist? Is it contrary to science to believe that the supernatural exists and is causally related to the natural world?

Methodological naturalism says that to be scientific a theory or hypothesis must not appeal to anything beyond nature and that nature includes only what can be conceptualized within the accepted canons of empirical science. Note that the definition of methodological naturalism runs the risk of falling into circularity: science is defined as the study of nature, and nature is defined as whatever is countenanced by natural science. The even more important point is that methodological naturalism is not a thesis about what exists or is real. It does not logically entail that only what science says exists really does exist. It does not entail that only the physical world is real, which would be metaphysical naturalism. A method of inquiry that stipulates *a priori* that only physical laws and processes are allowed to play a role in explaining natural phenomena cannot be expected to discover entities that transcend the natural world. Methodological restrictions required by scientific practice are not sufficient reason for thinking that only the natural world exists. To infer that only nature exists, from the fact that natural science is conducted in accordance with a method that stipulates that appeal to anything beyond nature is not considered legitimate science, is justified only if natural science is assumed to be the only source of knowledge of objective reality. That is to assume scientism, the view that natural science is the only rational way of knowing objective truth.

Although methodological naturalism does not logically entail metaphysical naturalism, many scientists and philosophers believe that if scientific explanation must appeal only to strictly natural causes, it is unscientific and contrary to the canons of rational inquiry to believe that anything beyond nature is real. Many scientists and philosophers of science embrace both methodological and metaphysical naturalism. For instance, Sidney Hook asserts that "there is only one reliable method of reaching the truth about the nature of things ... [and] this reliable method comes to fruition in the methods of natural science."[1] The booklet *Teaching about Evolution and the Nature of Science,* produced by the National Academy of Sciences, provides a clear statement of methodological naturalism: "Because science is limited to explaining the natural world by means of natural processes, it cannot use supernatural causation in its explanations. Similarly, science is precluded from making statements about supernatural forces because these are outside its province."[2] According to Paul Kurtz, methodological "naturalism is committed to a methodological principle within the context of scientific inquiry; i.e., all hypotheses and events are to be explained and tested by reference to natural causes and events. To introduce a supernatural or transcendental cause within science is to depart from naturalistic explanations. On this ground, to invoke an intelligent designer or creator is inadmissible."[3]

The insistence that science should not invoke a creator does not entail that God does not exist. Some Christian thinkers, such as Francis Collins[4] and Howard Van Till,[5] insist that the proper conduct of natural science does require methodological naturalism but that this does not entail metaphysical naturalism. As a purely methodological principle, methodological naturalism is neutral on the question of whether the supernatural exists. Accordingly, science under the assumption of methodological naturalism says nothing affirmatively or negatively about the existence of the supernatural. Although Christian thinkers who are inclined toward methodological naturalism believe that God created the universe, they agree that reference to God has no place in science. Many such Christian thinkers are opposed to the Intelligent Design movement for its claim that a scientific inference to an intelligent designer of life is possible. Although they do not think that science rules out the existence of God, neither do they think that appeals to God should be used to explain any natural phenomena. Science should remain neutral on metaphysical and religious issues.

However, many scientists and philosophers are naturalists who do think that methodological naturalism makes belief in the supernatural untenable. One such philosopher of science is Michael Ruse, who sees methodological naturalism as part of the definition of science and regards science as the only legitimate source of objective knowledge of the real world. Ruse

---

1. Hook, *The Quest for Being,* 185.
2. National Academy of Sciences, *Teaching About Evolution and the Nature of Science,* 124.
3. Kurtz, "Darwin Re-Crucified," 17.
4. Collins, *Language of God.*
5. Van Till, "Partnership."

states that science "by definition deals only with the natural." He further writes, "I argue that methodological naturalism is true in the sense that it embodies the proper procedure for acquiring knowledge.... The world does run according to law, and increasingly we know the nature of those laws and how they operate."[6] If the only proper procedure for acquiring knowledge is natural science, and if science rules out reference to the supernatural, then there is no way that theistic belief can be justified.

Most scientists think that methodological naturalism is a requirement for good science, and many think that it logically supports metaphysical naturalism. Can it not be legitimately asked whether either of these claims is true? Let us consider first the claim that natural science requires methodological naturalism. Many scientists and philosophers of science think that methodological naturalism is part of the definition of natural science, but this view has the unfortunate implication that most of the great scientists before the nineteenth century were not really scientists, since they sometimes invoked supernatural causes to explain what they observed. Newton, for instance, famously invoked God to explain why universal gravitation did not result in the collapse of the universe. Biologists before Darwin invoked God to account for the origin of life. One can disagree with the views of such scientists without declaring that they were not doing science, as would be implied by the view that methodological naturalism is part of the definition of science.[7]

An objection to the view that methodological naturalism is part of the definition of science is that those who defend the claim that it is have typically not adequately explained exactly what the definition of science is. As J. P. Moreland[8] argues, there isn't an agreed-upon set of necessary and sufficient conditions that define science and distinguish it from non-science. The issue of the definition of science is itself a philosophical issue, not a scientific one, and like most philosophical issues, this one has not produced a consensus answer.

Another objection to the view that good science requires commitment to methodological naturalism is that even contemporary scientists often deviate from it. Scientists describe the Big Bang, and presumably their descriptions are considered part of science. If the Big Bang is the beginning of the universe (nature), it cannot be explained by a law of nature. The fundamental constants of nature are "givens" that cannot be explained by laws

---

6. Ruse, "The Naturalist Challenge to Religion," 427–37.

7. This argument is made by Moreland in "Intelligent Design and the Nature of Science."

8. Moreland, "Intelligent Design and the Nature of Science."

of nature.⁹ There is no scientific proof that methodological naturalism is true. Methodological naturalism is not itself a proposition about the natural world; it is a methodological principle for the conduct of science. It cannot be "true" in the sense of corresponding with reality. Whatever "truth" it has must be measured in terms of its utility as a heuristic principle for practicing scientists.

Methodological naturalism does not seem to be a necessary requirement for scientific inquiry. However, the more serious issue is whether or not methodological naturalism supports metaphysical naturalism. The argument from the combination of scientism (the view that all genuine knowledge is scientific knowledge) and methodological naturalism is weak because it seems to rule out the supernatural by fiat. Science is declared to be the only legitimate source of real knowledge, and by definition science rules out the possibility of knowledge of anything beyond nature. So while scientism and methodological naturalism might leave open the possibility of the existence of God and other supernatural entities, they rule out the possibility of knowledge of God or the possibility that God could play any role in our understanding of reality. So God becomes irrelevant to rational thought. This seems too strong a claim to be justified by the adoption of a certain methodology.

A much stronger argument for the claim that methodological naturalism entails metaphysical naturalism is offered by Barbara Forrest, who admits that supernaturalism is not logically impossible and cannot be proven scientifically to be false. She sees the problem for supernaturalism to be that "from both an epistemological and a methodological standpoint, supernaturalism has not proved its mettle, whereas methodological naturalism has done so consistently and convincingly. Supernaturalism has not provided the epistemology or the methodology needed to support its metaphysics, whereas naturalism has, although the invitation to supernaturalism to do likewise is a standing one." Metaphysical naturalism justifies itself not by "disproving supernatural claims—methodological naturalism has neither the means nor the obligation to disprove either the existence of the supernatural or its causal efficacy. Rather, methodological naturalism enables us to accumulate substantive knowledge about the cosmos from which ontological categories may be constructed." Metaphysical naturalism is not justified *a priori*, but on the "basis of the explanatory success of science and the lack of explanatory success of supernaturalism."[10] This is

9. Moreland, "Intelligent Design and the Nature of Science," 52–53.

10. Forrest, "Methodological Naturalism and Philosophical Naturalism." Forrest uses the term *philosophical naturalism* rather than *metaphysical naturalism*. The two terms are synonymous.

a procedural or pragmatic justification of metaphysical naturalism. Naturalistic explanations yield results in science and supernatural explanations are abject failures at providing successful explanations or knowledge of the cosmos.

It is true that theism does not provide explanations of particular phenomena in the universe that compete with explanations offered by natural science. Forrest has declared the victory of naturalism over supernaturalism in a contest in which supernaturalism does not compete. To think of God as providing causal explanations of particular natural phenomena that natural science cannot explain is to treat God as a finite entity within the natural world rather than the transcendent ground of the existence of the universe. There are, however, things in the world that resist explanation in terms of the categories of a materialistic naturalism, which conceives of nature in terms of the categories of physics—spacetime, matter, energy, fields, etc. Contemporary naturalists express hope that science conceived along naturalistic lines will eventually be able to explain the origin of life, consciousness, and mind. Especially in the cases of mind, persons, and values, it seems that it is impossible for materialistic naturalism ever to deliver adequate explanations, and here the advantages of theism are most apparent. Theism does not provide the kind of explanations that natural science seeks. Supernatural entities are unobservable, and we will not get empirical support for theories about how God creates persons, minds, and values. A metaphysical framework that recognizes the reality of an omnipotent, supernatural, creative mind can provide a better framework for making sense of how and why the world contains minds and values than a metaphysics that requires that everything be explained in terms of physical laws and processes.

Michael Ruse[11] thinks that a strong argument for naturalism's superiority to supernaturalism is the fact that the human tendency to believe in the supernatural is explainable by evolutionary psychology. Such an argument commits the genetic fallacy. Even if religious belief can be explained by natural causes, this would not necessarily undermine the truth of religion. Presumably if naturalism were true, the capacity for scientific thought could also be explained by evolutionary psychology, but no naturalist would take this as evidence against the truth of naturalism.

Forrest is right that naturalism has a better track record than supernaturalism in explaining a wide range of natural phenomena, because theism does not attempt to do this. Materialistic naturalism has difficulty in explaining certain features of human beings, especially those that are of central concern to religion—such things as consciousness, personhood,

---

11. Ruse, "The Naturalist Challenge to Religion," 428.

values, moral agency, and autonomy. Michael Peterson[12] argues that theism has greater explanatory power than naturalism because in a theistic world it is far less improbable and surprising than in a materialistic world that these personal and moral characteristics should arise and flourish in the world. Thomas Nagel[13] argues that materialistic naturalism has no chance of explaining how Darwinian evolution could produce beings like us with rational minds and the ability to reason about objective moral values. If the world was created by an omnipotent spiritual being, it makes sense that he would create a world with persons who have rational minds. How our existence emerged from mindless, purposeless interactions of particles of matter is quite inexplicable. Forrest is also right that supernaturalism has no methodology for producing scientific explanations of phenomena in the natural world in terms of supernatural causes. However, as a metaphysical framework that makes intelligible how the universe could evolve from the Big Bang to a world that contains rational beings who can comprehend logic, mathematics, the mathematical order of the universe, and moral values, theism is more successful than naturalism. It does not do so by describing in detail the process by which God creates such aspects of the world. In some respects it leaves these phenomena having to do with persons, minds, and values as mysterious as does natural science. However, theism at least provides a metaphysical framework in the context of which it makes sense that the world contains persons whose lives can be oriented in a meaningful way by values that have a transcendental source. Naturalism must implausibly explain away these personal, rational, and spiritual aspects of ourselves as something radically different than what ordinary experience makes them seem to be. Theism can take them at face value and think of them as real and fundamental.

The commitment to natural science does not require a commitment to methodological naturalism, but more importantly methodological naturalism does not entail or require metaphysical naturalism. Forrest's argument that commitment to methodological and metaphysical naturalism is essential to the success of science loses much of its force when we look at areas of inquiry where the constraints of metaphysical naturalism seem unnecessarily restrictive. A worldview that acknowledges the reality of the mental and spiritual may lead to a more comprehensive understanding of the world that eludes a purely materialistic metaphysic.

---

12. Peterson, "The Encounter between Naturalistic Atheism and Christian Theism," 438–49.

13. Nagel, *Mind and Cosmos*, 6.

THEISM, NATURALISM, AND MIND

Among the things we seem to experience, which some people believe exist, but which are not obviously made of matter, are things such as the following: consciousness, experiences, beliefs, desires, ideas, emotions, feelings, meanings, purposes, motives, preferences, ambitions, affections, numbers, values, virtues, laws, and principles. Mental states, such as thoughts and ideas, don't take up space, have mass, or have shape. Consciousness does not seem to be a physical object or purely physical process. These items belong to what Paul Churchland,[14] a prominent naturalist philosopher and neuroscientist, calls "folk psychology." Churchland defends eliminative materialism, a version of strict naturalism applied to theory of mind, which denies the existence of mental states or properties. Folk psychology includes a vocabulary of terms that we use to talk about our inner mental states in a way that makes it seem that we are referring to things that really exist. The word *feeling* is used as though it refers to something that people can possess and talk about, but of course, a feeling is not really a thing. Folk psychology is regarded by Churchland as a primitive, prescientific way of talking, akin to talk about other "spooky things" like ghosts, demons, and vital spirits. A scientific approach to the mind would discard folk psychology in favor of talk about the brain and brain processes. Consciousness and mental states do not really exist as such. What is called a pain is a C-fiber firing, which causes an exclamation of "ouch!" and possibly some writhing. Depending on the circumstances, it might lead also to subsequent change in behavior.

Strict naturalism has the advantage of being theoretically lean and parsimonious. There are no "spooky things," like ghosts and feelings, to clutter one's ontology. The problem is that this extreme form of naturalism seems to deny the obvious. It is one thing to deny the existence of souls construed as immaterial substances that somehow mysteriously interact with the physical body. Immaterial substances are theoretically problematic, and it is not obvious that they really exist. Consciousness is another matter; it seems plausible to think that thinking exists. Anyone can introspectively recognize the undeniable fact of one's own consciousness. I cannot introspectively intuit my own or anyone else's mind as an immaterial substance, but I can know introspectively that I am conscious, that I feel pleasure and pain, and that I can think about myself, my surroundings, my past experiences, and other people (even if I am not sure what the "I" is). I also have goals, make plans, deliberate about how best to execute them, and finally decide on a course of action. Most people acknowledge that beliefs and desires have

---

14. Churchland, *Matter and Consciousness*, 30–34.

some effect on their behavior. The cause of my actions is sometimes my own beliefs and desires. I can have a purpose for what I do; I can act for the sake of an end. My desire to fulfill a purpose plays a causal role in bringing about the desired result. This is all too obvious, but it does not fit into the strict naturalist metaphysics.

A slightly less extreme naturalistic theory of mind is identity theory, or reductive materialism. Reductive materialism affirms the existence and causal efficacy of consciousness and mental states, but regards them as reducible to, or identical with, physical processes in the brain and nervous system. Reductive materialism admits the existence of mental states but not an immaterial mental substance, such as the mind or soul. Consciousness and mental states exist, but every mental state is identical with some process in the brain. A feeling of pain or a thought about something is just the same thing as a specific brain process. Mental states not only exist, but since they are identical with brain processes, they are physical and have causal powers.

A major difficulty with attempts to reduce consciousness to something more fundamental is that consciousness has a way of always reappearing, like the monsters in old horror movies. Reduction is a way of showing that something is explainable in terms of something more fundamental, and so it really is that more fundamental thing and not what it appears to be. For instance, the phenomenon of light is explainable in terms of electromagnetic waves of a certain range of frequencies and wavelengths. So light is not really what it appears to be in our perception of it; it is really electromagnetic waves. The way light appears to us, which seems much different than electromagnetic waves, is not how it really is—it is rather how it appears to our *consciousness*. If a biochemist reduces the phenomenon of love to a complex set of neurological processes in the brain, she is saying that love is not really that "crazy little thing" that you experience when you "fall in" it. Love is really a complex set of neurological and electrochemical processes, not what it appears to be in one's conscious experience. Now if one tries the same trick with consciousness, by reducing it to brain processes, then what does one say about what is left after the reduction is accomplished? Consciousness is a set of brain processes, not really what it appears to be—that rich, multifaceted complex of phenomena, which seems to exist in *consciousness*? Now, what is the thing that takes consciousness to be something other than brain processes? After consciousness is reduced to physical processes in the brain, what can be said about that something or other, to which it seemed that consciousness is something other than brain processes? Isn't it precisely to consciousness that consciousness appeared to be something different from a physical process? Without consciousness it is hard to make sense of what it is to which the brain processes appeared to be something nonphysical.

Identity theory faces other problems. One is that some naturalists are skeptical that there must be, or that we can possibly know that there is, a one-to-one correspondence between every mental state and a specific process in the brain. A more serious problem is the manifest difference between mental states and physical processes. Mental states do not take up space or have mass, and they are not measurable. Mental states are private; each conscious individual has privileged access to her own private thoughts and feelings. We can observe another person's brain processes but not her mental states. First-person subjectivity, a hallmark of the mental, is irreducible to third-person descriptions of neurological events. Knowledge of a complete description of the neurophysiological processes involved in vision is not the same thing as seeing. A person born blind who had complete knowledge of the neurophysiology of vision would not thereby know what it is like to see.[15] If such a person were to gain vision, she would thereby gain new knowledge not already possessed. Complete knowledge of the neurophysiology of a bat's brain and sensory organs does not constitute knowledge of what it is like to be a bat from the bat's subjective point of view.[16]

Many naturalists recognize the difficulties associated with the rejection of the existence of consciousness as anything beyond brain processes, even if they are unwilling to countenance the existence of God or the soul. Naturalists who admit the existence of irreducible mental states are sometimes called "broad naturalists."[17] There are various versions of broad naturalism that acknowledge that consciousness is not reducible to brain processes, that irreducible mental states really exist, and that they are fundamentally different from physical properties. One problem with views of this kind is that once the mental is not identified with physical processes in the brain, in the context of naturalism, it loses its causal powers. For naturalism, all causes are physical. If mental states are not reducible to something physical, like brain processes, then they are causally impotent. In the context of naturalism, without a mental substance, thoughts, beliefs, and desires are mere epiphenomena. They are produced by physical processes in the brain, but they do not affect the brain, and thus do not affect behavior. The causal interaction between mind and brain is a one-way street; the brain affects consciousness, but consciousness does not affect the brain.

This is a problem for naturalism. If mental states lack causal powers, their claim to existence is called into question, since for naturalism

---

15. This point is similar to that made in Frank Jackson's famous knowledge argument. See Jackson, "What Mary Didn't Know."

16. Nagel, "What Is It Like to Be a Bat?"

17. See Goetz and Taliaferro, *Naturalism*, 50–52.

everything that exists must be causally interconnected. According to naturalism, consciousness, if it exists, is the product of evolution. Natural selection would select and preserve consciousness only if consciousness somehow improves an organism's chance of surviving long enough to reproduce. It is hard to see how consciousness contributes to survival if it has no effect on an organism's behavior. The neurological processes that affect behavior could do just as well without the organism being conscious of anything, if consciousness is not really doing any of the work of adapting to the hazards of the world. Why would brains evolve in such a way as to become conscious if consciousness does not causally contribute anything? And how can nature produce effects that cannot themselves become causes? Consciousness becomes, on this naturalist view of it, a causal cul-de-sac, which would be inconsistent with the complete causal interconnectedness of everything in nature. An existing phenomenon in the natural world that plays no causal role in the course of nature seems not only incompatible with naturalism but also incompatible with any view of reality that regards it as a rationally ordered, causally interconnected whole.

One of the difficulties with substance dualism (the view that the mind is an entity distinct from the brain), which is supposed by materialists to be fatal, is the problem of two-way causal interaction of mind and brain. If mind is a mental substance with no properties in common with matter, then it is difficult to see how mind and matter can causally interact. How can mental states such as beliefs and desires possibly affect anything in the brain? The radical difference between mental substance and physical substance seems to preclude causal interaction. On the other hand, if two-way causal interaction between the mental and the physical is impossible, how is one-way causal interaction possible? How can the purely physical brain cause consciousness to come into existence? If consciousness is not physical, then how it can be produced by brain processes (or any other physical process) seems just as problematic for naturalism as the interaction problem is for substance dualism. This is one reason that strict naturalists think that their version of naturalism is more defensible than broad naturalism, for it dispenses with the real existence of consciousness as a thing to be explained. For the theist, on the other hand, the denial of the existence of mental states altogether seems more drastic and problematic than affirming the reality of an immaterial mind. In the context of a theistic worldview, which holds that the ground of being is a spiritual reality, the existence of a spiritual aspect of the human person is not implausible. Science does not prove that an immaterial reality cannot exist, and the naturalist's strongest reason for denying the supernatural is the success of science in providing naturalistic explanations and the alleged failure of supernaturalism to provide any explanations at all. Even so, naturalism has thus far failed to explain mind and seems unlikely ever to do so. The fact that theism, which Forrest admits is a logically possible view, affirms the reality of a supernatural, spiritual being, the existence of which would explain the possibility of human persons having immaterial minds, would seem to negate the defect that Forrest alleges supernaturalism to have, and constitute a major advantage of theism over naturalism as a worldview.

PLANTINGA'S ARGUMENT AGAINST NATURALISM

Alvin Plantinga[18] has argued that naturalism is self-refuting because its claims about the cognitive faculties of human beings undercut the possibility of rational justification of truth claims generally and the naturalistic thesis in particular. The naturalist's story about how human beings came into existence involves biological evolution governed by random variations and natural selection. The cognitive faculties of human beings were selected because they made them more competitive in the struggle for survival in an environment of limited resources. However, the adaptation to the environment of our cognitive faculties does not necessarily coincide with the truth conduciveness of their use. The behaviors and faculties that enable an organism to acquire food, protect itself against predators, attract mates, and move about in its environment, need not at all have the tendency to generate beliefs that accurately represent reality. So if our cognitive faculties were the product of evolution, there would be no justification for thinking that they are reliable mechanisms for the formation of true beliefs.

The naturalist who believes that her own cognitive faculties are the product of Darwinian evolution thus has a defeater for her belief that naturalism is true. A defeater of a belief is a proposition that is such that if the holder of the original belief became aware of it, she would no longer hold the original belief. Plantinga argues that if our cognitive faculties are the product of unguided evolution, we are not rationally justified in believing that they are reliable. The combination of naturalism and evolution entails that our cognitive faculties are unreliable. So anyone who accepts naturalism and evolution has a defeater for all of her beliefs that are produced by her cognitive faculties, including her belief that naturalism and evolution are true. Here is Plantinga's argument:

1. The probability that our cognitive faculties are reliable, given naturalism and evolution, is low.

18. Plantinga, *Where the Conflict Really Lies*, ch. 10.

2. One who accepts naturalism and evolution and recognizes that they imply that the probability that our cognitive faculties are reliable is low has a defeater for the assumption that her cognitive faculties are reliable.
3. This defeater cannot be defeated.
4. One who has an undefeated defeater for the belief that her cognitive faculties are reliable thereby has a defeater for any belief that is produced by those same cognitive faculties, including the belief that naturalism and evolution are true.
5. Therefore, naturalism and evolution are self-defeating and cannot be rationally accepted.[19]

The basic point of the first premise of the argument is that if our cognitive faculties—our senses, memory, reasoning ability—were the product of Darwinian evolution, governed by purely natural processes, the probability of the faculties being reliable mechanisms for forming true beliefs would be low. The cognitive faculties are, according to the naturalistic story, identical with or caused by neurological processes in the brain and nervous system, but it is the neurology that determines behavior and plays the adaptive role required by evolution. The cognitive content of mental states, such as beliefs that could in principle be true or false, plays no causal role in determining behavior. Neurological processes produce behavior that is favored by natural selection insofar as it enables the organism to survive and reproduce. Whether the beliefs that are also the product of those neurological processes are true or false is irrelevant to whether the behavior produced by them improves the organism's chances of survival. So there is no rational justification for thinking that cognitive faculties produced by Darwinian evolution would be reliable instruments for arriving at true beliefs. The truth of beliefs is irrelevant to the effectiveness of neurological processes for producing adaptive behavior. The causal chain from neurology to adaptive behavior does not include reliably truth conducive belief forming processes. So from the standpoint of naturalistic evolution, the probability of our beliefs being true is low. If we believe that the probability is low that our belief forming faculties are reliable in leading us to truth, then that belief is a defeater of all our beliefs, including the belief that naturalism and Darwinian evolution are true. Belief that naturalism is true becomes a defeater for all our beliefs, including the belief that naturalism is true.

Plantinga defends the critical first premise of the argument by emphasizing that natural selection selects for adaptive features and behavior,

19. Paraphrased from Dennett and Plantinga, *Science and Religion*, 17.

not truth conduciveness. He writes, "But natural selection doesn't give a fig for true beliefs as such. It rewards adaptive behavior and punishes maladaptive behavior, but it doesn't care about truth of belief; as Patricia Churchland says, 'Truth, whatever that is, definitely takes the hindmost.'"[20] If our belief-forming faculties were produced by purely naturalistic, non-purposive processes involved in Darwinian evolution, there would be no reason to think that the beliefs produced by such processes are likely to be true. So the naturalist is not justified in believing that naturalism is true; her commitment to naturalism is self-defeating. It should be emphasized that Plantinga's argument is not an argument against evolution—it is an argument against naturalism.

Critics of Plantinga's argument argue that true beliefs are more beneficial than false beliefs, but this is not always the case. While it is true that a true belief about whether a certain plant is nutritious or toxic will improve an organism's chance of survival, in a wide range of circumstances false beliefs may be no less advantageous. An attitude toward an object that increases an organism's chance of survival—to eat it, flee from it, mate with it, kill it, hide behind it—need have little to do with describing it accurately, much less knowing its essential nature. Natural selection selects for changes that increase the odds of survival. Survival, not truth, is the goal of evolution. The interest in evolutionary explanations of religion and religious belief shows that evolutionary naturalists recognize that truth conduciveness is not on natural selection's agenda. A theory that religious beliefs and practices were selected by evolution because they increase a group's tendency toward behaviors that have survival value does not tempt the typical evolutionary biologist to cite this benefit as evidence of the truthfulness of religion. To the contrary, such theories are typically cited as explanations of religion that have the effect of debunking it. Daniel Dennett's elaborate evolutionary explanation of religion recognizes the survival value of religion, but he takes the success of the evolutionary explanation to be more of a debunking of religion than a justification of its truth.[21] The same point could be made about an evolutionary account of our cognitive faculties. Oddly enough, an explanation of the evolutionary origin of the human sense organs, brain, and cognitive faculties does not typically result in a science-debunking argument that these faculties were selected for their survival value and not for their tendency to generate true beliefs about the real world.

---

20. Quoted by Plantinga in Dennett and Plantinga, *Science and Religion*, 19. It is worth noting the Churchland is a strict naturalist.

21. See Dennett, *Breaking the Spell*.

It is true that most scientists seem to find no reason to be skeptical of the veracity of our cognitive faculties on the basis of an evolutionary account of their origin. Like everyone else, they accept the reliability of our senses and reason at face value. Even if they recognize a difficulty in fully explaining how evolution selected characteristics that enable us to do science, the lack of an explanation, they believe, is no cause for skeptical alarm. I agree that they should not become skeptics about our cognitive faculties, but they would be well advised to become more skeptical of naturalism. Naturalism teaches that blind nature governed by nothing but the laws of nature is the creator of our cognitive faculties, and it is very difficult to see how our faculties would be reliable engines for producing true beliefs if naturalism were true.

Materialistic naturalism makes it impossible to account for the possibility of knowing that naturalism is true. Naturalism implies that rational thought is ultimately explainable entirely in terms of physical processes in the brain. Physical processes in the brain are, according to materialists, governed by physical laws. When a scientist ventures beyond his scientific investigations to make an argument for materialism, he will present some premises and deduce a conclusion from them. He might construct an argument like the following:

1. All things that exist are governed by the laws of physics.
2. All things that are governed by the laws of physics are made of matter.
3. Therefore, all things that exist are made of matter.

Perhaps this is not a great argument, but the point is not to suggest that this is the best argument a materialist has for materialism. It is simply to have an example on hand to make a point. This is an argument; it has two premises and a conclusion. The materialist who uses this argument, or any other, to arrive at the belief that materialism is true, is proceeding from premises to a conclusion by a process that is governed by the laws of logic, not the laws of physics. No doubt the processes going on in our materialist's brain, which admittedly are governed entirely by physical laws, are somehow correlated with the logical deduction that she is consciously thinking through. Clearly, the process of thinking through a logical deduction and arriving at a conclusion that is entailed by other statements that serve as premises of an argument follows different rules than the physical laws that govern the processes involved in the firing of neurons in the brain. The rules of the syllogism that determine the validity of the inference and lead the arguer to arrive at the correct conclusion are very different from the physical laws that govern the processes in the inquirer's brain. The attempt to reduce rational thought to brain processes fails to recognize the crucial role of the normativity of the rules of logic to determine the validity of the inference and to cause the drawing of the conclusion. Believing that materialism is true because one has reasoned through a logical argument for it is fundamentally different from believing that materialism is true solely because certain neurons fired in the brain. The validity of the inference and the justification of the belief based on it are not determined by the physical process in the brain that is governed entirely by the laws of physics. If one arrives at a belief as the result of a logical inference, one has mental states consisting in beliefs that the premises are true, awareness of a logical connection between the premises and the conclusion, the inference to the conclusion, and the resulting belief that the premise is true. This mental process is a very different kind of process, governed by a different kind of rules, than physical processes in the brain, even though the mental process is correlated with brain processes.[22]

If the complete explanation of the materialist coming to the belief that materialism is true, as it must be according to materialism, is the process in her brain that is purely physical and governed by the laws of physics, then there is no reason to think that the belief arrived at by that process is true. Of course the same point can be made about any belief arrived at by a rational inference. Why does the materialist believe that materialism is true? According to the materialist's own belief about the causes of belief, it is because certain neurons firing in his brain caused him to form the belief that materialism is true. Of course, if Darwinism is correct, the brain's capacity to do what it does is the product of millions of years of evolution governed principally by random variation and natural selection. Additionally, what natural selection favors are processes that increase the capacity of an organism to adapt to its environment so that it can survive long enough to reproduce. The long evolutionary story that explains our materialist's brain process that caused the belief that materialism is true would have no necessary or probable connection to the truth of the statement affirming materialism or to the logic of a valid argument for materialism. If knowledge is rationally justified true belief and if materialism is true, it is hard to see how anyone could be justified in believing that materialism is true, or anything at all, for that matter. The belief that materialism is true, according to materialism itself, would be caused by neurological processes in the brain that are the product of biological evolution. There is little reason to think

---

22. This argument is essentially a version of the argument from reason, which has roots that go back to Plato. For modern versions see Lewis, *Mere Christianity*; Reppert, *C. S. Lewis's Dangerous Idea* and "The Argument from Reason"; and Goetz and Taliaferro, *Naturalism*, 117–22.

that this kind of process would reliably track the logical structure of a rigorous argument for the truth of materialism.

There is a certain irony in the fact that many scientific naturalists accuse religious believers of arriving at their beliefs by nonrational processes, given that naturalism undercuts the possibility of the rational justification of any belief, including the naturalist's own belief that naturalism is true, while theism provides a metaphysical framework that helps us make sense of the fundamental reality of mind, and hence the possibility of the human mind arriving at beliefs by processes governed by reason and not reducible to physical processes subject to only physical causation.

Michael Ruse, in responding to Plantinga, admits that if our cognitive faculties are the product of Darwinian evolution then we cannot be rationally justified in believing they reliably give us knowledge of objective truth about what the world is like. He writes, "all our knowledge comes through our human faculties. If they distort reality, so be it. The best we can have is some kind of coherence theory of truth rather than strict correspondence theory—the best we can do is make all our judgments hold together coherently."[23] I appreciate Ruse's recognition that naturalism cannot account for the possibility of knowledge of propositions that correspond to reality. If the brain processes that give rise to scientific thinking are determined entirely by physical laws, I do not think we can count on them tracking the logical laws that are required for coherence any more than we can count on them producing beliefs that correspond to the way the world is. If we cannot be justified in thinking that our beliefs correspond with reality, then we cannot know that reality is as naturalism says that it is. Naturalism makes it unexplainable how knowledge of objective truth about the world is possible. Barbara Forrest celebrates the superiority of naturalism over supernaturalism in explaining natural phenomena within the world, but it seems that naturalism fails to explain how its explanations can be true.

Metaphysical naturalism suffers from the deficiency of being unknowable, given its own account of the source of our cognitive faculties. So it must ultimately be an article of faith for the scientifically oriented thinker who accepts it. Theism and naturalism are both worldviews that we cannot justify scientifically. Both are to some degree articles of faith. This might seem to put them on equal footing. We are faced with two theoretical frameworks, neither of which can be proven. I contend that theism is actually in the more favorable position. Both theism and naturalism stand as presuppositions that cannot be proven scientifically, but which provide theoretical frameworks through which one can pursue rational inquiry and make some

---

23. Ruse, "The Naturalist Challenge to Religion," 432.

sense of the world. Both are essentially articles of faith for those who accept them, but the theist acknowledges that her belief in God is accepted by faith and not ultimately provable. However, it need not be a blind faith. Explicitly rejecting scientism and naturalism, the theist is open to other possible sources of reason-giving to support her belief system. She is open to moral experience, religious experience, aesthetic experience, and a wide range of cultural and spiritual resources to find insights that may provide support for her beliefs. Theism enjoys support in virtue of its explanatory power in helping make sense of how these spiritual aspects of our experience are possible, while naturalism is helpless in accounting for them being other than illusory. What the naturalist has is a worldview that cannot be rationally justified by science, that as a matter of ideological commitment denies itself any other intellectual resources, and that fails to explain aspects of ourselves that are essential and central to our humanity. Naturalists are committed to a worldview that cannot be justified by scientific evidence, the only way of justifying belief that is acceptable to the naturalist. The naturalist's self-imposed restrictions deny her access to sources of insight beyond science, to which the religious believer may avail herself without deviating from her basic epistemological or metaphysical assumptions. So the theist is in a much more favorable and rational position.

THEISM AND MORALITY

Perhaps the areas in which a theistic worldview enjoys the greatest advantage over naturalism are those that have to do with providing a context for making sense of personhood and the normative dimension of human existence, including morality. Of course metaphysical naturalists have theories about how moral values are explainable in terms of evolution. It is easy to see that moral behavior has an adaptive advantage for groups whose survival depends on cooperation and social solidarity. Evolutionary psychology may provide plausible evolutionary explanations of the moral beliefs and behavior, but it is hard to see how such theories can explain the normative dimension of moral values. They cannot explain the sense in which moral judgments can be objectively true. The truth of the normative judgment that murder is wrong is more than just the fact that social groups that find ways to reinforce the prohibition of murder are more likely to survive.

Ruse sees the difficulty that naturalism has in explaining morality. He acknowledges that naturalism cannot explain the objective truth of moral statements, and the most about morality that it might accomplish is to explain in terms of evolutionary psychology the adaptive advantage of moral beliefs. He writes, "So in a sense, morality is an illusion—or at least our sense that morality is objective is an illusion, because my feelings are certainly not illusory. But why all of this? Because if we did not think morality is objective, before long it would break down as we began cheating.... the objectivity of morality that is—is an illusion put in place by our biology to make us social animals, because social animals are selected over nonsocial animals."[24] Ruse realizes, along with G. E. Moore, that objectively real moral values are not natural entities. They are not made of matter. They are nonnatural in the sense that they are not explainable in terms of purely materialistic natural processes and laws. As Hume argues, you cannot logically derive statements about what one ought to do from statements about matters of fact. In rejecting the supernatural, naturalism rejects moral values as anything more than illusions that improve our chances of surviving long enough to reproduce.

Neuroscientist and naturalist Sam Harris claims to have a naturalistic account of objective moral values. For him morality is a matter of promoting human well-being, which can be described with objectively true statements. He writes, "Questions about values—about meaning, morality, and life's larger purpose—are really questions about the well-being of conscious creatures. Values, therefore, translate into facts that can be scientifically understood." Harris argues that the scientific study of morality must be possible because the subject matter of morality is reality. "[H]uman well-being entirely depends on events in the world and on states of the human brain. Consequently, there must be scientific truths to be known about it."[25] Harris writes that "in speaking of 'moral truth,' I am saying that there must be facts regarding human animal well-being."[26] "Questions about values ... are really questions about the well-being of conscious creatures."[27] Well-being is defined hedonistically as pleasure and satisfaction of desires and needs. Science can tell us what human well-being consists of and what kinds of actions promote human well-being. Morality is about acting in ways that promote well-being. Thus morality does not require a nonnatural foundation.

It is true that science can tell us what kinds of actions promote human well-being, but unfortunately for Harris's theory, science does not justify the proposition that anyone is morally obligated to promote the well-being of other human beings. Harris has not solved the "value problem." He has not shown how facts about conscious beings, brains, and behavior can logically

24. Ruse, "The Naturalist Challenge to Religion," 431.
25. Harris, *The Moral Landscape*, 2.
26. Harris, *The Moral Landscape*, 31.
27. Harris, *The Moral Landscape*, 1.

generate propositions about what is morally right and wrong and what persons are morally obligated to do, or account for the ground of moral obligation. Of course a naturalist like Ruse denies that there is objective moral truth for which we need an account. For the theist, this is too high a price to pay. Once again we see that naturalism compels a rejection of what seems obviously true to common sense.

So morality is yet another important aspect of human experience that makes more sense in the context of theism than naturalism. A Christian theistic worldview provides a philosophical framework that has more explanatory power than naturalism for dealing with a "range of important phenomena," and which are very difficult to explain within the confines of naturalism. Michael Peterson lists the following examples: consciousness and self-consciousness, mind and rationality, truth, personhood, free will and responsibility, morality, agency, value, biological evolution, and science.[28] It is very difficult to see how mind can be explained in terms of the movements of particles of matter. Even a naturalist like "Searle frankly admits that the biological sciences have no idea how consciousness arose from non-conscious matter."[29] The existence of life, mind, persons with free will and moral agency, etc. is improbable and surprising in a world of nothing but matter and energy. From the standpoint of theism it is not at all surprising that God, acting through nature, should produce beings like us, with the intellectual and spiritual characteristics we have. Theism has more explanatory power than naturalism insofar as theism provides a metaphysical framework that makes it less surprising (than does naturalism) that we should find in the world these marvelous features that intractably resist naturalistic explanation and the existence of which seem vastly improbable from the perspective of naturalism. Theism does not explain in detail particular phenomena in the way that natural science does, but the richness of its ontology provides a plausible candidate for the cause of the features of the world that naturalism seems incapable of explaining.

FAITH AND REASON

One of Richard Dawkins's main criticisms of religion is that it grants permission to believe doctrines without evidence. Dawkins defines faith as

---

28. Peterson, "The Encounter between Naturalistic Atheism and Christian Theism," 444.

29. Peterson, "The Encounter between Naturalistic Atheism and Christian Theism," 446.

believing propositions to be true without evidence,[30] and much of his hostility toward religion is due to his moral condemnation of this irrational aspect, which he attributes to all religious belief. For Dawkins one of the reasons science is incompatible with religion is that the scientific method is committed to basing its conclusions on evidence, while religion is based on faith, which is the willingness to believe irrationally, without evidence. Dawkins argues that the scientific commitment to rationality, empirical inquiry, and the open quest for truth is fundamentally opposed to the religious mind-set, which is based on blind faith, dogmatism, reliance on the authority of sacred texts, and closed-minded commitment to one point of view. For Dawkins, science represents enlightened, objective, open-minded rational pursuit of truth, and religion represents the opposite—blind faith and irrational clinging to a closed system of belief for the sake of emotional comfort and self-satisfaction. Religious belief is based on a refusal to be an adult and think for oneself. Religion is a major impediment to human progress, which depends on the rational pursuit of truth. Of course, the implied normative claim here entails objective values that are difficult to account for in the context of naturalism.

Dawkins greatly exaggerates the difference between science and religion with respect to the issue of faith and the reliance on evidence. David Hume argued that all our beliefs of matters of fact rest on assumptions that we cannot rationally justify, such as the principle of cause and effect and the reliability of induction.[31] As is now well understood by philosophers of science since the publication of Thomas Kuhn's *The Structure of Scientific Revolutions*,[32] scientific thought is never purely objective and always involves a commitment to fundamental assumptions that are not rationally justified or based on evidence. Scientists and religious believers alike are subject to irrational bias and a reluctance to be open to alternative points of view. Some religious believers are narrow-minded and dogmatic; others are relentless in their examination of arguments that challenge their faith. Many scientists are religious, and many religious believers are fully committed to the scientific enterprise and open to the rational examination of the intellectual problems. The frequently heard charge that religious belief is based on blind faith is based on a lack of knowledge of how many religious believers come to their faith, which often involves serious intellectual reflection. On the other hand, many scientists and nonscientists impressed with the prestige of science are quite committed to propositions accepted by the

---

30. Dawkins, *The God Delusion*, 347–48.
31. Hume, *Enquiry Concerning Human Understanding*, 31–37.
32. Kuhn, *The Structure of Scientific Revolution*.

scientific community, for which they themselves lack understanding of the rational grounds. In some instances these commitments are articles of faith in philosophical presuppositions that lack scientific justification. Some of these philosophical assumptions, such as the assumption of naturalism and materialism, are not only held as articles of faith without rational justification, but are incompatible not only with religious realism, but also with scientific realism.[33]

As many religious thinkers have pointed out, faith need be neither blind nor devoid of evidence. Many religious believers engage in vigorous intellectual examination of the grounds and implications of their faith. All the great religions of the world have robust intellectual traditions. Consider Thomas Aquinas's *Summa Theologica*, which is not a credo of personal beliefs accepted by blind faith, but is a colossus of arguments and counterarguments offered in support of answers to a long series of serious questions that confront the thoughtful Christian believer. Its scope, rigor, sophistication, and profundity dwarf the critiques of religion offered by Dawkins, Dennett, and Harris.

Religious believers can, should, and often do engage in intellectual reflection on the intellectual issues that challenge their belief system. There is nothing about the five essential core propositions of Christianity listed by Ratzsche that is contradictory to science, and there is nothing about a person's believing them that would indicate irrationality on the part of that person. Finding support for the coherence and credibility of a system of beliefs that includes them is a complicated business, and a great deal of intellectual energy has already been expended toward that end over the history of Christian thought. Given that naturalism is unprovable, its adoption is an article of faith as surely as is the adoption of a theistic perspective. The adoption of an article of faith is more unfortunate for the naturalist than for the theist, since it is the naturalist who so emphatically disparages reliance on faith, while the theist acknowledges its unavoidability. Both naturalism and the theistic worldview can be intellectually tested by considering how well they help us make sense of a wide range of human experiences. Naturalism, naturally, scores very well in explaining aspects of the world that are explainable in naturalistic terms. The theistic worldview is more successful in providing an intellectual framework and background beliefs that enable us to make sense of aspects of our experience that seem to involve something other than matter in motion.

33. By "religious realism" I mean the view that at least some of the main concepts of religion, such as God, refer to something that actually exists independently of the human mind. By "scientific realism" I mean the view that good scientific theories attempt to describe the real nature of things, which exist independently of the mind.

The methods of natural science have difficulty in accounting for the justification of normative judgments, including judgments about moral rightness and wrongness, justice, beauty, and even the norms that are necessary for the conduct of science itself. Science can tell you how to make a bomb but not whether it is morally justified to use it. Science cannot justify normative claims. Hume, a favorite philosopher of naturalists, argued that it is impossible to justify a statement about what one ought to do from empirical statements about what is the case.[34] Science cannot tell us what we ought to do. So the view that only science gives us knowledge excludes not only religion, but also morality and values, some of which are necessary conditions of the possibility of science itself. If the naturalist rejects religion because it falls outside of science, she presumably thinks that she *ought* to reject it, and that others should too. Indeed, naturalists are often quite emphatic in their insistence that everyone ought to reject religion. This is a normative judgment, not scientifically justified. Consistency would require that the naturalist also reject the objective truth of moral statements generally and the idea that one ought to follow the evidence where it leads, which is itself a normative judgment and a favorite maxim of scientists. Of course this argument assumes the value of consistency as a canon of rationality and the epistemic obligation to think rationally. Science presumably must accept the laws of logic and the requirement of logical consistency as essential to the scientific enterprise. However, the laws of logic and the claim that scientific propositions must be logically consistent with each other are not themselves subject to scientific verification by sufficient empirical evidence. They can be justified philosophically as necessary conditions of the possibility of science, but they are not justifiable by empirical science itself.

The complaint against the religious believer that she bases belief on blind faith rather than evidence assumes that believers ought to base belief on evidence. This is a normative judgment; it is based on the assumption that one *ought* to be reasonable, one *ought* to have support for one's beliefs. This is the kind of statement that Hume said could not be justified by inference from the factual statements of science. Value judgments cannot be justified by scientific evidence. When one condemns the religious believer for believing without having evidence, one is assuming a normative standard that cannot be justified within the limits of the epistemic resources of natural science. The critic of religion is assuming a normative standard for which she does not have scientific justification. The critic thus believes without sufficient evidence that the religious believer has committed an epistemic violation, but in so doing commits the same violation of which she accuses

---

34. Hume, *A Treatise of Human Nature*, 468.

the believer. Now this does not show that the religious believer is warranted in her belief, but it does show that the scientist is not justified on the basis of scientific methodology in claiming that there is something wrong with religious affirmation of the existence of things beyond natural science, for indeed the scientist must do so as well. The religious believer need not be guilty of the charge of blind faith (although admittedly some may be), but the scientist is, insofar as she makes assumptions that are necessary for her critique of religious belief, and which are themselves not scientifically justifiable.

Science by itself, without the assumptions of naturalism, is not incompatible with religion. Science does not require naturalism; indeed, naturalism is not only incompatible with religion, but also with science. Science neither shows that religious belief is irrational nor that supernatural entities do not exist. Science does not rule out the possibility that there exists some ultimate, transcendent, sacred reality that is the ultimate ground of all that exists and to which human beings may become related in some way in order to attain the greatest good that is possible for them to attain.

Worldviews are not provable, but they are subject to rational assessment. Naturalism is also a worldview, which is not provably true, and it is not required by science. The view that the universe is intelligible and comprehensible to human reason is consistent with the claim that the universe was created by an all-powerful, supremely intelligent God. The possibility of science is consistent with theism. Naturalism as a worldview is much more difficult to harmonize with the intelligibility of the universe and the comprehensibility of the universe to us than is theism. Atheist and naturalist philosopher Thomas Nagel thinks that a purely materialistic form of naturalism of the sort that is currently fashionable has no chance of explaining the origin of life, consciousness, cognition, and the existence of objectively real values.[35] Nagel argues that in order to make sense of how nature could produce beings like ourselves we need a teleological form of naturalism. We need a conception of nature that sees in nature a "bias toward the marvelous," an inherent tendency to produce life, mind, and value. The purely materialistic conception of nature, governed solely by the laws of physics, cannot account for this inherent teleological aspect that is required in order to explain the bias toward the marvelous. Nagel considers theism as an alternative to materialism, but he thinks that theism fares no better than materialism in making intelligible our connection to nature and how nature produced us. He admits that theism provides an explanation of how nature produced us, but he thinks that theism

---

35. Nagel, *Mind and Cosmos*, 91.

does not do so in the form of a comprehensive account of the natural order. Theism pushes the quest for intelligibility outside the world. If God exists, he is not part of the natural order but a free agent not governed by natural laws. He may act partly by creating a natural order, but whatever he does directly cannot be part of that order. A theistic self-understanding . . . would not be the kind of understanding that explains *how* beings like us fit into the world. The kind of intelligibility that would still be missing is intelligibility of the natural order itself—intelligibility from within.[36]

Nagel hopes for "a completely different type of systematic account of nature, one that makes [the marvelous features of universe, such as life, consciousness, reason, and values] neither brute facts that are beyond explanation nor the products of divine intervention."[37] He admits that this is his "ungrounded intellectual preference."[38] I can understand why someone with naturalist impulses would prefer a theory of nature that was able to reveal the intelligibility of nature from within and without appeal to anything beyond nature. Nagel also admits that we are a long way from any such theory. It might well be that nature is not fully intelligible in itself without conceiving it as dependent on a transcendent ground. As Stephen Barr emphasizes, theism is not only already here, but it has been around for millennia. Why not avail ourselves of the explanatory resources that theism gives us?

Nagel famously admits in *The Last Word* that he is afflicted with a fear of religion. He writes, "I want atheism to be true and am made uneasy by the fact that some of the most intelligent and well-informed people I know are religious believers. It isn't just that I don't believe in God and, naturally hope that I'm right in my belief. It's that I hope there is no God! I don't want the universe to be like that."[39] So Nagel has a personal preference for atheism and an account of nature that conceives of nature as completely intelligible in itself without dependence on a transcendent ground. If one does not share this personal preference for atheism over theism, then the greater explanatory power of theism over materialistic naturalism would make theism a more plausible option. There is virtually no prospect for materialistic naturalism explaining how nature produced beings with life, consciousness, rational minds, and moral values. Until an alternative form of naturalism

36. Nagel, *Mind and Cosmos*, 26.
37. Nagel, *Mind and Cosmos*, 26.
38. Nagel, *Mind and Cosmos*, 26.
39. Nagel, *The Last Word*, 130.

comes along, the available alternatives seem to be materialistic naturalism and theism, and of these, theism seems to be preferable.

Nagel's self-admitted hope that God does not exist helps explain his preference expressed in *Mind and Cosmos* for a nontheistic teleological form of naturalism over theism, which he acknowledges lacks strong rational support. This preference supports the claim that materialistic naturalism is an article of faith rather than a requirement of good science. An even more striking illustration of the faith component of worldview assumptions is the famous passage from Harvard geneticist Richard Lewontin's review of Carl Sagan's last book.

> Our willingness to accept scientific claims that are against common sense is the key to an understanding of the real struggle between science and the supernatural. We take the side of science in spite of the patent absurdity of some of its constructs, *in spite* of its failure to fulfill many of its extravagant promises of health and life, *in spite* of the tolerance of the scientific community for unsubstantiated just-so stories, because we have a prior commitment, a commitment to materialism. It is not that the methods and institutions of science somehow compel us to accept a material explanation of the phenomenal world, but, on the contrary, that we are forced by our a priori adherence to material causes to create an apparatus of investigation and a set of concepts that produce material explanations, no matter how counter-intuitive, no matter how mystifying to the uninitiated. Moreover, that materialism is absolute, for we cannot allow a Divine Foot in the door.[40]

The unwillingness to allow a Divine Foot in the door is a worldview choice, not a demand of science or rationality. Given that is not justified by science, commitment to it is a matter of faith as defined by Dawkins—belief in the absence of scientific evidence. There is no reason that a theist should feel compelled by logic to follow in this arbitrary choice to refuse to allow a Divine Foot in the door and keep God out of one's worldview.

---

40. Lewontin, "Billions and Billions of Demons," 31.

4
God and Big Bang Cosmology

One of the ways that adherents of diverse religions can dialogue with each other to work out the disagreements between them about the nature of the sacred, transcendent reality is to bring modern science into the discussion and consider the capacity of different religions to respond to science as well as to each other. Science is an enterprise that, while not culturally neutral, does cut across the boundaries between religions. Buddhist and Christian thinkers have engaged modern science and with each other about issues arising from modern science. While science does not directly address issues concerning God or a sacred, transcendent reality, some scientific discoveries have implications that are relevant to some religious doctrines, and some of these cut differently for different religions.

One of the most important scientific developments in the twentieth century that many scientists and philosophers believe has religious implications is the discovery of evidence suggesting that the universe began to exist some 13.8 billion years ago. Since before Aristotle, the dominant assumption of science with respect to the question of the origin of the universe has been that the universe is eternal, with no beginning and no end. The Law of Conservation of Energy, that matter/energy is neither created nor destroyed, seems to imply the eternal existence of the universe. If the universe exists eternally, with no beginning or end, then there is no need for a creator to account for its existence. However, the Big Bang theory calls into question the eternal existence of the universe and suggests that its existence did have a beginning.

Hugh Ross is an astronomer and Christian apologist who writes that his conversion from atheism to Christianity was triggered in part by his discovery that of all the sacred texts of the world religions, the Bible is the only one that is consistent with modern science.[1] Ross claims that the Bible is unique among sacred texts in explicitly teaching a doctrine of creation by a transcendent creator. Ross finds the doctrine of creation not only in the book of Genesis, but also in Job, Isaiah, and more than twenty other passages.[2] He notes also several passages in the Bible that speak of God spreading the heavens, which he interprets as anticipations of the discovery that the universe is expanding.[3] The doctrine of creation can be interpreted variously, and according to some interpretations creation may be thought of as radical dependence of the universe on God and not necessarily that the universe has an absolute beginning. However, a more straightforward reading of the idea of creation would be that it involves the universe being brought into existence by the creator in the finite past. Ross interprets creation as implying a beginning of the universe and argues that the Big Bang theory supports this. It can be argued that a beginning of time and the universe does not imply the absurdity of a time and an event before the beginning of time, but instead that the past is of finite duration and that there are no temporal events before the beginning of time. As Ross and William Lane Craig argue, this is consistent with the claim that the beginning of the universe must have been caused by a nontemporal, transcendent cause.

THE KALAM COSMOLOGICAL ARGUMENT

The classical "proofs" of the existence of God are widely assumed to have been decisively discredited since the days of Hume and Kant, but they have made a comeback in the last half of the twentieth century. There has been a resurgence of Christian philosophy since the 1960s, which has benefitted from scientific developments in the last hundred years that seem to be consistent with the idea that the universe was created by a supremely powerful, intelligent being. One of the most prominent atheist philosophers of the last half of the twentieth century, Anthony Flew, announced in 2004 that although he was still religiously agnostic, recent scientific discoveries had convinced him that the universe was probably created by a supremely powerful, intelligent being. Hugh Ross points out[4] that "Paul Davies has moved from promoting atheism to conceding that 'the laws [of physics] . . . seem themselves to be the product of exceedingly ingenious design.'"[5] He further

1. Ross, *The Creator and the Cosmos*, 18–19.
2. Ross, *The Creator and the Cosmos*, 24.
3. Ross, *The Creator and the Cosmos*, 24–25.
4. *Journey toward Creation*, DVD.
5. Davies, *Superforce*, 243.

testifies, 'There is for me powerful evidence that there is something going on behind it all . . . it seems as though somebody has fine-tuned nature's numbers to make the Universe. . . . The impression of design is overwhelming.'[6]

New life has been breathed into cosmological arguments for the existence of God by Christian responses to the Big Bang theory, the standard model of which entails that the universe began to exist in the finite past. William Lane Craig has resurrected a version of the cosmological argument first developed by medieval Islamic theologians, al-Kindi, Saadia, and al Ghazali.[7] Craig dubbed it the *kalam* cosmological argument, using the Arabic word for Islamic scholasticism. The *kalam* argument, unlike most other versions of the cosmological argument, has as one of its premises that the universe began to exist. Historically most Christian philosophers have not wanted to use the beginning of the universe as a premise for a cosmological argument because they did not think that this could be proven. Thomas Aquinas, who believed as an article of faith that the universe was brought into existence from nothing in the finite past, did not think this could be proved by natural reason, so he formulated his three versions of the cosmological argument without the premise that the universe began to exist. Mortimer Adler argues that the strongest version of the cosmological argument should grant the possibility that the universe is eternal.[8] On the other hand, Craig makes several arguments for the premise that the universe did begin to exist, one of which appeals to the Big Bang theory.

Here is Craig's formulation of the *kalam* cosmological argument.

1. Whatever begins to exist has a cause of its existence.
2. The universe began to exist.
3. Therefore, the universe has a cause of its existence.[9]

The universe includes the totality of nature—space, time, matter, energy, fields, and whatever else science might discover as components of the universe. Therefore, if the beginning of the universe needs a cause, that cause must be something other than the effect, so it must be something that transcends the totality of the universe itself. It cannot be a part of nature—matter, space, dark energy, the quantum vacuum, or some other exotic physical something—for all such things are components of the universe

---

6. Davies, *The Cosmic Blueprint*, 203.
7. Craig, *The Kalam Cosmological Argument*, 19–49.
8. Adler, *How to Think About God*, 40–42.
9. Craig, *Reasonable Faith*, 116.

and do not exist until the universe exists, and thus cannot be the beginning cause of the universe.

The *kalam* argument is a valid categorical syllogism. The first premise is hard to argue for, mainly because it seems so obviously true that any proposed argument to support it is likely to be less plausible than the premise itself. Even Hume, who famously challenged the possibility of knowledge of the principle of cause and effect and insisted that nothing prevents us from conceiving an "un-caused-coming-to-be of an object,"[10] wrote to John Stewart in 1754, "But allow me to tell you that I never asserted so absurd a Proposition as *that anything might arise without a cause* . . . ."[11] Although he held that the causal principle could not be proved either rationally or empirically, he believed that it was true. Craig thinks that it is self-evident and confirmed by ordinary experience that something cannot just come into existence without a cause. A person accused of murder will have little success in convincing the police that the weapon in the glove compartment of his car just came into existence without a cause. Scientists generally concede that things in the empirical world do not come into existence without causes, but some seem not so sure that the causal principle applies to the universe as a whole, especially if it is suggested that the universe came into existence from nothing.

Of course, in saying that everything that begins to exist has a cause for its existence, we don't mean to suggest that there is exactly one cause of each thing that begins to exist. By the cause of something beginning to exist we mean the totality of the necessary and sufficient conditions of the thing beginning to exist. Some critics of the *kalam* argument think that the first premise is undermined by the fact that causality is a very complicated notion and that the entire universe is a complex, causally interconnected matrix that encompasses the whole universe.[12] Of course the credibility of the *kalam* argument does not depend on there being just one cause of anything that begins to exist. Jonathan M. S. Pearce argues that this "ever morphing matrix of causality" encompasses the whole universe and is the cause of everything in the universe. When this fact about causality is taken into account, Pearce thinks that we get this transformation of the *kalam* argument, which is obviously circular:

1. Everything which begins to exist has *the universe as the causal condition for its existence.*

---

10. Mackie, *The Miracle of Theism*, 94.
11. Hume, *The Letters of David Hume*, 1:187.
12. See Pearce, *Did God Create the Universe from Nothing?*, ch. 1.

2. The universe began to exist.

3. *Therefore, the universe had the universe as a causal condition for its existence.*[13]

Pearce correctly states that this argument is "entirely circular and even incoherent," but is wrong in saying that "causality itself renders KCA [the *kalam* cosmological argument] problematic."[14] Even if we grant the questionable assumption that everything in the universe that begins to exist has the entire universe as its causal condition, it would not follow that the whole universe is self-caused—that the whole universe is the cause of the universe beginning to exist.

It might be argued that there is an important difference between things like houses and cars beginning to exist and the universe beginning to exist. The coming into existence of cars and houses involves a transformation of matter such as wood or steel into a different form; it does not involve a transition from nothing to something. So there may be an equivocation in the concept of beginning to exist as we move from cars and houses to the universe, if it is claimed that the universe originated from nothing. Furthermore, fans of Hume will emphasize the idea that our knowledge of cause and effect depends on experience, and while we have a lot of experience that supports our belief that cars, houses, and weapons do not come into existence without causes, we have no experience of universes coming into existence, so we may not be justified in saying "whatever begins to exist must have a cause of its existence." Maybe we are justified in saying this only about things within the material universe. If a beginning to exist that is a transformation of matter into a different form requires a cause, it is hard to see how the origination of something from nothing would not also require a cause. We will have more to say about this issue later; for now let's assume that whatever begins to exist must have a cause, whether the beginning involves transformation of matter to a different form, or the origination of something from nothing, and that the first premise of the *kalam* argument applies to the universe.

The second premise of the *kalam* argument is much more difficult to justify. Our primary interest here is the scientific evidence for the second premise based on the Big Bang theory, but Craig also gives a philosophical argument based on the claim that an actual infinite is impossible. If the universe did not begin to exist, is eternal, and has always existed, then there has already occurred an actual infinite number of past events. Craig argues

---

13. Pearce, *Did God Create the Universe from Nothing?*, 22. Emphasis in original.
14. Pearce, *Did God Create the Universe from Nothing?*, 23.

that this is impossible because if you assume the possibility of an actual infinite, various absurd consequences follow. Craig notes that the medieval Muslim theologian al Ghazali observed that the planet Jupiter orbits the sun in about twelve years while it takes Saturn about thirty years.[15] So in a given block of time, Jupiter will have orbited the sun more than twice as many times as Saturn. However, if the universe has no beginning and Jupiter and Saturn have been orbiting the sun forever in the past, then the number of orbits for each is infinite and thus equal to each other. This is paradoxical.

Another argument involves Hilbert's Hotel, the thought experiment devised by the mathematician David Hilbert. Suppose the hotel has an infinite number of rooms, and all the rooms are occupied. So it would seem that there is no vacancy, but another person arrives at the hotel in need of a room, and the clever clerk divines a way of accommodating the new guest. He asks the guest in room no. 1 to move to room no. 2, which allows the new guest to take room no. 1. The guest who was originally in room no. 2 moves to room no. 3, the guest who was in room no. 3 moves to room no. 4, and so on. Since there are an infinite number of rooms, we will never run out of rooms into which to move the guests. And it is not just one new guest that can be accommodated—any number of new guests up to infinity will be able to find a room in Hilbert's Hotel. Suppose an infinite number of new guests want a room in the hotel. Move the guest in room no. 1 to room no. 2, the guest in room no. 2 to room no. 4, the guest in room no. 3 to room no. 6, the guest in room no. 5 to room no. 10, and so on. The infinite number of original guests are thus moved to the infinity of even numbered rooms, leaving the odd numbered rooms for the new guests. As there are an infinity of even numbers and an infinity of odd numbers, there are plenty of rooms for everyone! Now suppose a few nights later the guests in even numbered rooms decide to move out. There are still an infinite number of guests in the odd numbered rooms, so there are no fewer guests in the hotel than before the infinite number of guests in the even numbered rooms move out. Obviously this is absurd, and the absurdity arises from the assumption that it is possible to have a hotel with an infinite number of rooms. So there cannot actually exist a hotel with an infinite number of rooms, and likewise there cannot be an actual infinite number of past events. Therefore the universe cannot be past eternal; the universe began to exist in the finite past.

Even if actual infinities were possible, there could not be an infinite number of past events. This is because an infinite collection cannot be formed by adding one member after another. Such addition could be potentially infinite insofar as the addition of one member after another could

---

15. Craig, *Reasonable Faith*, 80.

continue without end, approaching infinity as a limit, getting ever closer to but never reaching infinity. An actual infinity of items in the series would never be reached. If the series of events in the past has no beginning, then it would have already reached infinity, which is impossible.

Or consider the case of Tristram Shandy, the meticulous but extremely slow autobiographer who takes a whole year to write about each day of his life. But suppose he is eternal, and his life has no beginning. He has already been writing for an infinite number of years, so he already has had a year to write about each of his many days and should be finished. At least he could have written about each day up to the current day. Of course it also seems that the longer he lives, the further behind in the writing of his autobiography he gets. We seem to have another absurdity arising from the assumption of the possibility of an actual infinite.

If there cannot be an infinite number of past events, then the universe began to exist. It seems that both premises of the *kalam* argument are plausible, and since the argument is valid, the conclusion that there is a cause of the universe is plausible. If the universe is the totality of physical reality, spacetime, matter, and energy, then it seems that the cause of the universe must be a transcendent being of some sort. At least it must be something other than anything that is part of the universe itself or the existence of which depends on the universe.

Craig also argues that the second premise of the *kalam* argument is supported by the Big Bang theory, which is interpreted by many scientists to entail that the universe began to exist about 13.8 billion years ago. If the Big Bang is the beginning of spacetime, matter, and energy, then there would be no prior physical "something" to cause it. Some Christians regard the Big Bang theory as a threat to theism, thinking that it constitutes a scientific explanation of the origin of the universe that replaces divine creation. However, the Big Bang theory itself does not explain what caused the universe to come into existence. It may well support, however, the claim that the universe did indeed begin to exist, leaving open the question what caused it. So the theory leaves us free to inquire into the question of what caused the universe to begin to exist.

Someone might object that this cause of the universe need not be an uncaused entity, and so the existence of a first cause of everything is not established. However, if the cause of the universe is itself caused by something else, then either that something else is uncaused or not. If it is not uncaused, then a regress of causes is resumed, and if it is not stopped by an uncaused first cause, then we are stuck again with an actually infinite series of causes. We can avoid the problems of the actual infinite only by reaching an uncaused first cause. So the ultimate cause of the universe must be uncaused.

If whatever that cause is—empty space, the quantum vacuum, dark energy, the Tao, or the Force—itself had a beginning, then we would once again be faced with the question of what caused it, and the infinite regress would again ensue. We would not have an ultimate explanation of the existence of the universe. God would seem to be a prime candidate for the transcendent first cause.

If the universe had an absolute beginning, that beginning would be a boundary of the natural order, and if anything exists beyond that boundary, it cannot be known by natural science. If the beginning of the universe had a cause, and if that cause can be known, such knowledge requires philosophical or theological reasoning (or perhaps religious experience or faith) that goes beyond the limits of natural science. If the totality of physical reality began to exist, the cause must be transcendent; it cannot be something that only exists within the physical universe. The cause of spacetime must be spaceless and timeless. It must be immaterial, since matter is a constituent of the material universe. It must be unchanging, because if it were changing, it would have to exist in time. These are attributes that theists ascribe to God. If the argument up to this point can be sustained, it would support the existence of a transcendent, eternal, immaterial cause of the universe.

Craig also argues that the cause of the universe must be a personal being with will.[16] If the cause of the universe were some sort of eternal, impersonal, changeless being or state, it would be inexplicable why the effect of this cause is not eternal. We should expect that if this proposed eternal, impersonal cause is the necessary and sufficient condition of the existence of the universe, then the universe which is supposed to be its effect would also be eternal. At any moment in the finite past, this alleged cause of the universe would have already existed for an infinitely long time. If it is a sufficient cause for the existence of the universe, why did it take an infinitely long time for the universe finally to come into existence? This problem is solved if the cause is a personal agent who decides to bring the universe into existence *ex nihilo* (out of nothing). Philosophers distinguish agent causation from event causation and state/state causation. Event causation involves an event being caused by prior events, as when a ball is caused to move by being hit with a bat. Events take place in time. The Big Bang is the event that initiates the expansion of the universe from the initial singularity, the point at which all known physical laws break down. It is the beginning of the universe that can be described by the laws of physics, and thus cannot be caused by a prior event. There is no time before the Big Bang (since time begins with the Big Bang), so there can be no event in time that caused the

---

16. Craig, *Reasonable Faith*, 117.

Big Bang. So it seems that the ultimate explanation of the existence of the universe cannot involve only event causation. It also seems not to involve only state/state causation. An example of state/state causation is the temperature being below 32 degrees Fahrenheit causing water to freeze. If the temperature on earth were below 32 degrees since the beginning of its existence, we would not observe water starting to freeze only a few years ago. If the cause of the universe were an eternally existing state, such as a quantum state, as some scientists have suggested, the universe would not have come into existence a finite length of time ago. So it seems that the universe coming into existence is not the result of state/state causation. It seems plausible to suggest that it involves agent causation.

Agent causation occurs when an event is triggered not just because of prior events that cause it, but when part of the explanation of the event is that an agent acted to make it happen, as when a ball is hit because the batter decided to swing. Agent causation involves a personal agent who intentionally decides to act to make some event occur. Persons who have will are the agents who can be causes by acting to bring about a change in the world. If the cause of the beginning of the universe were not a personal agent, what could it be? It could not be some sort of physical energy with the potential to spontaneously produce some sort of fluctuation that could bring the universe into existence, because before the beginning of the universe there are no energy fields, and there is no time for an event to occur, such as the actualization of a potential. If the cause were an eternal, impersonal being or state, then we would be confronted with the question of how it could be that this eternally existing cause brought the universe into existence only a finite length of time before now. Given an eternal cause of the universe, we should expect that the universe itself would be eternal. If that cause of the universe is not a personal agent, then we would expect the universe not to have a finite age. So it seems that the action of a personal agent is a plausible explanation of the beginning of the universe. If the cause of the universe were something other than a personal agent it would be mysterious how the cause could be a timeless, eternally existing reality that produces an effect that exists for only a finite length of time. The *kalam* argument makes plausible the existence of a transcendent, eternal, personal agent that created the universe. This is still a far cry from the God of Abraham, Isaac, and Jacob, but it is much closer to the God of the monotheistic religions than to a quantum fluctuation or some sort of indeterminate potentiality.

It seems plausible, therefore, to conclude that if the beginning of the universe was caused, the cause was a personal agent, and agent causation is the kind of causation that best explains the beginning of the universe. Let us now consider in more detail the question whether the Big Bang theory supports the premise that the universe began to exist.

THE BIG BANG THEORY AND THE BEGINNING OF THE UNIVERSE

One of the implications of the theory of relativity with which Einstein struggled is that its equations predict either an expanding or contracting universe. Given the equations as Einstein originally proposed them, if the universe were not expanding, then gravity would force it to contract. Obviously, if the universe were contracting, it would have collapsed by now, so Einstein had to reject contraction as an option. On the other hand, if the universe is expanding, the expansion would have begun in the finite past, suggesting that the universe had a beginning of its existence. Committed as he was to the standard assumption of an eternal and static universe, Einstein reluctantly introduced an antigravity factor, the cosmological constant, in order to prevent cosmic collapse and maintain the universe on the razor's edge between contraction and expansion. Although it was an inelegant addition to his theory, Einstein thought it was necessary in order to avoid the more disturbing consequence of an expanding universe. After meeting Edwin Hubble and seeing his evidence for the expansion of the universe, Einstein came to regard the cosmological constant as the greatest scientific blunder of his life, for had he stuck with the original form of the equations, he could have predicted the cosmic expansion. Ironically, it eventually turned out that the cosmological constant was not such a blunder after all, but was rather a useful idea for the standard cosmological model.

The first empirical evidence that the universe began to exist was the discovery by Vesto Melvin Slipher, announced at the meeting of the American Astronomical Society in 1914, that about a dozen galaxies that he had studied were receding from the earth at the rate of, according to his calculations, two million miles per hour.[17] In the 1920s Russian mathematician Alexander Friedman, and Belgian astronomer and priest Georges Lemaitre, were independently able to formulate relativity equations that predict an expanding universe.[18] This finding was soon confirmed by Hubble, who was able to measure the distance of galaxies from the earth. Hubble was also able to establish what is now called Hubble's Law, that the recessional velocity of galaxies is proportional to their distance from earth.[19] The evidence

---

17. Barr, *Modern Physics and Ancient Faith*, 38.
18. Barr, *Modern Physics and Ancient Faith*, 43.
19. Barr, *Modern Physics and Ancient Faith*, 39.

that galaxies are receding is the red shift of the light that is observed from those galaxies. Spectral analysis of the light from distant galaxies reveals a slight shift toward the red end of the spectrum, the degree of which is proportional to the distance of the star or galaxy from the observer. The red shift is explained by the expansion of the universe. The space through which the electromagnetic waves propagate is literally being stretched by the expansion of the universe, resulting in a lengthening of the wavelength. Distant galaxies are moving further from the earth because the universe is expanding. Hubble's Law, which says that the rate of expansion is proportional to distance, is explained by the fact that cosmic expansion is due to the expansion of space itself, not the movement of galaxies from each other in space. If you think of all stars and galaxies moving continually farther from earth, it will seem as though earth is the center of the expanding universe. However, earth is not in a special position; an observer situated anywhere in the universe would see the stars and galaxies moving away from her, just as observers anywhere on the surface of a spotted balloon would see the spots moving away as the balloon is increasingly inflated and becomes larger.

If the universe is expanding, then it was smaller and denser in the past. If we go back far enough in the remote past, to the limit of the universe's contraction, presumably we arrive at the beginning of the expansion of the universe, estimated to be about 13.8 billion years ago, when the total matter and energy of the universe is condensed to a point of zero volume, infinite density, and infinite temperature. Because of the infinite density and temperature of the universe at this point, the universe is a singularity where the mathematical equations associated with the laws of physics break down. Some physicists believe that at the singularity we get to time $t = 0$. Some say that, since at singularity the known laws of physics break down, at this point the universe is absolutely nothing. Others call the singularity the limit of our knowledge, where the universe is in principle unknowable by scientific means.

Further support for the proposition that the universe began to exist is provided by the second law of thermodynamics, according to which entropy increases over time. Entropy means disorder, and the second law of thermodynamics explains why on average the universe becomes progressively more disordered over time. Cars rust, but rusty cars never become less rusty. Organisms die and their bodies decompose, but decomposed flesh never recomposes. In particular finite regions, such as a building site, a quantity of matter can become temporarily more ordered, but only at the cost of greater disorder being produced elsewhere. The high rise can be erected, but at the cost of burning fuel and spewing waste into the air. In the long run, as we move forward in time, the overall average level of disorder increases. If the universe had no beginning, then the past is infinite, and the progression of increasing entropy has already been proceeding for an infinitely long time, and we would have already reached equilibrium—complete disorder. Since the universe has not yet reached a state of maximal entropy, it cannot have been moving toward that result for an infinitely long time. So it seems that the second law of thermodynamics implies that the universe must have begun to exist in the finite past, providing additional support for the second premise of the *kalam* cosmological argument.

The standard cosmological model has been refined to deal with various difficulties encountered. One problem for the standard Big Bang model is the horizon problem. Today the universe extends at least 46 billion light years in all directions from earth (the same would be true for any other location in the universe). The problem is that the universe is not old enough for light from any given location to have enough time to traverse the distance to all other parts of the universe. According to the theory of relativity, it is impossible for two objects to causally interact if light from one cannot reach the other. Assuming the standard Big Bang model, the universe is too big and too young for light to traverse the entire universe, which would seem to render impossible the notion that everything in the universe is causally interconnected. If the whole universe is not causally interconnected in some way, it is difficult to account for the degree of uniformity we find.

In order to solve a number of problems confronted by the standard model of the Big Bang theory, the inflation theory was proposed by Alan Guth.[20] According to the inflation theory, the universe underwent a period of exponential expansion, called "inflation," in the first fraction of a second of its existence. Inflation began after the age of the universe had reached Planck time, 10^{-43} seconds, when the temperature of the universe was 10^{32} K. At such a high temperature, protons and neutrons cannot exist as separate particles. According to Grand Unified Theories (GUT), at this ultrahigh temperature the four fundamental forces of the universe are united as one force. As inflation winds down at 10^{-33} seconds and the universe cools to 10^{27} K, symmetry is broken and the one universal force breaks into four forces of very different magnitudes and ranges. Quantum fluctuations during inflation produce tiny irregularities (non-homogeneities) that are responsible for the eventual large-scale structure of the universe that is observed today.

The first of the problems solved by the inflation theory is the horizon problem. The inflation theory explains how regions that are too far apart for light from one to reach the other could nevertheless be causally interconnected. Before inflation, when the universe was smaller than a single

---

20. Barr, *Modern Physics and Ancient Faith*, 54.

atom, the whole universe was causally interconnected. Regions that are now separated by more than the critical distance required for causal interaction became separated during inflation, when space was expanding at a rate far greater than the speed of light. If regions of space for a moment in the past moved away from each other faster than the speed of light, then they could become separated by a distance that is so great that even after expansion slows to the normal, noninflationary rate, light from one region will never be able to make up the distance to the other regions. So inflation solves the problem of how all regions of space can be causally interconnected despite the universe being too big for light from any one region to reach all other regions within the time span available since the end of the inflationary epoch.

A corollary to the horizon problem is the smoothness problem—how can we explain the degree of smoothness in the universe. When viewed from a very large scale, the universe is incredibly smooth throughout. It is obviously not perfectly smooth, because in some local regions we find massive bodies, such as galaxies, stars, planets, and black holes. However, a broader perspective on a cosmic scale reveals that overall the universe is very uniform, or smooth. Now the question is why this should be. This is related to the horizon problem, because if the universe as a whole is smooth, then it must as a whole be causally interconnected (it being too much of a coincidence that it just happened by chance to be uniform). Furthermore, the smoothness issue is more than just a question of why the *whole* universe is smooth, it is also a question of why, no matter how interconnected everything is, the universe is *smooth*. The expansion of the universe is, after all, essentially a cosmic explosion of incredible magnitude. One would not expect the debris falling after a nuclear explosion to be arranged in a smooth, orderly pattern. Even slight irregularities in the initial Big Bang conditions would be greatly magnified in the course of billions of years of continued expansion. Deviations from smoothness are amplified over billions of years by gravitational attraction; this is how the large-scale structure develops. Some deviation from perfect smoothness is necessary for a world such as ours. A perfectly smooth universe would never produce galaxies, stars, and planets. So how do we account for the degree of smoothness that we find? The answer given by the inflation theory is that the rapid expansion of inflation smooths out whatever "wrinkles" might exist prior to inflation, much like rapidly inflating a wrinkled balloon would smooth the wrinkles one would see prior to its inflation.

The third problem solved by inflation is the flatness problem. According to relativity theory, the mass of matter causes the curvature of space. The overall curvature of the universe could in principle be positive, negative, or flat. Locally there are galaxies, stars, and planets that curve space positively (according to relativity theory, gravity curves space), but data from the Planck Probe have enabled scientists to produce a thermal map of the universe that shows that the curvature is very nearly flat.[21] If the geometry of the universe as a whole were positive, the universe would ultimately collapse. If the geometry is flat or open, the universe expands forever. In order for the universe to expand for the billions of years that ours has, it must at least be very nearly flat.[22] Inflation explains the flatness of the universe in much the same way that it explains smoothness. During inflation the volume of the universe expands almost instantly by a factor of 10^{75}, making it essentially indistinguishable from flat.[23]

Now the idea that the universe began to exist is not a welcome conclusion for some scientists. If there was no time before the beginning of the universe, how could there be a time in which there was the event of causing the universe to come into existence? If there was not a cause of the beginning of the universe, why does the universe exist? Another question arises as a consequence of the second law of thermodynamics. Since the universe is still relatively ordered (life is still thriving on earth, and the sun still provides us with useful energy), and the universe has been becoming progressively more disordered for 13.8 billion years, the initial condition of the universe must have been extremely ordered, which means extremely low entropy. Roger Penrose[24] has calculated the probability of the extremely low entropy of the early universe to be one chance in $10^{10^{123}}$. Since there are no laws of physics at singularity, how are we to account for the extremely low entropy among its initial conditions? The idea that the universe began to exist with highly ordered initial conditions already in place is very hard to explain, leading many cosmologists to welcome a theory that allows the Big Bang not to be the absolute beginning of the totality of physical existence.

There are a variety of theories that attempt to explain how the Big Bang is not the beginning of the universe. One theory proposed in order to avoid the thesis that the universe began to exist at the Big Bang is the oscillating universe, or bouncing universe model, according to which our world is one of a series of cycles that the totality of nature has undergone. According to this model, the Big Bang was the beginning of just one of many cycles of the universe. Each cycle begins with a Big Bang, followed by a period of expansion. The expansion continues until gravity halts and reverses the expansion, causing the universe to contract. Contraction continues until the

21. Spitzer, *New Proofs for the Existence of God*, 84.
22. Adams, *Origins of Existence*, 43–44.
23. Guth, "Inflation and the New Era of High Precision Cosmology."
24. Penrose, *The Emperor's New Mind*, 344–45.

universe collapses with a "big crunch," which brings about a transition, or bounce, to another Big Bang, beginning a new cycle. Such cycles of the universe repeat, without beginning or end. Such a scenario is warmly received by advocates of the several religious traditions that teach a cyclical universe.

The bouncing universe model was popular a few decades ago, but there are serious problems with it. First, there is no empirical evidence for the theory, and it is perhaps in principle impossible for there to be empirical evidence for it. It seems likely that possible experience is confined to our own universe. Second, there is no known possible mechanism by which the transition from big crunch to Big Bang could be accomplished.[25] Certainly there is no evidence or viable theory about how the Big Bang 13.8 billion years ago was preceded by a collapse of a previous universe. Third, it has recently been determined that the expansion of the universe is accelerating,[26] due to dark energy, which causes gravitation to become a repulsive force. For at least 5 billion years the mass/energy of the universe has been dominated by dark energy, which causes an acceleration of cosmic expansion. Given what is now believed it is hard to see how the expansion of the universe could be reversed. Recently discovered evidence supports the view that the geometry of space is flat, which implies that expansion will not reverse. The final fate of the universe is not known, but it seems extremely unlikely that there will be a reversal of its expansion.

Another problem is that the second law of thermodynamics would entail that each bounce of the universe would lose energy, and eventually the process would fizzle out, and the universe would be devoid of useful energy. If it is suggested that this may happen in the future but has not happened yet, the obvious reply is that the cyclical model implies that if there is no beginning of the process of universe generation, there would have already been an infinite number of cycles, and so the process should have already run down. The theory of the bouncing universe also leads to the radiation paradox. Right now it is estimated that 1 percent of the electromagnetic radiation in the universe is light from stars. The other 99 percent is cosmic background radiation left over from the Big Bang. Stars are formed during the expansion of the universe. If the universe were to contract and collapse, stars would be destroyed and the starlight would be folded into the cosmic background radiation. If the universe has been cycling through Big Bangs and big crunches forever, it would have converted much more of the starlight to cosmic background radiation than it has, presumably all but an infinitesimal portion. Given that there is currently "only" about 100 times

---

25. Craig, *Reasonable Faith*, 130.
26. Spitzer, *New Proofs for the Existence of God*, 27.

more cosmic background radiation than starlight, there could not have been much more than a hundred previous bounces.[27]

One final problem is also a consequence of the increase in cosmic radiation that would result from a series of cosmic expansions and contractions. Richard Tolman discovered that increased radiation would result in increased pressure that would make each subsequent cycle longer, resulting in each subsequent phase of the universe being greater in volume, with more time required for each new cycle.[28] This means overall cosmic expansion moving forward in time, and so looking back in time we would see overall contraction with each previous cycle. Consequently, even if the universe is cyclical, there would still be a beginning of the universe and a first cycle.

There is no longer much interest in the bouncing universe model, but there are other versions of the cyclical universe that are being developed. It remains likely, however, that any cyclical theory will entail a cosmic beginning. Three leading cosmologists, Arvind Borde, Alan Guth, and Alexander Vilenkin, published a theorem in 2003 that says that any universe or multiverse that has been expanding throughout its history cannot have an infinite past and thus must have a past spacetime boundary. In other words, any expanding universe or multiverse must have begun to exist at some time in the finite past. To quote Vilenkin, "It is said that an argument is what convinces reasonable men and a proof is what it takes to convince even an unreasonable man. With the proof now in place, cosmologists can no longer hide behind the possibility of a past-eternal universe. There is no escape: they have to face the problem of a cosmic beginning."[29] The BGV theorem implies that any universe or multiverse that has an average expansion over its entire history must have a beginning in the finite past.

Numerous theories about what existed before the Big Bang, in order to avoid an absolute cosmic beginning, have been proposed. The BGV theorem applies to any universe that has an overall expansion throughout its existence. Two ways of getting around the theorem involve describing the existence of the universe prior to the Big Bang such that the whole history of the universe does not involve overall expansion. One way of doing this is for the pre-Big Bang phase to involve contraction, so that the overall expansion is not positive. The other way is for the pre-Big Bang phase to involve an infinitely long period of non-expansion. An infinitely long period of non-expansion without a beginning would counterbalance the finite period of expansion that is currently underway, so the overall average expansion

---

27. Spitzer, *New Proofs for the Existence of God*, 28.
28. Spitzer, *New Proofs for the Existence of God*, 29.
29. Vilenkin, *Many Worlds in One*, 176.

of the universe would not be positive. The suggestion is that the first Big Bang was preceded by an eternally existing static state, sometimes called the cosmic egg, which finally cracked to produce the Big Bang. The problem with this was demonstrated by Vilenkin and his student, Audrey Mithani.[30] If the static state was stable, it would never crack to produce a changing universe. Furthermore, if it were both stable and eternal in the past, it would never transition to a changeable universe. On the other hand, in order for the cosmic egg to crack and produce the Big Bang, it must be unstable or metastable (not perfectly stable), in which case it would collapse or crack after a finite time, implying an existence of a finite period of time, and hence a beginning of the universe. As Craig and Sinclair argue, the cosmic egg implies contradictory attributes.[31] In order to be beginningless it must be perfectly stable. In order to be capable of transitioning to the Big Bang it must not be perfectly stable. So the cosmic egg theory does not provide a way to avoid a beginning of the universe.

What about an infinite pre-Big Bang contraction phase to offset the post Big Bang expansion? According to this kind of theory, our universe begins with a bounce rather than a Big Bang. Sean Carroll suggests that the universe could be beginningless and past eternal if there is an infinitely long contraction phase and an infinite expansion phase and the low entropy point in the middle.[32] From the infinite time before the big bounce the universe contracts from infinite volume to a small enough size to make the universe subject to quantum effects. The universe contracts from the infinite past, continues to contract until it bounces, whereupon it enters its expansion phase, which has been underway for 13.8 billion years. The expansion will continue forever into the future. According to this model, the universe does not begin to exist and is eternal in both the past and future. The expansion in the future never ends; there is only one bounce.

A major difficulty with this theory is dealing with the problem of entropy and the second law of thermodynamics. The extremely low entropy at the beginning of the expansion phase of the universe would seem to imply, given that entropy increases over time, that the contraction phase before the bounce requires that entropy was even much lower in the extremely remote past. It seems absurdly improbable that an infinitely long period of decreasing entropy, proceeding from a low entropy state in the remote past, could end with the extremely low entropy that we see at the beginning of the current phase. For the contraction phase to be infinite and to end in

---

30. Vilenkin and Mithani, "Did the universe have a beginning?"
31. Craig and Sinclair, "The Kalam Cosmological Argument," 101–201.
32. Carroll, *From Eternity to Here*.

the very low entropy of the beginning of the expansion phase, the entropy of the period infinitely prior to the bounce would presumably be infinitely low. Another suggested possibility is that entropy decreases in the contraction phase prior to the bounce. This would imply that the contraction phase proceeds from an infinitely distant high entropy past to the low entropy bounce. The universe moves from high entropy at time t = minus infinity to a low entropy at time t = 0, and to high entropy at time t = plus infinity. This seems to involve either a violation of the second law of thermodynamics, with entropy decreasing with the passage of time, or else the arrow of time going in reverse during the contraction phase. It seems that this model could not possibly be realistic. A more realistic description of what Carroll is suggesting, which is consistent with the second law of thermodynamics, is that there are two arrows of time proceeding from time t = 0 involving movement from low entropy to high entropy. Craig argues in a debate with Carroll that such a model would be tantamount to the affirmation that time t = 0 would still be the beginning of the universe, with two temporal series proceeding from it.[33] Carroll insisted that the model does not a have a temporal beginning but rather a bounce at a low entropy moment between two temporal series, one in which the universe contracts and one in which the universe expands. Carroll does not insist that the model is true; he admits that it is a proposal with details that are yet to be worked out. The model shows that it is possible to develop models according to which the universe has no beginning and is past eternal, and which is consistent with observations and allows us to make accurate predictions. However, it seems that such models do not describe reality.

Stephen Hawking's "no boundary model" is supposed to offer a way to deny that the universe began to exist without making it past eternal. According to the no boundary model, prior to Planck time (when the age of the universe is 10^{-43} seconds), since the laws of classical physics break down, quantum effects make it impossible to distinguish distinct moments of time or even to distinguish space and time. Hawking's position is that in the very early universe the distinction between space and time breaks down, so instead of past time reaching a singularity that is a definite beginning point of time, the point is "rounded off," and the distinction between present and future becomes fuzzy. Instead of imagining the beginning of the expansion of spacetime to be like the point of a cone, think of the cone as rounded off, like a badminton shuttlecock. There is no definite point that can be specified which is the precise moment at which the universe begins to exist—a precise, definite first moment of time. The universe did not come into existence

---

33. Craig and Carroll, "God and Cosmology."

at a definite moment, and so it did not begin to exist. The universe just is. Although the past is finite, there is no beginning. As Hawking writes, "So long as the universe had a beginning, we could suppose it had a creator. But if the universe is really self-contained, having no boundary or edge, it would have neither beginning nor end, it would simply be. What place, then, for a creator?"[34]

As ingenious as Hawking's proposal is, it does not really succeed in avoiding the need for a beginning of the universe. According to the model it is still true that the past is finite and the universe began to exist, even if it is impossible to specify a precise moment that marks the beginning. To say that the universe has a finite past and began to exist a finite number of years ago seems to imply that the universe came into existence out of nothing. If the past is finite we can still say that the universe began to exist and ask for an explanation of the beginning of the universe.

Yet there are many scientists who are uncomfortable with the idea of a transcendent cause of the universe and of the idea that the universe was created out of nothing. There are several models being developed that permit the universe to be past eternal. Time will tell whether any of them are successful in making predictions and being consistent with observation. For the time being, the best scientific evidence supports the claim that the universe began to exist.

In the next chapter we will consider some other attempts to avoid the conclusion that the universe needs a transcendent cause in order to exist.

---

34. Hawking, *A Brief History of Time*, 156.

5
Eternal Inflation and the Multiverse

The Big Bang singularity is regarded by many cosmologists not as the beginning of the universe, but rather the point at which the equations of relativity theory break down, which may be preceded by a state that is governed by laws of quantum physics. At times earlier than Planck time, 10^{-43} seconds, the universe is smaller than an atom and thus subject to quantum physics, not classical physics. An adequate theory of quantum gravity, which cosmologists do not yet have, is needed in order to understand the universe at the earliest moment of its existence. This is why many cosmologists do not think that we are able to know anything about the universe at singularity, at time t = 0, just prior to the Big Bang. Many cosmologists believe that the theory of inflation offers the best account of the universe and its evolution from the Big Bang. Perhaps what we call the Big Bang is not the only Big Bang, nor the beginning of the entire universe. Perhaps what began to exist 13.8 billion years ago is only one part of a much larger multiverse.

One important multiverse scenario is a version of the inflation theory based on quantum gravity theory. Some, but not all, quantum gravity theories imply a huge number of universes produced by quantum fluctuations. Russian cosmologists, Andrei Linde and Alexander Vilenkin,[1] proposed the eternal inflation model, according to which random quantum fluctuations have been generating universes from time immemorial. Linde refers to his model as chaotic eternal inflation. According to this theory, inflation is an eternal process, which can endlessly generate universes.

Quantum theory says that in the energy field that pervades the quantum vacuum virtual particles can spontaneously pop into existence.

---

1. Davies, *Cosmic Jackpot*, 80.

The quantum vacuum is empty space that is devoid of ordinary particles of matter but contains vacuum energy or dark energy, thought to be the energy that propels the expansion of the universe. It has been suggested that quantum theory allows bubbles of spacetime to spontaneously pop into existence from the space energy contained in the quantum vacuum. A patch of spacetime created by a vacuum fluctuation is a discrete universe if it is a "self-contained space having some non-zero volume and possibly filled with matter of some sort."[2] It is imagined that such a patch of spacetime could pop into existence out of nothing, and the dark energy of the vacuum could permit it to expand exponentially. Most of space will continue expanding exponentially forever. In the span of unlimited time, countless universes are spawned when random quantum fluctuations allow dark energy to decay in certain patches of space. In such regions of space expansion settles to the slower rate that characterizes pocket universes such as ours. Our observed universe is the result of a small section of a vast inflationary bubble that was pinched off from the whole by slamming on the brakes of inflation's exponential expansion and settling into the ordinary cosmic expansion that we now observe. Vacuum or dark energy is a cosmological constant, meaning that the energy density must remain constant. As space expands, the amount of energy must increase in order to maintain constant density. Over time countless quantum fluctuations produce energy decays that result in more bubbles collapsing into ordinary expansion, creating more pocket universes. Most of space continues its inflationary expansion forever, and so the space between the discrete pocket universes increases much more rapidly than the space of the pocket universes, ensuring that they will not collide or interact in any way. The totality of this ensemble of universes is the multiverse. The totality of the multiverse extends vastly beyond the horizon that we can observe with the most powerful telescopes. Beyond the outer limits of the pinched off bubble segment that comprises our observable universe, faster than the speed of light inflation continues without end. Even more remarkably, this incredibly vast cosmic bubble of which our universe is but a tiny part is itself only one part of a countless ensemble of other cosmic bubbles, each of which may be generating other universes that pinch off and resume ordinary expansion. Cosmic bubbles can be produced from segments of the spacetime fabric of which our universe is a part, or from regions of the eternal quantum vacuum that are totally unconnected to our universe.

    If the inflationary multiverse is eternal in the future, can it be eternal in the past? Does eternal inflation imply that the multiverse did not begin

---

2. Barr, *Modern Physics and Ancient Faith*, 274.

to exist? The BGV theorem implies that cosmic expansion of a multiverse must have had a beginning. Did the multiverse come into existence from nothing? If it did, would it have to have been created by God? Or could it have come into being from nothing all by itself? And what exactly do we mean by "nothing?"

A UNIVERSE FROM NOTHING?

In the last decade some physicists have suggested that the universe could have come into existence out of nothing without the help of God. Lawrence Krauss argues that physics can provide a naturalistic explanation of how the universe came into being out of nothing.[3] A major gap in physical theory today is the lack of a theory that unifies general relativity and quantum physics. The theory of relativity is about spacetime, gravity, and large objects, such as galaxies, stars, and planets. Quantum physics governs the behavior of smaller things, such as protons, electrons, and quarks. Currently there is no consensus theory that resolves mathematical inconsistencies between the theory of relativity and quantum theory. One implication of the Big Bang theory is that what is today the biggest thing, namely the universe, was once very small and subject to the rules of quantum physics, thus intensifying the need for a theory that will unify relativity and quantum physics. It is hoped that a quantum theory of gravity will accomplish the unification of the theory of relativity and quantum physics. It is also hoped that a quantum gravity theory can explain how our universe might have come into existence from a quantum fluctuation.

When Krauss talks about the universe coming into existence out of nothing, he is not using the word *nothing* as philosophers do, to mean absolute non-being, the total absence of anything whatsoever. He and others talk about nothing as the quantum vacuum, which is seething with energy that can randomly and spontaneously give rise to virtual particles. Krauss says that this nothing is unstable and has a tendency to produce something—quantum fluctuations that are perhaps capable of inflating into universes.[4] It turns out that the positive mass energy of the universe is counterbalanced by the negative energy of gravity. If the overall geometry of the universe is flat, then the total negative energy of gravity plus the total positive mass energy would equal zero. Since the total energy of the universe is zero, it is

---

3. Krauss, *A Universe from Nothing*.
4. Krauss, *A Universe from Nothing*, ch. 10.

possible for it to exist without a cost in energy—the ultimate "free lunch," a universe from nothing.[5]

Clearly Krauss has not explained how the universe can have come into being *ex nihilo*, without a sufficient cause of its existence. When philosophers ask why the universe exists, why there is something rather than nothing, they mean by "nothing" absolute non-being. Absolute non-being is not empty space or a quantum vacuum seething with energy and virtual particles. Absolute non-being has no properties or potentiality. Krauss says that nothing must be defined scientifically (since everything that is serious must be!), not as philosophers define nothing, in some weird abstract way that cannot be tested scientifically. Krauss manifestly is not answering the question why anything at all exists. He is, rather, explaining how the universe we see today emerged from some very primordial something, like the energy in empty space. A quantum vacuum, though frequently referred to as "nothing," is not actually absolute non-being. It assumes the existence of space, and thus a universe, or at least something, which already exists. A quantum vacuum must be in some sort of state and contain some sort of energy in order to have the potential to produce a fluctuation. A fluctuation requires something to fluctuate. If whatever state or field that exists prior to the quantum fluctuation has the potential to have a universe emerge from it, it must *be* in some way or other. We want some explanation of why it exists. So an account of the universe arising from a vacuum fluctuation would not constitute an ultimate explanation of the existence of the universe. If the quantum vacuum has a beginning, then we want an explanation of its coming into existence.

The question how the universe developed from empty space is an important scientific question and may lead to very interesting theories that help us understand how the universe evolved. However, it will not answer the philosophical question of why the universe exists—what the sufficient reason for its existence is. Whatever the "nothing" is that Krauss has identified, if it actually is something and not absolute non-being, it will still lead to the question, why does *that* exist? It will not explain why a universe exists rather than nothing. Naturalists such as Krauss may be content with the fact that scientific explanations always produce answers that push the question "why?" back another step without ending the need for further inquiry. Krauss admits that we may never find a final explanation: "maybe we will never find a theory that describes why the universe has to be the way it is."[6] The progress that has been made so far by scientists in understanding

---

5. Krauss, *A Universe from Nothing*, ch. 6.
6. Krauss, *A Universe from Nothing*, 138.

the universe has produced "some of the most beautiful and also the most complex ideas with which humanity has ever had to grapple. It is a picture whose creation emphasizes the best about what it is to be human—our ability to imagine vast possibilities of existence and the adventurousness to bravely explore them—without passing the buck to a vague creative force or to a creator who is, by definition forever unfathomable."[7]

Krauss recognizes that the empty space of quantum physics is not exactly the "nothing" intended in Leibniz's question, but he seems convinced that physics offers the only meaningful way to think about and answer the question, even though he admits that final answer might be forever beyond our grasp. He writes,

> When I have thus far described how something almost always can come from "nothing," I have focused on either the creation of something from preexisting empty space or the creation of empty space from no space at all. Both initial conditions work for me when I think of the "absence of being" and therefore are possible candidates for nothingness. I have not addressed directly, however, the issues of what might have existed, if anything, before such creation, what laws governed the creation, or, put more generally, I have not discussed what some may view as the question of First Cause. A simple answer is of course that either empty space or the more fundamental nothingness from which empty space may have arisen, preexisted, and is eternal. However, to be fair, this does raise the possible question, which might, of course, not be answerable, of what, if anything fixed the rules that governed such creation.[8]

Here Krauss admits that he is not addressing the ultimate question of why anything at all exists, and that that question might not be answerable. I would argue that it definitely is not answerable by physics, and physics is not justified in proscribing philosophy or religion from attempting to answer it. Any scientific theory about a natural process that produced empty space and the energy therein, and a theory about whatever produced that which produced empty space, would clearly just push the regress of causes back another step, as would the question of the source of the laws by which these processes are governed. Only a necessary being could end the regress, and a necessary being that is also an intelligent, personal being and law-giver, offers a plausible explanation of the source of the causal laws involved.

---

7. Krauss, *A Universe from Nothing*, 138–39.
8. Krauss, *A Universe from Nothing*, 174.

Although the principle *ex nihilo, nihil fit*—from nothing, nothing comes—cannot be proven, the vast majority of philosophers since the pre-Socratic philosopher Parmenides have regarded the principle as self-evident. When we consider the question of the origin of the universe, there seem to be two options—either a First Cause or a universe that came into existence uncaused out of nothing. Many people find belief in God problematic because God is supernatural and beyond the bounds of ordinary experience or science. However, if the existence of God is logically possible, this option would seem to be less problematic that the spontaneous, uncaused coming into existence of a universe out of nothing. If prior to the beginning of the universe there is nothing, then the coming into existence of a universe would be sheer magic. This seems more problematic, and more at odds with science, than the existence of a transcendent, eternal personal agent.

Obviously Krauss disagrees. According to Krauss, "the metaphysical 'rule' which is held with ironclad conviction . . . that '*out of nothing, nothing comes*,' has no foundation in science. . . . All it represents is an unwillingness to recognize the simple fact that nature may be cleverer than philosophers or theologians."[9] One wonders whether nature is cleverer than scientists. Krauss is somewhat careless about his use of the term *nothing*. His "nothing" can be empty space or the more basic nothing from which empty space comes. He is suspicious of philosophical arguments about absolute nonbeing, where "lies the intellectual bankruptcy of much of theology and some of modern philosophy. For surely 'nothing' is every bit as physical as 'something,' especially if is to be defined as the 'absence of something.' It then behooves us to understand precisely the physical nature of both these quantities. And without science, any definition is just words."[10]

With or without science, definitions are just words. But words mean things, and defining them is not the prerogative of physics. And "nothing" does not mean "something." Krauss is wrong in saying that nothing is a physical something. If it were a physical something, then showing how the universe came from it would not answer the fundamental question why anything at all exists. The question would arise why this physical something exists. It is the business of philosophy, not science, to define "nothing." When Leibniz raised the question why anything exists rather than nothing, he did not mean by "nothing" some sort of physical something. He meant absolute nonbeing—the total absence of anything whatsoever, including any kind of physical something. "Nothing" is not something physical, and defining the concept of "nothing" is not something for physical science to accomplish.

9. Krauss, *A Universe from Nothing*, 174.
10. Krauss, *A Universe from Nothing*, xiv.

If the nothing that Krauss is talking about is really something—some kind of primordial physical state or energy—then whatever that something is, it either began to exist or not. If it began to exist, it either came from absolute nonbeing, or not. If it came from absolute nonbeing, we are back to the problem of how something can come into existence from absolute nonbeing. If it came into being from something, then we are back to the regress of causes. If the primordial source of the universe did not begin to exist, then it is eternal. If it is eternal, then according to the second law of thermodynamics, it would have reached maximal entropy by now.

Krauss is right that the metaphysical rule, *ex nihilo, nihil fit* has no foundation in science. It is the other way around—the principle is foundational to science. Science cannot prove it, but science must presuppose it, for to deny it would entail the complete negation of a rational order in nature. Following Hume, some scientists[11] say that the principle of cause and effect is an empirical principle that only applies to empirical phenomena within the order of natural phenomena. Hume would say that we have no rational grounds for saying that the beginning of the universe must have a cause, since we have no experience of universes coming into existence. Contrary to the Humean view of causality, the principle of cause and effect is not an empirical principle based on science. The principle of cause and effect is a condition of the possibility of science, not a conclusion derived from science. Most philosophers since Parmenides have held that it is a necessary truth of reason that something cannot come into existence without a cause. This is an *a priori* principle, not an empirical generalization. The principle of cause and effect is a form of the principle of sufficient reason, which says that for everything that exists, there must be a sufficient reason for its existence, either in itself or some other being. This principle applies to the universe, whether or not the universe began to exist. For events in the physical world, the sufficient reason involves a set of causal conditions, which are typically other events or states in the physical world. However, if we ask for the sufficient reason for the existence of the whole universe, the sufficient cause must be something transcendent to the whole universe. The sufficient reason for the existence of the universe cannot be in the universe itself, for the existence of the universe is contingent. The existence of the universe is not a necessary truth, so it is meaningful to ask why it exists.

Krauss objects to the claim that God is the ultimate explanation of the existence of the universe, that it immediately raises the question why God exists. Who or what created God? If something created God, then God is not the first cause of everything. If we cannot find a cause of God, then we are

---

11. Page, "On God and Cosmology."

stuck with an unexplained being, which leaves us no better off than we were when we were wondering what caused the Big Bang. Krauss has a problem with assigning God the task of being the First Cause of the universe. He writes, "the declaration of a First Cause still leaves open the question, 'Who created the creator?'"[12] However, if God is a necessary being, a being that cannot possibly not exist, as theism has traditionally held, then the question why God exists does not arise, and God's existence does not require that he be created by some other being. Indeed, that is what it means for God to be the first cause.

Krauss says that, "those who argue that out of nothing, nothing comes seem perfectly content with the quixotic notion that somehow God can get around this."[13] This statement shows Krauss's misunderstanding of the notion of God as a necessary being. The theist holds not that God somehow came into being out of nothing or created himself out of nothing, but rather that God did not begin to exist, precisely because God is a necessary being—without beginning or end. Krauss says that if "the notion of true nothingness requires not even the *potential* for existence, then surely God cannot work his wonders, because if he does cause existence from nonexistence, there must have been the potential for existence. To simply argue that God can do what nature cannot do is to argue that *supernatural* potential for existence is somehow different from regular natural potential for existence."[14] However, creation *ex nihilo* does not mean that God actualizes the potential of nothing to become something. The nothing has no properties or potentialities at all, so there is nothing there for God to actualize, and the absurdity of God actualizing a potential of something that has no potential is not involved. To say that God creates the universe out of nothing means that he calls the universe into existence without constructing it from a pre-existing material. The nothing referred to in *ex nihilo, nihil fit* is not a pre-existing indeterminate something with the potential to become a universe. The reason that God can do what nature cannot is not that supernatural potential for existence is somehow different than natural potential for existence. It is rather that prior to the existence of nature, nature does not exist, and it therefore lacks both natural and supernatural potential for existence, while God is an omnipotent creator with the power to bring into existence what does not already exist.

Jim Holt argues that the theist, who complains that the naturalist fails to explain adequately why the universe exists, is no better off because the

12. Krauss, *A Universe from Nothing*, xii.
13. Krauss, *A Universe from Nothing*, 174.
14. Krauss, *A Universe from Nothing*, 174–75.

theist is left with God as an ultimate, unexplained brute fact.[15] Naturalists sometimes ask, if an uncaused God can exist, then why can't the universe exist as an uncaused "brute fact"? If the universe began to exist, its non-existence is a possibility. Its existence, therefore, is contingent, which raises the question why it exists. Atheists were sometimes willing to accept the existence of the universe as an unexplained "brute fact" back in the days before the existence of the universe was thought to have a beginning. Now that it is widely believed that the universe did begin to exist, the "brute fact" option is harder to accept. Is it really any easier to accept the existence of God as a brute fact?

The answer to this question is "no," but the theist need not say that God's existence is a brute fact. Rather, God is a necessary being. As such, God exists by his own nature. God's existence has no beginning and no end; it is impossible for God not to exist. The question why God exists is answered by the fact that it is impossible for God not to exist. The question, "who created God?" is misguided. God does not need to be created, nor did God create himself. Asking for the cause of something is appropriate only for what exists contingently. We appropriately ask why something exists, or what caused it to exist, only when its non-existence is a possibility. In the case of a necessary being, the question of why it exists simply does not arise, for the simple reason that it is not possible for it not to exist.

Krauss grants that God as First Cause ends the regress of causes to explain the existence of the universe, but he dismisses it out of hand. "The apparent logical necessity of First Cause is a real issue for any universe that has a beginning. Therefore, on the basis of logic alone one cannot rule out such a deistic view of nature. . . . If one takes the view of God as the cause of all causes, and therefore is eternal even if our universe is not, the *reductio ad absurdum* sequence of 'why' questions does indeed terminate, but as I have stressed, only at the expense of introducing a remarkable all-powerful entity for which there simply is no other evidence."[16] Well, the fact that God would be a sufficient causal explanation of the existence of the universe is itself a considerable bit of evidence, but I would challenge the claim that there is no other evidence. We shall consider below the fine-tuning of the universe as further evidence of an intelligent creator. A number of thinkers have found evidence from the fact that theism provides explanations of the complexity of life, the possibility of consciousness, the existence of persons, the existence of abstract entities, such as numbers and the laws of nature, and the existence of values. Thinkers such as Richard Swinburne, Stuart Hack-

---

15. Holt, *Why Does the World Exist?*, 105–6.
16. Krauss, *A Universe from Nothing*, 173.

ett, C. S. Lewis, C. Stephen Evans, and William Lane Craig[17] make moral arguments for the existence of God, finding evidence for God's existence in the moral dimension of human existence. Krauss boasts that his conclusions are "based on the remarkable and exciting developments in empirical cosmology and particle physics *and* have not come from philosophical or theological musings about morality or other speculations about the human condition."[18] I grant that cosmology is exciting, but so is philosophy, and philosophical arguments showing the insufficiency of physics to explain why there is something rather than nothing are more than mere "musings." Neither are they motivated solely by a desire for consolation, as Krauss is wont to say. Furthermore, as we have seen, theism enjoys the advantage over naturalism of not being self-referentially incoherent.

Another thinker who has no sympathy for efforts to argue that God is the cause of the Big Bang is Adolf Grunbaum,[19] one of the greatest philosophers of science today. Although Grunbaum admits that the universe has a finite past, he thinks it is nonsensical to say that the universe came into existence out of nothing. To say the universe came into existence out of nothing presupposes that once upon a time the universe did not exist. Since time itself exists only when the universe exists, to speak of a time before the beginning of the universe is to imagine a time before there was time, which is absurd. There can be no time before the universe exists, so the universe has always existed, even though its age is finite. The universe always existed in the sense that there was never a time in which it did not exist. To say that there must be a cause for the beginning of the universe is misguided because such a cause would have to exist before (at earlier times than) the universe, and its act of creating the universe would be an event at a time prior to the beginning of time. Before time exists there is no time in which events can take place, so there can be no event that causes the universe to come into existence.

According to this line of reasoning, that the past is finite does not mean that the universe began to exist out of nothing. To ask what was happening before the Big Bang is misguided in the same way that asking what is south of the South Pole is misguided. Questions such as "what was happening before the Big Bang, what existed before time t = 0, and what caused the Big Bang?" are nonsensical. The Big Bang cannot have a cause because there was no time before the Big Bang when the supposed cause could exist and do the

---

17. Swinburne, *The Existence of God*; Hackett, *The Resurrection of Theism*; Evans, *Natural Signs and Knowledge of God*.
18. Krauss, *A Universe from Nothing*, 143.
19. Grunbaum, "Creation as a Pseudo-Explanation in Current Physical Cosmology."

causing. The problem of why the universe exists is a pseudo-problem. It is not the business of science to concern itself with pseudo-problems, including this one.

Grunbaum denies that there could have been a cause of the Big Bang because there could not be an event before the beginning of time that could be the cause. According to Craig, the theist can argue that the act of creation of the universe exists simultaneously with the beginning of the universe, not at some moment in time before the beginning of the universe. God can exist and act ontologically and causally prior but not temporally prior to the beginning of the universe.[20] Grunbaum assumes that a cause must exist temporally before its effect, but he does not argue for the impossibility of causes existing simultaneously with their effect. Augustine held that there was no time before the beginning of the universe, and that creation is an instantaneous act that initiates time rather than an event that occurred in time.[21]

Grunbaum declares that he cannot understand this idea, but he does not show that it is incoherent. Admittedly, the idea of God creating the universe *ex nihilo* is beyond human comprehension, but no more so than the idea of an absolutely necessary, absolutely perfect being itself, or of the idea of the universe coming into existence without a cause. Grunbaum cannot understand the idea of God creating the universe not temporally before, but simultaneous with the universe coming into existence. I assume he means that he cannot understand how creation in this sense could happen, for the idea of two things existing simultaneously is not particularly difficult to understand. Christians say it is a mystery, but it does not seem unintelligible or self-contradictory. If one denies that the universe came into existence, and says instead that it just is, then I cannot understand how the universe could just be, have a finite age, and yet not have a beginning of its existence. If the universe encompasses everything other than God, the coming into being of the universe would have to be *ex nihilo*. As difficult as it is to understand how a God could create the universe from nothing, it seems more difficult to understand how the universe could come into being from nothing without a cause, or how it could just be and yet have a finite age. As far as the coming into being out of nothing is concerned, it is at least as hard to understand how it could happen without a cause as to understand how it could happen as the result of a cause, even if the kind of causation involved is radically different from anything in our ordinary experience. Either way—with or without a cause—the universe began to exist from nothing. However, to say

---

20. Craig and Sinclair, "The Kalam Cosmological Argument," 195–96.
21. Augustine, *Confessions*, 229–32.

that the universe came into existence from nothing uncaused adds another layer of difficulty, because it requires suspension of the principle of sufficient reason and causality. That seems to make things considerably harder to understand.

Those who deny that the principle of cause and effect applies to the whole universe have to rely on a Humean argument that cause and effect is an empirical principle, and we have no experience of universes coming into existence. True enough, but we do now have good scientific reasons to believe that this universe came into existence (which Hume never dreamed of), and I know of no reason to think that it is easier for universes to come into existence without a cause than it is for tigers or guitars to come into existence without a cause. The need for a cause would seem to be at least as great for the creation of a universe out of nothing as for the cause of the origination of a tiger from already existing matter. The simultaneity of the cause and the effect in the case of God's creation of the universe, which Grunbaum claims not to understand, seems no harder to understand than the uncaused origination of the universe.

The Big Bang singularity is a point at which the laws of physics break down, including causal laws. This situation has been taken by some atheist thinkers to imply that there cannot be a cause of the Big Bang. In the absence of physical laws, does it even make sense to talk about a cause of the Big Bang? For atheist philosopher Quentin Smith the breakdown of the laws of physics implies that the Big Bang is an uncaused event and not the product of divine creation.[22] However, while there cannot be a causal explanation of the Big Bang in terms of natural laws, or a physical cause of the beginning of the universe, this does not rule out the possibility of a transcendent agent cause. A transcendent agent cause of the universe is more plausible than no cause at all, given that the intellectual repugnance of something coming into existence without a cause is greater than the repugnance of the possibility of a transcendent or supernatural cause.

Sean Carroll asserts that science seeks explanations of phenomena in the universe, but it is inappropriate for science to seek a cause for the whole universe. He says that "the notion of cause isn't part of an appropriate vocabulary to use for discussing fundamental physics. Rather, modern physical models take the form of unbreakable patterns—laws of nature— that persist without any external causes."[23] When you ask for a cause of the universe as a whole, you are operating at a level beyond nature and hence beyond any laws or principles that we can understand or apply to the object

22. Smith, "The Uncaused Beginning of the Universe."
23. Carroll, "Big Picture Part One."

in question. Carroll argues that the question of the cause of the universe is not a scientific question. When science gets a model that is logically consistent, makes accurate predictions, and explains observation, then science has done all it can do and all that it is reasonable to expect from it. It makes no sense to seek an answer to the question why the universe as a whole exists. We established the principle of cause and effect in the course of dealing with the world we experience, and extending the principle to the whole universe is misguided. Well, even if is true that science is not concerned with the question of whether there is a cause of the universe, it is not a meaningless question. If we have to step outside of science into metaphysics to raise it and attempt to answer it, so be it. Carroll says that Hawking's "no-boundary proposal" allows the universe to be completely self-contained and not requiring a cause. Actually, the proposal does no such thing; it simply allows a description of the earliest moments of time without a singularity and definite first moment of time. The finite age of the universe remains, and thus a beginning, even if a precise first moment is not identifiable.

Carroll claims that to assert that God is the cause of the universe is worthless because God is an ill-defined concept.[24] It does not allow us to make reliable predictions. Without giving us the ability to make good predictions, the concept of God plays no useful role in our thinking. What predictions we would expect to be entailed by theism turn out to be false. There is a lot of evil in the world, religious people are not happier or more moral than unreligious people, prayer doesn't work, etc.

Carroll is quite right to recognize the difference between causes that science can discover and a putative cause that transcends natural science, but his rejection of the value of a philosophical explanation of the existence of the universe in terms of a transcendent cause seems arbitrary. It is true that the idea of a transcendent cause of the whole universe is not scientific and does not contribute to the development of models that explain the details of the evolution of the universe. However theism as a worldview does provide a philosophical framework that helps in making sense of the relation between scientific understanding of nature and other areas of human concern, such as values and our sense of meaning and purpose. That religious ideas do not play a significant role in the development of models to explain the evolution of the universe does not diminish the value of religious ideas. That the idea of God can play a significant role in our overall philosophical understanding of reality, and that in particular the idea of God as creator of the cosmos plays such a fundamental role in Christian thought, helps make plausible the thought that God is the transcendent cause of the universe. If it

---

24. Carroll, "Big Picture Part One."

turns out that the most plausible cosmological models favor a universe that began to exist, the thought that it was created by God seems more plausible than the idea that, although the universe is contingent and not past eternal, it somehow just exists as a brute fact with no possible ultimate explanation. The fact that some scientific cosmologists do not see an intellectual need to go beyond that and seek a philosophical or theological explanation other than what science can provide does not entail that the question why anything at all exists is a meaningless or pointless question, unless one imposes on oneself arbitrary naturalistic restrictions.

Again, the principle of sufficient reason is an *a priori* principle, the rationality of which does not depend on our interactions with the empirical world. Many people have an interest in the question why the universe exists insofar as that question has implications for one's worldview and sense of the meaning and purpose of one's life. It is certainly true that for people who believe in God the role of that belief in their worldview goes far beyond satisfying a desire for an answer to the philosophical question why the universe exists. Carroll himself has an intense interest in questions of human values, meaning, and purpose. That the role of the concept of God is limited in its scientific fecundity need not prevent one from being open to the value of a religious worldview for enriching human endeavors that go beyond scientific inquiry.

It is worth noticing the ethical and quasi-religious motivation behind Krauss's preference for naturalism over theism. He seems to be saying that living meaningful lives in a world without a purpose given to us from on high requires courage, and this atheistic stance is obviously nobler than that of the religious person who needs a cosmic comforter. Krauss repeatedly reveals that he thinks the main motivation for affirming the existence of God is the need for comfort and consolation. In responding to theists who appeal to the Big Bang Theory to support belief in a creator Krauss writes, "You can choose to view the Big Bang as suggestive of a creator if you feel the need, or instead argue that the mathematics of general relativity explain the evolution of the universe right back to its beginning without the intervention of any deity. But such a metaphysical speculation is independent of the physical validity of the Big Bang itself and is irrelevant to our understanding of it."[25] Krauss may be right that the mathematics of general relativity explains the evolution of the universe all the way back to the beginning of the universe, but it does not explain the cause of the Big Bang itself. Although metaphysics seems to be a dirty word for Krauss, the question of the cause of the beginning of the universe is indeed a metaphysical question. Scien-

---

25. Krauss, *A Universe from Nothing*, 5–6.

tists have a tendency to try to divorce scientific theory from metaphysical inquiry, but if science leads us to the conclusion that the universe began to exist at the Big Bang and does not lead us to an ultimate explanation of the Big Bang itself, then a further quest for a plausible candidate for a First Cause is appropriate. Yes, this is metaphysical speculation, but as such it is beyond the scope of empirical science, and so the scientist, qua scientist, has no grounds for dismissing it as illegitimate. It is certainly false that the only motivation for such speculation is the need for comfort in the face of the bleakness and purposelessness of the universe that Krauss finds.

The question whether the universe exists because it was created by God is a straightforward philosophical question. Science cannot answer it. There are emotional and religious overtones of both the theistic and naturalistic answers. Scientific atheists find emotionally attractive the idea that there is no ultimate meaning and purpose of human existence beyond what they can forge for themselves in a purposeless world. Philosophical theists and other religious believers find more attractive the idea that human beings were created by a good God for a purpose, and that the purpose is ultimately good. To the extent that these two attitudes are based on emotion and personal preference, they do not provide a reason for preferring one worldview over the other. There is no scientific justification for ruling out as irrational the thought that God is the transcendent cause of the existence of the universe.

Krauss says that the God arrived at by cosmological arguments is far from the God of religion. He writes, "It is vital to realize that this deity bears no logical connection to the personal deities of the world's great religions, in spite of the fact that it is often used to justify them. A deist who is compelled to search for some overarching intelligence to establish order in nature, will not in general, be driven to the personal God of the scriptures by the same logic."[26]

Christian theologians such as Thomas Aquinas, who defend the cosmological argument, readily admit that the argument does not entail many of the attributes of the Christian God. Obviously an argument that God is the necessary First Cause of the universe entails only what is required in order to be the First Cause of the universe. That one line of argument fails to support everything that theists believe about God is hardly a serious objection to the cosmological argument as being relevant to theistic belief. The theist has other arguments to support other beliefs about God. The design argument suggests that God is also an intelligent being. Moral arguments suggest that God is morally good. Many theologians and religious

---

26. Krauss, *A Universe from Nothing*, 173.

philosophers believe that there are important religious reasons for thinking that it is religiously appropriate that the knowledge of God that is available by reason apart from revelation be very meager and by no means sufficient for religious faith. The deistic God of the philosophers and the God of Christianity are not two different entities, but rather two different descriptions of the same entity, the latter being far richer than the former, and both falling far short of the infinite greatness of God himself.

In summary, it seems that current science offers support for the second premise of the *kalam* cosmological argument—that the universe began to exist. The single Big Bang universe theory supports the universe beginning to exist 13.8 billion years ago. Whether the past timeline leads to a singularity point or rounded edge prior to Planck time, the universe would still have a finite age. To say with Hawking and Carroll that the no boundary model entails that the universe "did not pop into existence; it just is" seems like an evasion of the implications of the universe having a finite past and that a universe with a finite past needs a cause for its existence. The BGV theorem entails that even a multiverse must begin to exist if it has average overall positive expansion. It is hard to see how models that avoid the overall positive Hubble expansion can be realistic. If the pre-Big Bang scenario involves a contraction from an infinite past, it runs into the problem of how to explain the low entropy of the universe at the time of the Big Bang or bounce. If it tries to get around this problem by positing high entropy in the infinite past, then it must either deal with the problem posed by the second law of thermodynamics, which would entail that entropy must increase as the arrow of time moves forward into the future, or it must allow that somehow time can go in reverse "before" the Big Bang/bounce. However this would mean the so-called past period up to the Big Bang/bounce is not really past, but rather, relative to the moment of the Big Bang/bounce, an alternative future. So instead of avoiding a beginning of the universe, the model seems to posit a beginning with two arrows of time proceeding from it. The other possible way of getting around the BGV theorem is to posit an infinite static universe prior to the Big Bang. The problem then is that if the past eternal state is truly static, it cannot fluctuate to create our universe, and if it is not static, it cannot be past eternal; it cannot have existed for an infinitely long time without fluctuating before the Big Bang. Without that infinite period before the Big Bang it cannot compensate for the infinite expansion after the Big Bang in order to avoid an average positive Hubble expansion. So it seems that the most plausible view is that the universe began to exist.

If the universe began to exist, it seems plausible that there was a cause of its coming into existence. The principle that from nothing you cannot get something seems more plausibly to be an *a priori* principle of reason than a rule of thumb we got into the habit of believing as a consequence of dealing with everyday affairs. So both premises of the *kalam* argument seem more plausible than their contradictories.

6
Cosmic Fine-Tuning

As astrophysics developed in the twentieth century, a number of surprising discoveries were made concerning the precision with which the universe is constructed. Convincing evidence has been discovered that there are a variety of ways in which the structure of the universe must be very precisely set, or fine-tuned, in order to permit the existence of intelligent life forms, such as human beings. It turns out that a number of laws of physics, fundamental constants of physics, and initial conditions of the universe have been discovered to be fine-tuned in the sense that the range of life permitting values of such parameters is quite small in comparison with the range of values that are possible. The laws of nature, when expressed mathematically, involve certain constants, which have values that are not determined by the laws. For instance, Newton's law of gravitational attraction states that any two bodies attract each other with a force that is directly proportional to the product of their masses and inversely proportional to the square of the distance between them. This can be formulated as

$$F = \frac{G\, m_1 \times m_2}{r^2}$$

where F is the force between the two bodies, m is mass, and r is the distance between the center of the two bodies. G is the gravitational constant, which was eventually measured seventy-one years after Newton's death. The list of physical constants, in addition to the gravitational constant, include the cosmological constant, which helps govern the expansion of the universe, Planck's constant, the constants which determine the strength of the other fundamental forces (the strong and weak nuclear forces and the electromagnetic force), the constants that determine the masses of the fundamental particles, and the relative abundance of protons and neutrons in the early universe. It has been determined that if the numbers associated with the fundamental constants were only slightly different, the universe would be very different, so different that embodied intelligent life would be impossible. These parameters must be very finely calibrated, within very small tolerances, in order for the universe to exist long enough and get big enough to produce all the necessary physical ingredients to build complex organisms and a suitable environment to sustain the existence of living beings like ourselves.

The strength and range of the four fundamental forces of nature are critical for the possibility of life. The most familiar of these is gravity, the attractive force that not only keeps living organisms like ourselves attracted to planet earth and keeps the planet in its orbit around the sun, but is also necessary for the creation, continued existence, and orderly movement of the earth, sun, moon, stars, galaxies, and every physical body in the universe. Just as important is the strong nuclear force, which holds neutrons and protons together in the nuclei of atoms. Without that force, there would be no atoms or any of the elements that make up all the physical objects in the universe, including, of course, our bodies. The electromagnetic force is necessary in order for electrons to stay in their orbits around the nuclei of atoms. Without the electromagnetic force, atoms could not combine to form the molecules that make up all the compounds in the universe. The weak nuclear force governs the decay of many nuclear particles. The strengths and ranges of these four forces and their relationships to each other are all very finely tuned and of critical importance in order to allow the universe to contain galaxies, stars, planets, and living organisms with the kind of complex organic chemistry that we find on earth. Also important are the sizes and masses of the fundamental particles and their relationships to each other. It is very difficult to believe that this fine-tuning could be entirely due to blind chance. So it is not surprising that theists have used the evidence of fine-tuning to resurrect the design argument for the existence of God.

Here are some specific examples of fine-tuning.

1. The most extreme example of fine-tuning is the low entropy initial condition of the universe. Since entropy, or disorder, increases over time, in order for the universe to persist for the billions of years required for the creation of galaxies, stars, and planets, the entropy of the early universe must be very low. The probability of the early universe having the extremely low entropy of its initial condition was calculated by Sir Roger Penrose,[1] one of Britain's leading theoretical physicists,

---

1. Penrose, *The Road to Reality*, 343.

to be $1/10^{10^{123}}$. Penrose arrived at this number by first calculating the total entropy of the universe by multiplying the number of baryons (neutrons and protons) in the universe (10^{80}) by the total entropy of each baryon (10^{43}). The resulting 10^{123} represents the total phase-space of possible levels of entropy the universe could have. Given the age of the universe, the target level of entropy of the early universe consistent with the current actual level would be roughly one part in $10^{10^{123}}$. As Penrose puts the point, "This tells us how precise the Creator's aim must have been: namely to an accuracy of one part in $10^{10^{123}}$."[2] This means that the probability of the low entropy of the early universe existing by sheer chance is roughly one chance in $10^{10^{123}}$. As Robin Collins says of this improbability, "the precision required to 'hit' the right volume by chance is thus enormously greater than would be required to hit an individual proton if the entire visible universe were a dartboard?"[3] To write Penrose's number in decimal form would require vastly more zeroes than the number of baryons in the universe. Robert Spitzer writes that if the zeroes were written in 10-point type they would fill our galaxy.[4]

2. The cosmological constant, which governs the expansion of the universe, is said to be finely tuned to one part in 10^{120}. The cosmological constant governs the expansion of the universe. If the cosmological constant were too large, stars would be too hot and would burn up too quickly to produce the elements necessary for life. If it were too small, stars would be too cool to ignite nuclear fusion and no elements heavier than hydrogen would be produced.[5]

3. If the initial expansion of the universe had differed in strength by more than one part in 10^{60} life could never have been created. If the expansion rate were too slow, the universe would have quickly collapsed before creating suitable life sites. Were the rate of expansion greater by the critical degree, the universe would have thinned out before allowing the clumping that produces galaxies, stars, and planets, and hence, no life could have been created.[6]

4. Calculations by Brandon Carter indicate that the gravitational constant, which determines the strength of the force of gravity must be

---

2. Penrose, *The Road to Reality*, 343.
3. Collins, "The Fine-Tuning Evidence is Convincing," 38.
4. Spitzer, *New Proofs for the Existence of God*, 59.
5. Ross, *The Creator and the Cosmos*, 54.
6. Davies, *The Accidental Universe*, 90–91.

tuned to within a maximum deviation of 1 part in 10^{40} in order for the universe to produce stars.[7]

5. If the strong nuclear force, which binds neutrons and protons in the nucleus of atoms, had been about ten percent stronger, the result would be the production of nuclei of almost unlimited size, turning small bodies into mini neutron stars, which would not last long enough for life to evolve. If the strong force were too weak, protons and neutrons would not stick together, and no elements other than hydrogen would be produced.[8]

6. The weak nuclear force regulates the helium production process in stars. The energy from stars is produced by nuclear fusion of hydrogen atoms into helium. The weak force slows the process so that stars can burn continuously over a long period of time rather than exploding like hydrogen bombs.[9] If the weak nuclear force were too strong, "then the Big Bang's nuclear burning would have proceeded past helium all the way to iron."[10] This would mean there would be no carbon, oxygen, or most of the other elements essential to life. If the weak force were too weak, too little heavy matter for rocky planets would be produced in stars. The universe would be all hydrogen and helium, an unlikely prospect for the production of living organisms or suitable environments for them. In other words, if the weak force were not just right, the universe would be either mostly iron or mostly helium, neither outcome conducive to the possibility of life. Furthermore, the weak force is critical to the behavior of stars when they explode as Type II Supernovae, which are responsible for expelling the elements created in stars to locations where planets can be formed.

These are only a few of the examples of fine-tuning discussed in the literature, but they are some of the clearest and least controversial. They are often referred to as "anthropic coincidences." Hugh Ross lists thirty in the 2001 edition of *The Creator and the Cosmos*,[11] but many of them are controversial. Even if some of the examples are questionable, there are enough anthropic coincidences to support the claim that the conditions necessary for human life to exist are very tightly constrained. When one multiplies the probabilities of several of the fine-tuned parameters, one very

---

7. Collins, "A Scientific Argument for the Existence of God," 322.
8. Leslie, *Universes*, 34.
9. Davies, *Cosmic Jackpot*, 134.
10. Leslie, *Universes*, 36.
11. Ross, *The Creator and the Cosmos*, 221–27.

quickly arrives at a mind-bogglingly low probability of the existence of a life-permitting universe.

THE FINE-TUNING ARGUMENT

Many theists have argued that the fine-tuning of the universe is evidence of design. Robin Collins constructs a fine-tuning design argument for the existence of God. Collins bases his argument on the likelihood principle, or what he sometimes calls the prime principle of confirmation.[12] "Simply put, the principle says that whenever we are considering two competing hypotheses, an observation counts as evidence in favor of the hypothesis under which the observation has the highest probability (or is the least improbable)."[13] The likelihood principle is used by detectives, scientists, and automobile mechanics. For instance, suppose your opponent in a poker game is dealt a royal flush. Two hypotheses are considered. The first, the design hypothesis, Hd, is that the dealer cheated by arranging the cards in advance so that the opponent would be dealt a royal flush. Hc is the chance hypothesis; there was no cheating and the royal flush was dealt by chance. The question arises, which of these two hypotheses is the better explanation of why the royal flush was dealt? If we apply the likelihood principle, we must consider which hypothesis makes the observation—the dealing of the royal flush—more probable. Given Hc, it is very improbable that your opponent will be dealt the royal flush. Under Hd it is much less improbable. Suspicion of cheating would be quite justified. If several consecutive royal flush hands are dealt, threats of violence will ensue!

So here is Collins's argument:

Premise 1. The existence of the fine-tuning is not improbable under theism.

Premise 2. The existence of the fine-tuning is very improbable under the atheistic hypothesis.

Conclusion: From premises (1) and (2) and the likelihood principle, it follows that the fine-tuning data provide strong evidence to favor the design hypothesis over the atheistic hypothesis.[14]

This argument is not intended as a proof. Collins is very explicit that his argument shows only that fine-tuning is evidence for the existence of

12. Collins, "A Scientific Argument for the Existence of God," 47–75.
13. Collins, "A Scientific Argument for the Existence of God," 51.
14. Collins, "A Scientific Argument for the Existence of God," 53.

God. It does not prove that God exists or even that it is more rational to believe that God exists than not. The most it shows is that fine-tuning provides evidence that raises to some degree the epistemic probability that God exists. The argument does show that the fact of cosmic fine-tuning is evidence for the existence of God. One of the standard objections that science fans give against theism is that there is no evidence for the existence of God. Well, the fine-tuning argument shows that there is at least some evidence for the existence of God. It is possible that fine-tuning is the result of chance. However, the point is that the design hypothesis makes fine-tuning much more probable than does the chance hypothesis, and this means that fine-tuning is evidence of design.

The probability of fine-tuning being the result of chance alone is difficult to calculate, but we know that it is exceedingly low. If one considers only the low entropy condition of the early universe, the probability would be lower than one chance in $10^{10^{123}}$. It might be argued that the probability of fine-tuning by sheer chance is infinitesimal, because the range of possible values for the various finely tuned parameters, from which the "correct" one is selected, is infinite. On the other hand, Collins argues that if God exists, then fine-tuning is not at all surprising. If we consider some of the standard beliefs about the nature of God, for instance, that God is omnipotent and supremely good, then it is not at all surprising that if God exists, he would create a world that is highly complex, ordered, intelligible, and well suited for the existence of life, including intelligent life that enjoys the possibility of knowing about the universe and its creator. It is at least less surprising than that such an orderly world would exist purely by chance. Unless the existence of God is inherently more improbable than fine-tuning by chance, it would seem that fine-tuning is evidence supporting the theistic hypothesis.

To some critics of the fine-tuning argument it seems too much of a God of the gaps argument—bringing in God to explain the gaps in the scientific account. On the contrary, as John Lennox points out, the fine-tuning is not a God of the gaps argument because it is not based on gaps in our scientific understanding; it is based on scientific information about the universe.[15] There is no gap in the science that God is invoked to explain. If the universe began to exist at the Big Bang, the initial conditions are in place from the beginning of the universe, so it would seem that no scientific explanation for the initial conditions of the universe is in principle possible. If there is a cause that explains the initial conditions, it must be a transcendent, metaphysical cause.

---

15. Lennox, *God's Undertaker*, 73.

Some might argue that a more rational approach to the issue would be to hold off appeals to God and continue to search for a scientific explanation of fine-tuning. It might be expected that the fine-tuned parameters will be found to be based on more fundamental mathematically necessary laws. As Robin Collins, Bernard Carr, and Martin Rees[16] have noted, this would not really make it any less surprising that the fundamental constants of nature are fine-tuned for life. As Collins puts it, this "simply transfers the improbability [of fine-tuning] up one level: of all the laws and parameters of physics that could conceivably have been logically necessary, it seems highly improbable that it would be just those that are life-permitting."[17]

Paul Davies sees several problems with the inference to a designer God. First, the appeal to God does not really explain anything. When one is seeking a scientific explanation of some phenomenon, one wants to know the physical cause or mechanism. To be told simply that God did it is unilluminating. One would want to know why and how God did it. Second, the appeal to a designer will simply kick the question up another level and raise the question who designed the designer, and we are off on a regress. If the appeal to the designer was triggered by the complexity and fine-tuning of the universe, then the designer must be at least as complex, and thus in need of explanation. Third, the designer might not be God; it might be a natural being or some evolved "supermind."[18] A natural super-being would not provide an ultimate explanation of fine-tuning, for clearly we would want an explanation of how and why such a natural being acts as it does. And fourth, if the designer-creator is a transcendent God, which it seems it would have to be in order to have a chance of escaping the third objection, then it is unclear how this would provide a coherent explanation of why the universe is fine-tuned. God would be a necessary being who exists outside of time. Davies writes,

> It is far from clear to me whether such a conclusion is logically valid or conceptually coherent.... We are still confronted with the problem that, in spite of God's necessary existence and nature, God did *not necessarily* create the universe as it is, but instead merely *chose* to do so. But now the alarm bells ring. Can a necessary being act in a manner that is not necessary? Does that make sense? On the face of it, it doesn't. If God is necessarily as

---

16. Carr and Rees, "The Anthropic Cosmological Principle and the Structure of the Physical World," 605–12.

17. Collins, "A Scientific Argument for the Existence of God," 56.

18. Davies, *Cosmic Jackpot*, 265.

God is, then God's choices are necessarily as they are, and the freedom of choice evaporates.[19]

If God is a necessary being, then God cannot be free not to create the universe as it is. Then the universe turns out to be a necessary being. If the universe exists necessarily as it is, then the fine-tuning is accounted for without the appeal to God. God thus becomes redundant, and adds no explanatory power to the idea of the universe having its fine-tuned characteristics by virtue of necessary laws.

How might we respond to these objections? The first objection, that an explanation in terms of design is worthless unless we know how and why the designer operated, is simply false. We often explain phenomena in terms of design and designers without knowing how and why the designers did what they did, and such explanations are not worthless. If an archeologist finds elaborate markings on the side of a stone wall in the ruins of an ancient city, the explanation that the markings are the product of human action is not undermined by the lack of knowledge of how or why the marks were put on the wall, or what they mean. The explanation of why the top of Mt. Rushmore looks like four former presidents of the United States in terms of the actions of human agents who designed and carved the mountain according to a design plan of some sort is not worthless for lack of knowledge of why or how they did it. Of course, if we do know how and why they did it, our explanation is enhanced and our understanding increased. Although it would be nice to know how and why God created the universe as he did, the lack of such knowledge does not render the hypothesis that the universe is fine-tuned because a transcendent intelligent being designed and created it worthless or completely lacking in explanatory power. Rational belief that the universe exists because it was designed and created by a transcendent, immaterial, powerful, intelligent being who did so for a good purpose, whether we know what that purpose is, is more and better than sheer ignorance of why the universe exists.

What about the argument that the designer must also be complex and that there must be a designer of the designer? It does not follow from the complexity of the universe that a designer of it must be more complex. The traditional view of God is that God is immaterial mind or spirit and absolutely simple. If God is not a material being, then God is neither complex nor has parts. The traditional arguments about the nature of God lead to the idea that God cannot be a complex or material being if God is the ultimate ground of the existence of the universe. The great Christian theologians have long recognized that for God to be the ultimate ground and first cause

---

19. Davies, *Cosmic Jackpot*, 203–4.

of the universe, God must be immaterial, so of course a complex God is not the ultimate being. It remains difficult to understand how a simple, immaterial mind could cause physical phenomena or design and bring into existence a fine-tuned physical universe out of nothing, but is it any more difficult than understanding how the fine-tuning of the universe could have resulted from sheer dumb luck?

Another commonly heard objection to the fine-tuning argument is that there are other life-forms that could exist if the fine-tuned parameters were different, so we should not think that life could not exist if the parameters that we find in our universe were different. However, there is nothing about the fine-tuning argument that requires that the life forms that we find on earth are the only life-forms that are possible. It may well be true that a universe with different fundamental laws and constants might permit intelligent life to exist, but this would not undermine the fine-tuning argument. The fundamental constants are not determined by the laws of nature; they are put into the equations of the laws after the equations are formulated. Given the laws that do exist in our universe, the fundamental constants that are required for life are finely tuned and extremely improbable. This is the fact that needs to be explained. If the laws of nature were different, perhaps a different set of constants would be life-permitting. The issue remains why in this universe, with its physical laws, the fundamental constants should be just right for life. Even if a different set of laws and constants are compatible with the existence of other life-forms, the fact still remains that the life-forms that exist in this universe require a very high degree of fine-tuning. The claim that a fine-tuned automobile factory is necessary in order to build Buicks is not even slightly undermined by the fact that there could be other kinds of machines built in a very different kind of factory.

What about the objection that the designer responsible for fine-tuning might be a natural being that does not provide an ultimate explanation? The very fact that a natural being would not provide an ultimate explanation of the existence of the universe is a reason to think the designer of the universe is not a natural being. This objection, as well as the previous one that the designer would be complex and therefore in need of a further explanation, points toward the suggestion that the designer that is needed to explain the existence of a fine-tuned universe is a simple, immaterial, spiritual, transcendent, supernatural being—God, as traditionally conceived. It is the God conceived as natural and complex that fails to provide a final explanation, which is a reason to reject the natural God in favor of the transcendent one.

It is the traditional idea of a God who is transcendent and a necessary being that raises the problem of how a necessary being can have freedom of choice. Davies admits that there is a history of Christian thinkers struggling to make sense of the relation of a finite, contingent world to an infinite, eternal, transcendent, and necessary God. Davies also admits his lack of expertise to sort out these issues: "Confused? I certainly am. I am not an accomplished enough philosopher to evaluate these explanations."[20] Given Davies's admission, we should perhaps take his questioning of the coherence of a necessary God and a contingent creation as a question pointing to a problem to be wrestled with rather than a knock-down argument against the coherence of theism.

As we have already noted, Craig argues that the best way to explain how the universe could have a beginning of its existence and an eternal cause of that beginning is that it was created by a personal being with will. Both Craig and Davies agree that if God exists, God is a necessary being. Davies cannot see how a God who is a necessary being could have free choice and be the cause of a contingent universe. Craig's point is that the only way an eternal being could be the cause of a contingent universe that has a beginning in the finite past is for that eternal being to be an agent with free choice.

Who has the stronger argument? It does seem difficult to see how the universe could have a finite age if its cause is eternal. What about the other problem—reconciling God's necessity with his freedom? According to Davies the problem is that if God is a necessary being, all the attributes of God must be necessary. So God's being a creator must be a necessary attribute. Does that mean that God is not free? God could still be free in the sense that God is not constrained to create or limited in what he can create by anything other than himself and his own will. The universe is still contingent in the sense that its existence is entirely dependent upon God as its cause. *How* the universe is, as well as *that* it is, are entirely dependent upon God.

Davies has difficulty with the idea of a transcendent God, but he also sees that a natural God cannot provide an ultimate explanation of the existence of the universe, and he sees that the possibility of accounting for fine-tuning by showing that it is a necessary consequence of the laws of physics or mathematics is not very promising. Even if we could show that fine-tuning could be derived from pure mathematics, we would still need something to "breathe fire into the equations," to bring the fine-tuned universe into existence.

---

20. Davies, *Cosmic Jackpot*, 204.

THE MULTIVERSE EXPLANATION OF FINE-TUNING

The best alternative to the God hypothesis as an explanation of fine-tuning is the many worlds hypothesis. The most popular version of this approach is the inflationary multiverse. Suppose there are many worlds beyond the visible universe, different pockets of the multiverse, and the physical laws and constants vary across the different pockets of the multiverse. Suppose the physical constants and laws vary randomly over wide ranges of possible values across the different universes, so that it is probable that some of the universes will by chance have the conditions that are necessary in order for life to exist. No matter how improbable it is that any one universe should have just the right constants and physical laws that make possible the existence of intelligent life, it is quite probable that in a world ensemble or multiverse of many universes some will get it just right. Given enough chances, no matter how improbable the desired result is, sooner or later you will get it. This is another application of the idea that given enough time, anything that can happen, will happen. If it is possible for all the conditions necessary for life to exist, then given enough trials, eventually some will get exactly the right conditions.

Discussions of fine-tuning and the multiverse are usually associated with the anthropic principle. The anthropic principle is sometimes thought of as a teleological principle that indicates that the universe is somehow biased in favor of the production of life, but most scientists who use the principle think of it as a selection principle that removes teleological implications from the fact of fine-tuning. The anthropic principle was first introduced by Brandon Carter, who formulated both a weak and strong version of it. The weak anthropic principle is that "our location in the universe is *necessarily* privileged to the extent of being compatible with our existence as observers."[21] As many have noted, this principle is trivially true. All it says is that given that we living beings exist, the universe must have the conditions necessary for our existence. The strong anthropic principle says that our universe "must be such as to admit the creation of observers within it at some stage."[22] The basic idea is that in considering the issues raised by fine-tuning and attempts to reflect on the probabilities of the universe having the characteristics that are essential to life, we need to recognize that only such characteristics that are compatible with the existence of observers can ever be observed by us. Of course, this also is a tautology; we can only observe conditions that are compatible with our existence as observers. But

---

21. Carter, *Confrontation of Cosmological Theories with Observation*, 291.
22. Leslie, *Universes*, 128.

the anthropic principle is supposed to have implications for our assessment of the degree to which the improbability of fine-tuning calls for our being surprised or astonished and inclined to think that a special explanation is needed. The anthropic principle is supposed to have the effect of reducing the "wow factor." Suppose someone says, "look how fine-tuned the universe is; look how improbable it is that the universe would have all the requirements for the existence of life!" Armed with the anthropic principle someone might reply, "Well, it is not surprising that the universe is fine-tuned for life, because if it weren't, we wouldn't be here to notice that it wasn't fine-tuned. So the fact that we (observers) are here means that the universe must be fine-tuned, so it is not surprising that it is."

The anthropic principle functions as a selection principle. John Leslie tells the fishing story, which involves your catching a fish 23.2576 inches long.[23] Is such an exact length surprising? Of course not, because the fish had to be some length or other, so why not 23.2576 inches? Then you discover that the fishing apparatus will only catch fish that are 23.2576 inches long, plus or minus one part in a million. Is it now surprising that you caught the fish with a length within that narrow range? It depends. Suppose there are millions of fish in the lake of various lengths and plenty within the range of your fishing device. Then it is not at all surprising that you caught the fish. This is the many fish hypothesis, which corresponds to the multiverse or many worlds hypothesis. That any fish you catch must be very close to 23.2576 inches long does not mean the lake was designed to provide fish that you could catch. Your apparatus selects the fish that are the right length because only those fish can be caught by your apparatus. This is how the anthropic principle works. Only universes with observers can be observed, so observers select only universes that are fine-tuned for the possibility of observers, which requires life, since only living beings can observe anything. Another possible explanation of why you caught a fish that is almost exactly 23.2576 inches long is that your apparatus will only catch fish very close to that length, there is only one fish in the lake, but it was put there by a generous person who, knowing about your apparatus, wanted you to catch that fish. This is analogous to the God hypothesis. Without additional information, there is no reason to prefer the many fish explanation to the generous fish stocker explanation. You might think the generous fish stocker explanation is rather far-fetched, but that is only because we know that lakes typically have lots of fish, and it's a little weird to think that someone would stock a lake with one fish, fine-tuned to fit someone's fishing apparatus. But who knows? It is unusual to have a fishing apparatus that catches only fish

---

23. Leslie, *Universes*, ch. 1.

that are very close to 23.2576 inches long. The one explanation that will not seem at all plausible is that there is just one fish in the lake and by chance it happens to be within one part in a million exactly 23.2576 inches long and by chance your apparatus is suited to catch fish exactly that length. This is the situation we have with one universe that by sheer chance happened to be fine-tuned for life. It will not help to say, "Well, it's not surprising that the fish you caught was 23.2576 inches long because your apparatus can only catch fish that are that long." The apparatus qua selection principle reduces the surprising aspect of catching exactly the right-sized fish only if there were a lot of fish from which it could select. If there is just one fish, it is very surprising that it happened to be just the right size. So the anthropic principle only makes fine-tuning unsurprising if either there is a designer God or many universes.

Some are willing to attribute fine-tuning to chance and argue that there is nothing there that calls for special explanation because everything that happens is hugely improbable. It was enormously improbable that I would be born. The probability of all the factors required for me to be born is extremely low, and yet here I am. Is that evidence for the existence of God? Surely not! If I were not here, someone else would be, and the probability of her being here would be as low as that of my being here now. The universe had to have some set of constants and fundamental characteristics. If it didn't have the ones that it does, the ones that make life possible, then it would have some other set. We would not know it because we would not exist. No one would know it because there would be no observers. However, that state of affairs would be just as improbable as the fine-tuning that does in fact exist. Something had to happen; it might as well be this. Fine-tuning had just as good a chance as any other cosmic scenario.

Leslie argues that when thinking about whether it is plausible to attribute fine-tuning to chance we should take into account the value of life. The situation that exists as a result of the fine-tuning of the universe makes the world much better than it would be without observers or life. To illustrate the point Leslie gives the example of being dealt a Bridge hand of all spades. That hand is no more improbable than any other. Every possible hand is equally improbable, yet we are not surprised if we get random assortment of cards of different suits. What makes it surprising to get the hand of all spades is that such a hand has value in the context of the game of Bridge. For that reason we think it much more probable that the dealer was cheating than that the hand was fairly dealt. If a missile is shot 10 million light years into space and hits a target the size of a postage stamp, we are surprised and inclined to think that it was not sheer chance that the missile hit the target. The missile had to end up somewhere and the odds of it ending up on any particular spot are equally low. However, hitting a target has a special significance that we take into account when questioning why the missile landed there. We are justified in being surprised if on one firing of the missile we hit the target. Yes, every possible destination of the missile is enormously improbable and the target is no more improbable than any of the others, but the special significance we attach to hitting the target makes us suspect that if we hit it, more than chance is involved. And we would suspect cheating if the dealer serves up thirteen spades to our rival in Bridge. So too we have reason to be surprised at the fine-tuning we find in the universe. True, this combination of fundamental laws and constants may be no more improbable than any other, but the fact that the existence of life, especially intelligent life, is especially valuable makes the chance hypothesis less plausible.

Things change if there are a huge number of universes. If we play 15 billion rounds of Bridge, sooner or later someone will be dealt thirteen spades. If we launch our missile 10^{500} times, we will eventually hit the target. So given enough universes, eventually some of them will get all the fine-tuning parameters just right for life. The multiverse hypothesis is a formidable alternative to the designer God hypothesis. Given an infinite number of trials, anything that can happen, will happen. In an infinite number of universes, there will be occasions where Bridge dealers serve up 137 consecutive perfect hands. Paul Davies writes,

> A well-known aphorism says that in an infinite universe anything that can happen must happen. Subject to some mathematical pedantry, that is true. A simple example is coin tossing. The odds against flipping a coin and getting heads 1,000 times in a row is almost infinitesimally small (about one chance in 10^{301}). Nevertheless, if there are enough coins being tossed, it will happen somewhere. . . . If an infinite number of coins is being tossed, however, the getting 1,000 heads in a row is absolutely certain: infinity will beat any odds, however adverse. In fact, 1,000 heads will crop up not just once, but an infinite number of times.[24]

No matter how improbable fine-tuning is, if there are an infinite number of universes, the logical possibility that some of them are fine-tuned ensures that some will be fine-tuned.

Sean Carroll thinks that the God hypothesis to explain fine-tuning encounters a problem due to excessive fine-tuning. If the universe is finely tuned because God designed it for life, we would expect that it would be tuned just enough to get that job done. Carroll acknowledges that the

---

24. Davies, *Cosmic Jackpot*, 174

multiverse does not yet explain the extremely low entropy of our observable universe, but he is confident that science will figure it out. He says that the tuning of the

> low entropy of the early universe to one part in $10^{10^{123}}$ [is] a preposterous number. The entropy didn't need to be nearly that low in order for life to come into existence. One way of thinking about this is to note that we certainly don't need a hundred billion other galaxies in the universe in order for life to arise here on Earth; our single galaxy would have been fine, or for that matter a single solar system. . . . It is unclear why God would do so much more fine-tuning of the state of the universe than seems to have been necessary.[25]

This seems like a preposterous complaint. Why should we think that if an omnipotent God is the designer of the universe he would only create a universe that is just fine-tuned enough to permit the existence of human life? As for there being more galaxies than are needed for life to exist on earth, it may be that there are many other life sites in the universe. The theist who thinks that the universe is designed for life does not necessarily think that the universe is designed only for the sake of human life. God may have other projects underway as well. Efficiency is not a high priority for an omnipotent being, so the fact that the universe is more finely tuned than is necessary for us to exist is not a strong objection to theism.

PROBLEMS WITH THE MULTIVERSE

We have already seen that multiverse theories do not succeed in avoiding the need for the beginning of the universe. How do they fare in dealing with the fine-tuning issue? In the eternal inflation model, a universe is spontaneously generated when, after a small region of spacetime in the quantum vacuum for a fraction of a second undergoes exponential expansion, inflationary expansion collapses and ordinary cosmic expansion resumes, resulting in a new expanding universe. As the multiverse expands, more bubble universes can be created, like blisters on the surface of a balloon. Suppose a theory of eternal inflation can get around the BGV theorem and we can have a beginningless, eternally inflating multiverse. If the quantum vacuum universe generator has no beginning, then it has been producing universes for an infinitely long time. If this process has been going on eternally, there would

---

25. Carroll, "Does the Universe Need God?"

be an infinite number of universes within the multiverse. What if there are an infinite number of universes?

Several problematic consequences follow if there is no beginning, the past is infinite, and there are an infinite number of bubble universes. One problem is the logical absurdities that follow from an actual infinite, whether it is an actual infinite number of universes or an actual infinite number of past events in one universe (which would follow from a beginningless universe). There are also some additional weird metaphysical problems with an infinite number of universes, which have been described by Paul Davies. One is that if there are an infinite number of universes, then every possible state of affairs exists in some universe or other. This follows from the very plausible suggestion that we have previously encountered, that given enough time, anything that can happen, will happen. Given infinite time and an infinite number of universes, every possible state of affairs will exist in some universe. This means that any state of affairs that is logically consistent does actually exist in some universe.[26] Furthermore, if it is possible for something to happen once, it is possible for it to happen many, or even an infinite number, of times. So arguably, everything will happen an infinite number of times. This is modal realism, the view that every possible world, every possible state of affairs, actually exists. This would also imply Nietzsche's idea of eternal recurrence. Not only are there parallel universes in which you (or your counterpart) do everything that is possible for you to do, but all of those actions are repeated an infinite number of times.

If every possible state of affairs exists in some actual universe, then among the possibilities that will exist is the production of fake, or simulated universes.[27] Frank Tipler has proposed that in the future it will be possible for super-advanced civilizations to produce computers that can generate simulated universes that are indistinguishable from real universes.[28] It has been suggested that it may become so cheap and easy to produce simulated universes that they will become extremely plentiful, so plentiful that they may outnumber the real universes.[29] Nick Bostrom suggests this as a possibility, not an inevitability, but in an infinite universe scenario, it would be an inevitability. If the simulated universes outnumber the real ones, Borstrom suggests, then it would be more probable that the universe we are living in is a simulated one. If this is so, then for all we know, this universe is a fake. The possibility that this universe is a fake, (and that if it were, it would

26. Davies, *Cosmic Jackpot*, 210–12.
27. Davies, *Cosmic Jackpot*, 183–88.
28. See Tipler, *The Physics of Immortality*.
29. See Bostrom, "Are You Living in a Computer Simulation?"

be impossible to know that it is, since fake universes look exactly like real ones), means that it's impossible to know that our universe is not a simulation. If we cannot know that we are not living in a fake, computer-simulated universe, then scientific knowledge of the real world would be impossible. So Davies argues that the infinite multiverse model threatens the rationality of the scientific enterprise itself. It is a very serious mark against a scientific theory that it threatens to undermine the viability of science itself. Scientific theories should not undermine the possibility of science as a rational enterprise. It is another case where naturalism manifests a tendency to undermine itself and science.

Consider that every possible world that contains moral beings with free will and the ability to perpetrate evil has a certain admixture of good and evil. Modal realism would entail that every possible combination of good and evil, and every degree of evil that could possibly exist does actually exist in some actually existing universe. Every manner and degree of suffering that is logically possible actually exists in some universe or other. This is an extremely undesirable consequence of modal realism, to say the least. It seems that the multiverse theory, at least the infinite number of universes variety, has a problem of evil worse than theism's.

Davies's fake universe argument, however, only works if one assumes it is possible to produce a world simulation that is indistinguishable from the real world and that consciousness can be produced by computers. Both of these assumptions are very questionable. But even if we can escape the possibility of fake universes, we still have the problem of modal realism as a consequence of an actual infinite number of universes.

Another problem with the multiverse theory is the lack of empirical support. Given the lack of interaction between different universes, it is difficult to conceive how there could be any possible empirical test. Davies suggests some possible indirect empirical tests, but they are highly controversial and not now technically possible.

Yet another difficulty with the many universes hypothesis as an explanation of fine-tuning is that it doesn't really explain fine-tuning, or anything, for that matter. Instead of offering an explanation, it provides a way of attributing fine-tuning to chance. We wanted to know why the highly improbable conditions that are necessary for life to exist obtained, and the answer turns out to be that there are an infinite number of trials, so some of them get it right. If you survive the firing squad and want to know why, how much are you helped by the claim that there are an infinite number of universes and so no matter how improbable it is that anyone ever survives a firing squad, if it is even remotely possible, it does happen occasionally, and you were one of the lucky ones? That is not an explanation; it is merely an excuse for saying that it was just sheer dumb luck! If that passes for an explanation, then any improbable event could be explained by saying, "There are an infinite number of universes, so if x is possible, then in some universe or other x will be, and on this occasion, our universe happens to be the one in which x exists."

The one attraction of the theory is that it might explain fine-tuning without a designer. But does it really? Robin Collins argues that even if there were an infinite number of universes, the need for a designer would not be obviated. If the mechanism that generates universes is able to produce diverse universes that randomly vary the physical laws and constants such that every possible configuration is produced, then the universe generator itself would have to be fine-tuned, which would simply raise the question of the explanation of fine-tuning up another level. We would still need an explanation for the fine-tuning of the universe generator.[30]

Collins does not claim that fine-tuning can only be explained by an intelligent designer; he claims only that the God hypothesis is a better explanation than chance, whether there is one universe or an infinite number of universes. His argument is an inference to the best explanation and is intended only to show that fine-tuning is evidence that increases the probability that God exists. Collins does not even claim that the argument makes it irrational to deny the existence of God. The argument does show that fine-tuning is evidence that provides some support for belief that God exists and makes it possible for people to reasonably believe that God exists. So both cosmic fine-tuning and Big Bang cosmology provide evidence that God exists. Not only is Christian theism compatible with modern science, but two of the major developments in modern scientific cosmology provide evidence for the existence of God.

---

30. Collins, "A Scientific Argument for the Existence of God," 61–62.

7

The Challenge of Religious Diversity

The diversity of religions constitutes a serious challenge to the credibility of theistic belief in the current ultural climate. The issue is not new. All religions have developed in contexts that involved tensions between different belief systems. Buddhism developed out of a critique of what we now call Hinduism, which itself is a complex tradition comprised of many competing strands. Christianity arose from its parent tradition, which we now call Judaism, and developed in competition with Greco-Roman paganism. Throughout the period of medieval Scholasticism, Christian theology reached a high level of maturity in large measure through its response to Islamic and Greek thought, both of which had to be regarded as serious challenges to the Christian faith. From the very beginning of its history Christianity especially has been energized by the command to spread the gospel throughout the world, a motive that is intelligible only in the context of a world populated by people of faiths other than that taught by Jesus.

Religions make truth claims concerning matters of utmost importance, and they often explicitly or implicitly make claims that at least seem to contradict each other. Belief that certain propositions about the world are true is not the only, and some would argue not even the most important, aspect of religion, but most religions do involve their adherents holding some beliefs about ultimate reality that seem to contradict those held by adherents of other religions. Although the precise relation between religious belief and practice is one of the areas about which religions may disagree, it is a basic assumption of this inquiry that we must reject as false one of any pair of statements that blatantly contradict each other.

EXCLUSIVISM, INCLUSIVISM, AND PLURALISM

Christians have responded to the issues raised by the implications of religious diversity in a number of ways. Alan Race, in *Christians and Religious Pluralism*, coined the terms that are widely used in current discussions of the problem of religious diversity—*exclusivism*, *inclusivism*, and *pluralism*.[1] Throughout most of Christian history the dominant position has been exclusivism, but this can be said of most religions, since most religious believers of any faith tend to think their own beliefs are truer than the beliefs of other religions. The most straightforward approach to dealing with a set of conflicting belief systems is to say that at most one can be true, and any beliefs that conflict with the true ones must be false. In the case of religions we are dealing with complex sets of beliefs, which may contain complicated admixtures of truth and falsity. Presumably most religions involve not just a list of statements affirmed by their adherents, but at least fairly coherent systems of beliefs that more or less rise and fall together. So while admitting that all religions contain at least some truth claims that may be false, let us say that an exclusivist is one who believes that at least the most central or fundamental truth claims of her religion are true, and beliefs that conflict with them are false. In saying that Christianity is the one true religion, the Christian exclusivist does not necessarily mean that it is the whole truth and nothing but the truth and that all other religions are completely or mostly false. She means, rather, that the most important doctrines of Christianity are true, and the claims of any other religion that conflict with the most essential Christian doctrines must be false. This leaves open the possibility that other religions may teach many doctrines that are true.

Applied to the issue of salvation, exclusivism is usually taken to imply that one's own religion provides the one true account of salvation and the one and only way of attaining salvation. A Christian exclusivist holds that Christianity is the one true religion and that all other religions are false insofar as they conflict with essential Christian doctrine, and that salvation is available only through the means articulated by Christian teaching. Exclusivists differ among themselves on the question of whether one must be a Christian in order to receive salvation. Although many Christian exclusivists believe not only that salvation is made possible by the death and resurrection of Christ and that salvation is possible only for those who explicitly "accept" Christ by faith, some are hopeful that the salvation mediated by Christ is attainable through grace by persons of other faiths who have never been exposed to the gospel.

---

1. Race, *Christians and Religious Pluralism*, chs. 2–4.

Christian exclusivism is not only out of fashion today, but is widely regarded as an unwarranted and even morally repugnant view. Since religious truth claims are matters of faith, it is widely held that there are no rational criteria for determining the objective truth of any one religion, and so it seems unwarranted to hold that just one religion has *the* one absolute truth. It seems arrogant, intolerant, and unduly harsh to believe that only adherents of one's own faith can attain salvation. To opponents of exclusivism it seems morally repugnant especially for Christians to accept exclusivism, because Christianity teaches that many people do not attain salvation, and that those who are not saved are doomed to everlasting damnation. Thus a seemingly much more attractive and moderate position is inclusivism, which holds that, though one religion is the true one, many other religions are partially true, and salvation can be attained by adherents of other religions. One way of drawing the line between exclusivism and inclusivism is to hold that the latter acknowledges the possibility of salvation for non-Christians and the former does not. However, the matter is complicated by the fact that some Christian exclusivists allow the possibility of salvation for non-Christians. Insofar as some forms of exclusivism allow the possibility of salvation for adherents of other religions, it may seem that the difference between exclusivism and inclusivism is only a matter of degree. Some Christian exclusivists acknowledge the possibility of salvation for non-Christians and some Christian inclusivists hold that Christianity is the true religion, in the sense that the partial truth of the other religions is ultimately explainable in terms of Christian doctrine. So the gap between exclusivism and inclusivism is sometimes rather slight. Both can allow for the possibility of salvation for non-Christians.

Although Karl Rahner is widely considered the foremost proponent of Christian inclusivism,[2] Gavin D'Costa[3] holds that it is essential to inclusivism that other religions be regarded as *per se* means of mediating salvation to their adherents. Saved Buddhists are saved by being good Buddhists, not by being anonymous Christians. It is still Christ who saves them, not Buddha or their own disciplinary efforts to attain enlightenment or nirvana. Their Buddhist practice does not make them anonymous Christians, but it does open them to the possibility of receiving saving grace from the Christian God through Christ. The difference between moderate exclusivism and inclusivism depends on what and how much is made of the role of adherence to the practice of the non-Christian religion in mediating divine grace and revelation.

2. See Rahner, "Faith, Hope, and Charity."
3. See D'Costa, "The Impossibility of Pluralist View of Religions."

Let us call exclusivism which allows the possibility of salvation for non-Christians "moderate exclusivism." Is there a significant distinction between moderate exclusivism and inclusivism? The critical issue here is whether the salvation received by adherents of other religions is mediated by those other religions *per se* or solely through the Christian revelation implicit in the other beliefs and practice of the other religion. Put differently, the issue is whether the salvation received by the non-Christian is mediated through that person's own non-Christian religion, or whether it is mediated through some sort of tacit response of the non-Christian to the Christian revelation, which the non-Christian's own religion imperfectly expresses. Is the Buddhist who receives salvation saved by the practice of Buddhism, which is *per se* an avenue through which God's grace is mediated, or is the Buddhist saved by somehow tacitly participating, unbeknownst to her, in the church of Jesus Christ, and thereby receiving grace through the Christian revelation? Let us say that the moderate exclusivist is one who acknowledges the possibility of the salvation of the Buddhist, but holds that the Buddhist is saved by means of the Christian revelation, which is implicit in the Buddhist's beliefs and practice. The saved Buddhist is, to use Karl Rahner's term, an "anonymous Christian." She is tacitly a Christian, saved by Christ, without knowing the source of her salvation. Let us call one who holds that a Buddhist can attain salvation through Buddhist practice, which is *per se* a medium through which divine grace is received, an inclusivist.

Whether inclusivism is conceived as affirming the possibility of adherents of other religions being anonymous Christians, or as affirming that other religions *per se* can be legitimate, albeit inferior, avenues for receiving salvifically efficacious divine revelation, it is still regarded by some theologians and Christian philosophers as subject to many of the same objections as exclusivism. It is thought to be almost as arrogant to hold that a Buddhist is saved by Christ as it is to think that he is on his way to hell because he has never heard of Christ. Either way is to regard Christianity as superior to the other's religion. Thinking one's way is best is thought to be wrong because it denies the equal validity of the other's viewpoint, even if one believes that the other is saved through her own religious practice. It is not enough to believe that other religions may be partially true and salvifically efficacious; they must be regarded as equally valid means of attaining salvation. Religious pluralism is the view that all religions, or at least the great world religions, are, more or less, equally true.

There are several different versions of pluralism. The core idea in all forms of pluralism is that many religions are more or less equally true and equally effective in providing the means of attaining salvation. No one religion can claim to be closer to the truth than all the others. Many religions enjoy parity with respect to revelation of truth about ultimate reality and effectiveness in facilitating the attainment of salvation, the cultivation of moral virtue, and promotion of social harmony.

In the last several decades pluralism has become a widely held position among liberal Christian theologians. David Ray Griffin[4] identifies four major reasons for the move toward pluralism. The first is the tremendous expansion of knowledge of world religions that has become available in the last century. The second is a growing emphasis of some Christian thinkers on the primacy of the doctrine of divine love and the idea that Christian exclusivism conflicts with this doctrine. The third reason is ethical. There is a sense that Christian absolutism has for centuries been invoked to justify imperialism, oppression, and violence. Among many Christian thinkers recently there is a sense that the Christian command to love one's neighbor entails a respect for the neighbor's own religious tradition and recognition that "we cannot really love these neighbors if we, instead of listening to their religious witness, are trying to convert them to *our* religion."[5] The fourth reason for the increased support for pluralism is the widespread acceptance of the modern scientific worldview and rejection of theistic supernaturalism. Pluralist theologians do not deny the existence of a transcendent reality, but some do deny that there is a personal God who acts in the world on behalf of human beings. Griffin affirms a soteriological supernaturalism in the sense of the possibility of the attainment of an orientation of life toward the transcendent reality. However, he rejects the idea that God acts supernaturally in human affairs, and thus he rejects "the idea that God acted supernaturally in Christian origins."[6] This denial of Christian supernaturalism and revelation through unique acts of God in history are thought to be supported not only by modern science but also modern "historical consciousness," which sees all religions as the product of particular historical and cultural processes. All human thought is situated in a cultural context and conditioned by the conceptual framework that is the product of culture. Religious ideas, as all other ideas by which human beings make sense of the world, are the product of culture. Pluralists hold that the religious ideas of Christianity are not uniquely the product of direct divine revelation and thereby uniquely authoritative. Christianity is one religion among many, and all religions are social constructions.

Although religious pluralism might seem incompatible with commitment to any one religious tradition, pluralism is a widely held position

---

4. Griffin, "Religious Pluralism."
5. Griffin, "Religious Pluralism," 12.
6. Griffin, "Religious Pluralism," 15.

among Christian philosophers and theologians. Indeed, for some prominent Christian thinkers, pluralism is the position that best resonates with some central tenets of Christian theology, such as God's love for all human beings. One senses a great deal of moral fervor in the writings of Christian pluralists, who regard Christian absolutism as a main source of conflict between different religions and their adherents, against which Christians should be devoted to working. Given the magnitude of the problems that face humanity in the postmodern world, there is great need for people of all faiths to work together to seek solutions. To the extent that exclusivism is an obstacle to cooperation between persons of diverse religious beliefs, it mitigates against the attainment of some of the ends shared by many of the great religions, including Christianity. It is not surprising that some Christians should find religious pluralism an attractive position and one that is consistent with their religious values.

The obvious difficulty for pluralism is making sense of how religions that seem to contradict each other can be more or less equally true and equally valid means of attaining salvation. How can we regard all religions as equally true if they contradict each other? There are several possible responses to this question. One response is to regard each religion as having a part of the whole truth. They enjoy parity insofar as no one religion has a monopoly on truth or even a larger share then the others. Each religion has a small part of the truth, the whole of which is forever out of the reach of all. Genuine contradictions between religions are possible, and in cases where doctrines of different religions contradict each other, one of them must be wrong, but no one religion can lay claim to a greater share of truth than the others. Dialogue between religions is valuable since each has much to teach and learn from the others. There is ultimately one Truth, forever beyond the complete grasp of any one religion, but we get closer to it through dialogue between the religions—each having equally valuable approximations of the truth to share with the others.

One might argue that despite the obvious differences between religions, underlying those differences is a common core of essential truth that all share. The differences are less fundamental than what religions hold in common. They amount to different paths to the same destination. One way of articulating this idea is to say that there is one ultimate, sacred, transcendent reality, which all religions are talking about in their various ways. Religions are human attempts to know the sacred reality and attain a proper relation to it. Religions variously call this reality God, YHWH, Allah, Brahman, Nirvana, Śūnyatā or emptiness, or the Tao. For some religions the ultimate sacred reality is a personal being, and salvation is conceived as the attainment of a personal knowledge and relationship with this supreme, sacred, transcendent personal being. The monotheistic Abrahamic religions fall into this category. For other religions, the ultimate is an impersonal reality. Hinduism, Taoism, and Buddhism fall into this category. Salvation may be conceived as the attainment of a union with the impersonal absolute, the absorption of the self into a unity with the ultimate that overwhelms consciousness of self as a distinct identity. For Buddhism salvation is conceived as the extinction of the self as an ego that is distinct from the ultimate reality. For the pluralist all these schema are variations on a common theme, and it is the common theme that is most important. All religions, or at least the great world religions, are about the same project—responding appropriately to the ultimate sacred, transcendent reality, and attaining or restoring the proper relation with it, which is the ultimate end for human beings. This kind of theory is most fully developed by John Hick.

JOHN HICK'S PLURALISM

One of the most prominent and widely discussed versions of religious pluralism is that of Hick. Hick begins with the affirmation of the religious ambiguity of the universe, meaning that the universe is such that both religious and naturalistic interpretations of it are possible.[7] We cannot prove naturalism to be either true or false; the interpretation of the universe as nothing but matter and energy cannot be disproved. Naturalistic explanations of religious experience are possible and rationally defensible, but on the other hand, for many people religious experience is sufficient to render religious belief plausible. Persons from a wide range of religious traditions have experiences that they interpret as support for their religious beliefs. Hick advocates a critical trust principle with respect to religious experience. In the absence of good evidence that a religious experience is illusory, religious adherents are justified in taking their religious experiences as support for their beliefs.[8] Most religious experience occurs within the context of particular religious traditions, and there is no objective evidence for the superiority of one religion over another. The principle of charity should be extended across religious boundaries. The kinds of religious experiences that justify one in adhering to the doctrines of one's own religion are similar to the kinds of experiences that adherents of other religions have within the context of their own religious traditions. In the absence of culturally and religiously neutral criteria for adjudicating between apparently competing claims of different religions, we should allow that adherents of different reli-

---

7. Hick, *An Interpretation of Religion*, 12.
8. Hick, *An Interpretation of Religion*, 240–46.

gious beliefs are equally justified in holding them and remaining committed to their own faith traditions.

This is not an unfortunate situation from the standpoint of most religions since it ensures that the world does not present itself to us in a way that overwhelms our freedom to either respond religiously or not. It is essential to religion that a religious response to the world be voluntary and not compelled by irresistible evidence. Religious experience justifies but does not compel a religious interpretation of the universe. However, it does not justify propositional knowledge of the nature of the sacred, transcendent reality.

Hick's theory is based on a Kantian account of religious knowledge, according to which knowledge of ultimate reality as it is in itself is impossible for humans.[9] According to Kant, reality as it is in itself, independently of human conceptualization, is unknowable. We know the world as it appears to us in experience and as conceptualized by a framework that we impose on our experience. For Kant, the concepts by which we make sense of experience are universal, thus ensuring the objective validity of experience. By adopting a Kantian epistemological framework and applying it to religious experience, Hick argues that the great religions are interpretive frameworks that enable human beings to make sense of their experience of the transcendent reality and the totality of their experience in relation to the transcendent. Just as for Kant the *thing-in-itself* is unknowable, for Hick the transcendent reality that is the concern of the great religions is unknowable as it is in itself. Hick calls the sacred, transcendent reality that all religions seek "the Real." The Real is strictly ineffable—beyond human reason and concepts. Religions provide interpretations and representations of the Real that enable human beings in particular cultural contexts to make sense of their religious experience in ways that are appropriate for their social and cultural situations.[10]

Some religions interpret the Real as a personal deity, and in some religions this personal deity is regarded as the creator of the universe, perhaps omnipotent, omniscient, all-good, and eternal. Hick calls conceptions of the Real as one or more personal beings the "Personae" of the Real. The monotheistic religions, Judaism, Christianity, and Islam, are examples of religions that regard the Real as personal.[11] For some religions the Real is an impersonal absolute, the ground of being, but not an individual personal being or creator. Hick calls conceptions of the Real as impersonal the "Im-

---

9. Hick, *An Interpretation of Religion*, 210–28.
10. Hick, *An Interpretation of Religion*, 246–49.
11. Hick, *An Interpretation of Religion*, 252–75.

personae" of the Real. Taoism, some forms of Hinduism, and Buddhism are examples of religions that conceive the Real as impersonal.[12] Since the Real itself is beyond human conceptions of personhood, we cannot know that the Real-in-itself is either a personal being or an impersonal absolute. Since number is a human concept, we cannot even know whether the Real itself is either one or many. The truthfulness of religious conceptions of the Real are to be understood not in terms of correspondence to how the Real-in-itself actually is, but in terms of the appropriateness of the responses to the Real that various religions foster.

The religious ambiguity of the universe not only makes it impossible to prove that there is (or is not) an ultimate transcendent reality, but also impossible, if there is such a reality, to determine whether it is a personal God or an impersonal metaphysical absolute. Hence from the standpoint of the acceptance of the religious option, the interpretations of the Real as personal or impersonal are equally legitimate. All experience, including religious experience, is interpretive. The object of the experience is always "experienced as" something or other according to some concept that is imposed on the experience.[13] Hence the transcendental object of religious experience may be experienced as YHWH, Allah, Brahman, the Dharmakaya, or the Tao, depending on the cultural context within which the experience occurs.[14]

The point of religion is not merely to describe reality but to diagnose the human condition and offer a solution to the human predicament. The great post-axial[15] religions are those that emerged in the last few centuries before the beginning of the Common Era from the teachings of such figures as Confucius, Siddhartha Gautama, Zoroaster, the Hebrew prophets, and Jesus. What these traditions share in common is the teaching that the human condition involves a fundamental problem or defect with respect to our relation to the Real and that we have the prospect of a limitlessly better situation by correcting that defect. Human beings lack the capacity to attain conceptual knowledge of the Real, but religion teaches them how to be spiritually and ethically related to the Real in such a way as to make progress toward the attainment of the ultimate *telos* of human existence. The fundamental problem of human existence is diagnosed variously by different religious traditions, but although the fundamental problem and defect

12. Hick, *An Interpretation of Religion*, 278–95.
13. Hick, *An Interpretation of Religion*, 140–42.
14. Hick, *An Interpretation of Religion*, 294.
15. The term *axial age*, originally coined by Karl Jaspers and appropriated by Hick, refers to the period from around 800 to 200 BCE in which similar religious revolutions took place in Greece, the Near East, Persia, India, and China. See Jaspers, *The Origin and Goal of History*.

of human beings is described in different ways, the basic underlying idea common to all the major religious traditions is that human beings need to overcome self-centeredness. The solution is to overcome self-centeredness and become reality-centered. The Christian describes the problem as sin, which entails loving oneself more than God and making oneself rather than God the lord of one's life. The solution is attained by submitting to the will of God and allowing God to be the lord of one's life. The Buddhist speaks of extinguishing the clinging self. The core idea is the same—overcoming self-centeredness and becoming reality-centered—grounded in the ultimate reality that is ineffable and beyond our capacity to know intellectually, but which can be experienced, in a salvifically efficacious way, in the context of a particular religious tradition.

Hick is impressed by the fact that all major religions have similar ethical teachings, with an emphasis on the importance of love of others and overcoming self-centeredness. As a pluralist, Hick is concerned to account for the ethical and soteriological parallels of diverse religions and to explain why the apparent differences between them do not involve logical contradictions that render them incompatible. Hick achieves this resolution of the contradictions between diverse religions by denying that any religious descriptions of the Real can be literally true, since the Real is beyond human capacity to know, conceptualize, or describe in literal language. All the doctrinal teachings of the great religions that attempt to describe the Real are symbolic or metaphorical representations that are devoid of literal, cognitive significance. The truth of religion is understood pragmatically in terms of success in enabling individuals and societies to overcome self-centeredness and attain reality-centeredness.[16] The criteria for measuring this success are ethical. As is written in the New Testament, by their fruits you shall know them. Religious claims are judged by their tendency to produce human beings that exhibit moral virtues such as love, compassion, kindness, generosity, justice, patience, etc., which are marks of unselfishness and a genuine relation to the Real. Even though we cannot have objective, cognitive knowledge of the Real, we can be transformed by a relation to the Real into unselfish, compassionate, loving persons, which is the primary point of religion.

Seen as descriptions of the Real, all religious doctrines are literally false. Nonetheless, when understood as authentic responses to the ineffable Real within particular cultural contexts, all the great world religions are more or less equally true, in the sense that they are equally valid means of facilitating the attainment of the ultimate religious end, which is for persons

16. Hick, *An Interpretation of Religion*, 36–53.

to overcome self-centeredness and become reality-centered. Religious truth is judged pragmatically in terms of successful fostering of the attainment of salvation, liberation, enlightenment, etc. Hick's theory of religious truth is a species of pragmatic theory; religions are true insofar as they succeed in facilitating the transformation from self-centeredness to reality-centeredness among devotees of the religion. The criterion for judging this success is ethical.[17] Persons who have made progress in this transformation will be more humane, morally virtuous, just, compassionate, etc. Hick judges that all the great religions are more or less equally successful in facilitating the transformation of persons to reality-centeredness. Thus, the great religions are more or less equally true.[18]

It is important to appreciate that in spite of Hick's rejection of a correspondence theory of truth in favor of an ethically construed pragmatic theory, he says he is nevertheless committed to religious realism and the possible veridicality (truthfulness) of religious experience. The theory is realist in the sense that it affirms that the ultimate religious reality, the Real, does actually exist independently of religious concepts—the Real in-itself actually exists. Religious experience can be veridical in the sense that it can be a genuine, valid response to the Real. Although the Real is ineffable, Hick believes that the Real actually exists and that different religions respond to, interpret, and develop ways of living in accordance with the Real in different but equally valid ways.

Hick's project is an attempt to find a middle path between an overly absolutist form of realism on the one hand and relativism or antirealism on the other. Although Hick defends the view that religious statements about the Real are not literally true in the sense of accurately describing the Real as it is in itself, Hick resists the slide into the non-realist view that religious doctrines should be construed solely in terms of religious practice and values, with no connection at all to an actually existing, transcendent reality. Hick's view is that the Real does exist and that religious doctrinal beliefs are true insofar as they are based on experiences that are valid, transformative responses to the Real. The criteria for judging the validity of responses to the Real, since it is ineffable, must be pragmatic and ethical. The best way we have for judging whether religious beliefs are true is to look at the effectiveness of the religion in facilitating the transformation of persons to reality-centeredness. The great religions of the world agree that human beings are initially selfish and concerned primarily with their own welfare but have the potential to become unselfish and devoted to the well-being of others. Some

---

17. Hick, *An Interpretation of Religion*, 299–314.
18. Hick, *An Interpretation of Religion*, 372–76.

132   GOD, SCIENCE, AND RELIGIOUS DIVERSITY

version of the Golden Rule is taught by most of the great religions. Universal love and compassion and social justice are held up as supreme moral ideals in all major religious traditions. The truth of religious beliefs, construed in terms of their validity as responses to the Real, is best judged in terms of the efficacy of the religion in transforming people into moral saints. Hick's assessment of the success of religions in producing moral saints comes to the conclusion that all religions are more or less equally successful in this regard. Hence, all the great religions are more or less equally true.

PROBLEMS WITH HICK'S PLURALISM

Hick's version of pluralism has been subjected to a great deal of critical response. One strand of criticism focuses on the Kantian epistemology that provides the epistemological foundation of Hick's theory. If the Real-in-itself is unknowable and ineffable, then it is difficult to see how any religion can be known to be a valid interpretation and a salvifically effective response to it. If we can apply no human concepts to the Real, including the concept of good, then it is unintelligible how moral sainthood could be a criterion for assessing the validity of the adequacy of responses to the Real. There is no way of making sense of why moral virtue indicates a more satisfactory response to the Real than any other attribute, since no human concepts accurately characterize the Real as it is in itself. If we know that moral goodness is an indicator of being reality-centered but cruelty is not, then we must know that to say that the Real is good is closer to the literal truth about the nature of the Real than saying that the Real is cruel. This suggests that goodness is an attribute of the Real, which entails that at least the concept of goodness can be applied to the Real. The Real must not be entirely ineffable.

Further, Hick's emphasis on the ineffability of the Real-in-itself threatens to make Hick's theory indistinguishable from a wholly non-realist account of religious experience. It is hard to see that the Real-in-itself can make any genuine contribution to the content of religious experience if it is entirely ineffable. For instance, we cannot say that it plays a causal role in determining the content of religious experience, since we cannot apply the concept of causality to the Real. It is hard to see how, without playing some causal role in religious experience, a relation to the Real has anything to do with the content of religious experience.

Metaphysical problems arise when we inquire concerning the ontological status of the entities referred to in the various religions—YHWH, Allah, Brahman, Nirvana, the Tao, and the like. If they are taken to be merely metaphors and not real entities, then Hick's theory seems to become a form of religious non-realism, for the main objects of religious devotion for the various religions do not really exist. If, on the other hand, we say that the religious entities are in some sense real, then we seem to be left with polytheism. George Mavrodes has argued that Hick's theory does indeed entail polytheism.[19] The terms used in religions to refer to the sacred, function in relation to the concept of the Real-in-itself, in a way that is analogous to how empirical concepts function in relation to the thing-in-itself in Kant's framework. For Kant, tables, chairs, and dogs are empirically real objects of experience, but the perceptions of those objects do not inform us concerning the things as they are in themselves. Tables, chairs, and dogs are real objects, which are distinct from each other. Therefore, there is a plurality of empirically real objects in the empirical world. There would be no temptation to think that since the thing-in-itself is unknowable, empirical objects are not really distinct from each other, but are rather just different, equally valid responses to and interpretations of the ineffable, noumenal reality. Something analogous to this is what Hick is saying about the relation between the beings referred to in the different religions and the ineffable Real-in-itself. Thus it seems that the implication of Hick's theory is that either the various religious entities that different religions refer to have no relation to the Real-in-itself, in which case the theory collapses into non-realism, or, on the contrary, the names of diverse religious entities are grounded in reality, in which case there are many different, real entities—many gods. The theory entails either non-realism or polytheism.

If one emphasizes the plurality of religious ideas that can be valid responses to the Real, Hick's theory seems to entail polytheism. On the other hand, if one emphasizes that all religions are responding in equally valid ways to the same sacred reality, then Hick's theory begins to look insufficiently pluralistic. If one emphasizes the claim that all religions are referring to the same Real, and the equal validity of all the interpretations of that Real, then one loses the significance and richness of the diverse religious responses to the Real. The only truth contained in the various religions is explicated in terms of the fact that all the religions are responding to the same Real and that they are successful in producing moral saints. Thus Hick can be criticized for not being sufficiently pluralistic insofar as he denies that there is a plurality of religious truths. There are many different religious traditions, but they are fundamentally united in expressing the same religious truth, construed soteriologically in terms of their efficacy in fostering the transformation of persons from self-centeredness to reality-centeredness.

19. Mavrodes, "A Response to John Hick."

So where it counts, all religions are fundamentally of one voice. A more genuinely pluralistic position would recognize the real differences between religions in not only their conceptions of ultimate reality, but also in their conceptions of the ultimate soteriological goal of religion.

According to Hick, what is true in religion turns out to be the same for all religions (equally valid and salvifically efficacious responses to one Real), and what is distinctive about the different religions is not cognitively significant. So Hick's pluralism turns out to be not very pluralistic at all, since all religions turn out to be basically the same, at least with respect to their cognitive content. The rituals and practices may be different, and they differ in their ways of expressing religious truth, but the truth expressed is essentially the same. Ironically, given that religious pluralism is largely motivated by a high regard and respect for religious diversity, it turns out that Hick's version of pluralism seems to undermine the importance of attention to the specifics of diverse religions in favor of an abstract theory which melds them all into one.

Not only does Hick fail to deliver on one of the promises that motivates pluralism in the first place—sensitivity to distinctive contributions of different religions, but he also fails to deliver on another promise—overcoming the one-sidedness of exclusivism. Gavin D'Costa argues that Hick's pluralism is actually an exclusivist theory based on a specific and parochial conceptual framework characteristic of modern Western philosophy, which rejects the actual truth claims made by particular religions in favor of a grand metatheory.[20] Although Hick's theory operates at a higher logical level than that of specific religions, it is actually just one viewpoint among many, which rejects the claims of the others in favor of its own, and which is no less culturally relative than those of the particular religions. Pluralism makes a claim about all religions and what their doctrines ultimately mean. Pluralism arrogantly regards its own interpretation of the beliefs of other religions as superior to those religions' own interpretations of their beliefs. Logically, the pluralist is committed to rejecting the claims of religious believers who are exclusivists or inclusivists. If what is supposed to be repugnant about exclusivism is that it arrogantly affirms its own claims and dismisses competing claims as inferior, then Hick's pluralism must be guilty of the same offense, as it must also reject all truth claims made by particular religions in the terms that their own adherents understand them. A self-avowed exclusivist can say to a religious opponent, "I understand what you are saying, but I think it is incorrect and here are my reasons." The Hickian pluralist says, in effect, to the adherents of all religions, "I hear what you are

---

20. D'Costa, "The Impossibility of Pluralist View of Religions."

saying, but it does not really mean what you think it does. What you are saying is not wrong, but to see how it is true you have to see that it means what I say it means, which is radically different than what you think it means." This seems no less offensive than saying that someone's factual belief is false. If exclusivism is offensive to adherents of other faiths, Hick's pluralism seems at least as offensive.

In response to these difficulties one move that the pluralist can make is to give up the thesis that all religions refer to the same sacred, transcendent reality. David Ray Griffin[21] and S. Mark Heim[22] each argue that this thesis prevents Hick's theory from being genuinely pluralistic, since it maintains that all religions are in fundamental agreement about the ultimate reality to which they refer. Griffin, following Whitehead, argues for what he calls deep pluralism, which holds that religions are not united in their reference to the same transcendent object, but rather may refer to different Absolutes. Griffin calls the type of pluralism that holds that there is one sacred, transcendent reality referred to by all religions "identist pluralism." On the other hand, deep pluralism, according to Griffin, recognizes truths in religions that are genuinely distinct from truths in other religions. A deep pluralist "would . . . see truth in other religions in relation to aspects in which they are different from one's own tradition, as well as in relation to aspects in which they are similar."[23] John Cobb has developed a form of deep pluralism, which Griffin dubs "complementary pluralism," and which emphasizes "the different salvific implications of different aspects or dimensions of the total truth, [and] sees a central task of theological dialogue to be the discovery of how these various doctrines are complementary rather than contradictory."[24] Cobb does not share Hick's commitment to the claim that all religions express with equal success the same truth. By allowing religions to express different truths about different aspects of ultimate reality, Cobb's theory is able to be pluralistic while simultaneously permitting all religions a greater share of truth than countenanced by Hick's Kantian epistemology with its ineffable Real. Cobb's version of pluralism also does not require equal cognitive and soteriological success for all religions.[25]

Although both Cobb and Hick are Christians, Hick seems to be a pluralist first, and takes great pains to ensure parity among religions. For Cobb,

21. Griffin, "Religious Pluralism."
22. Heim, *Salvations*, 243–62.
23. Griffin, "Religious Pluralism," 29.
24. Ibid., 41.
25. See Griffin, "John Cobb's Whiteheadian Complementary Pluralism," 39–66; and Heim, *Salvations*, 243–62.

the commitment to pluralism is largely motivated by concerns arising from his Christianity and its belief that God loves all that exists and that Christ is the savior of all human persons, regardless of culture or geography. Cobb's theory also better accounts for the fruitfulness of religious dialogue than Hick's. Since different religions refer to different aspects of ultimate reality, they have much to teach and learn from each other. When a religion is confronted with the perspective of another religious tradition, it can attempt to accommodate the valid insights that the other brings to its attention and incorporate them into its own framework. Furthermore, Cobb's theory suggests a criterion by which the cognitive success of religions can be assessed. A religion is more successful to the extent that it is able to incorporate the truths revealed in other religions while remaining faithful to its own fundamental commitments. From the standpoint of a Christian theistic worldview that lays claim to objective truth, it is of upmost importance that its most important claims about God as creator, the nature of the world, and the human condition be defensible against doctrinal claims of other religions that are contradictory to them.

8

Byrne's Version of Religious Pluralism

Another interesting version of pluralism has been developed by Peter Byrne.[1] Byrne agrees with Hick's view that all the great religions of the world are more or less equally valid responses to the ultimate religious reality. But gone in Byrne's theory is the Kantian framework that leads to much of the difficulty with Hick's version of pluralism. The Kantian element in Hick is what allows all religions to be equally true and fundamentally in agreement, in spite of their obvious differences. In place of this maneuver Byrne offers a carefully balanced combination of realism, agnosticism, and appreciation of both the ubiquity and diversity of religious interpretations of reality.

Peter Byrne finds the ubiquity of religion throughout history to be evidence that there is a reality with which all religions are groping to connect.[2] Byrne argues that the diversity of religions and lack of criteria for adjudicating disagreements between them imply that we cannot know that any one religion is superior to the others with respect to its doctrinal claims. While Hick argues that no religious claims are literally and objectively true, Byrne argues that one religion might be objectively true, but because of religious diversity, we cannot know which or whether one is true. Byrne's position leaves open the possibility that future religious inquiry and dialogue might lead to a transition from pluralism to the affirmation that one religion is truer than others. For now Byrne recommends the view that the diversity of religions supports agnosticism about the doctrinal claims of specific religions.

1. Byrne, *Prolegomena to Religious Pluralism*.
2. Byrne, *Prolegomena to Religious Pluralism*, 124–25.

THE THREE MAIN THESES OF BYRNE'S RELIGIOUS PLURALISM

Byrne's proposal offers a subtle and sophisticated attempt to unite a view that affirms the equal truthfulness of all major religions and the view that religious truth consists in correspondence to a mind-independent sacred, transcendent reality. Byrne defends a realist understanding of religious truth, while at the same time holding that all religions enjoy equal cognitive and salvific success. Byrne's pluralist proposal is clearly inspired to some extent by the religious pluralism of John Hick but is in some ways an improvement upon Hick's pluralism. We will consider whether it succeeds in harmonizing the realistic interpretation of religious truth and the equality of all religions.

Byrne's religious pluralism is committed to three basic claims, which are formulated in three theses:

1. All major religious traditions are equal in respect of making common reference to a single transcendent, sacred reality.

2. All major religious traditions are likewise equal in respect of offering some means or other to human salvation.

3. All traditions are to be seen as containing revisable, limited accounts of the nature of the sacred; none is certain enough in its particular dogmatic formulations to provide the norm for interpreting the others.[3]

The first thesis implies the existence of one transcendent, sacred reality and asserts that all major religions are more or less equally successful in making cognitive contact with that reality insofar as their various descriptions of it succeed in making reference to it (if not, as we shall see, in accurately describing it). The core of Byrne's pluralism is the idea that all major religious traditions succeed equally well in referring to a common sacred, transcendent reality, but because we have no objective way to reconcile differences in the specific claims that religions make about that reality, or the nature of and means of attaining a salvific relation to that reality, no one religion is justified in claiming cognitive or salvific superiority over any others. Byrne rejects religious essentialism, the idea that religion has an essential core that all particular religions share in common. His pluralism does not hold that all religions agree on some common set of core beliefs, but does hold that the great religions all have some idea of a sacred, transcendent reality and some notion that the ultimate end of human endeavor involves

---

3. Byrne, *Prolegomena to Religious Pluralism*, 12, 57, and 191.

the attainment of an appropriate relation to that reality. This latter feature of religions is characterized differently by different religions, but Byrne uses the term *salvation* to cover the wide range of conceptions of the relation between human beings and the sacred, transcendent reality, and how that relation is attained.

Religions diagnose and respond to the basic deficiencies of human life stemming from our finitude and contingency, such as "the fact of death and the fact of frustration of our aims and projects."[4] The human quest for salvation is the quest for self-transcendence in order to ameliorate the fundamental deficiencies of our existence. Participation in "religious practices is constitutive to a great extent of salvation. . . . As systems of belief and practice [religions] enable a new conception of the good to inform our lives, one which involves seeking the ground of the point and worth of action in something transcendent of individual choice and eternal. They make possible a relation with that which is transcendent."[5] This rather generic notion of salvation does not necessarily involve the belief in an afterlife, but Byrne acknowledges that belief in an afterlife would support the possibility of the attainment of a perfected relation to the transcendent. His general agnosticism about doctrinal details of specific religions extends to the question of an afterlife. Byrne's notion of salvation as the attainment of a relation to the transcendent does not depend on either a knowable description of that reality or a definitely attainable eternal life in relation to it. The aspect of salvation that we can be more confident in affirming is the moral transformation that constitutes self-transcendence. Byrne suggests that in order to avoid conceiving salvation in a way that is too thin, "we must hold out for the idea that salvation *finally* consists in a *perfected* relationship to the sacred and transcendent."[6] Whether or not there is agreement among diverse religions about the nature of an afterlife, or even whether an afterlife is possible, religious practice and morally virtuous action fostered by religion constitute a kind of self-transcendence that is constitutive of salvation. "An afterlife . . . might be seen as making possible a more perfect relation to the transcendent, but the engagement in appropriate practices with heart and mind of itself effects the decisive self-transformation."[7] Byrne states that "virtuous actions are capable of becoming ends in themselves because the practice of the virtues is a means of having one's life informed by goods which lend

---

4. Byrne, *Prolegomena to Religious Pluralism*, 99.
5. Byrne, *Prolegomena to Religious Pluralism*, 101–2.
6. Byrne, *Prolegomena to Religious Pluralism*, 101.
7. Byrne, *Prolegomena to Religious Pluralism*, 102.

value to the very business of their pursuit."[8] Religious practices constitute being related to "values [that] have a worth which transcends contingency" and are "such as to enable human life to transcend the temporal."[9] Byrne acknowledges that a "*perfected* relationship to the sacred and transcendent ... may indeed only be possible if a true set of beliefs about its object is present and if perhaps we enjoy an existence where an undiluted, undistracted concentration upon it is feasible,"[10] but his pluralism entails that all actual religions are partial failures as the means of attaining such a relationship and "none will have *the* complete truth about the transcendent."[11] Thus, no one religion can claim cognitive or soteriological superiority over the others or sufficient certainty in its doctrinal claims to provide the norm for interpreting the others.

Byrne seems to be saying that we cannot, at least at this time in the history of religion, be sure that any one religion teaches us the final truth about the sacred, transcendent reality or whether there is an afterlife in which a perfect relation to that reality is attainable. Even if such a perfect form of salvation is not available to us, religions nevertheless offer an important and valuable kind of salvation that entails a degree of transcendence of our self-centeredness and temporality, and an improvement of our relation to the sacred. The ubiquity of religion throughout the world and the partial success that religions enjoy in providing means of attaining at least a partial kind of salvation (as evidenced by the apparent ethical efficacy of religion) make plausible the affirmation of the existence of a sacred, transcendent reality to which all the great religions refer. The positive contribution to human progress made by religions justifies belief that they enjoy at least some degree of cognitive success in referring to a sacred, transcendent reality. While no one religion enjoys sufficient cognitive success to justify belief that its specific doctrinal claims are true, the broad agreement among the many diverse religions about the existence of the transcendent and the central importance of love and social justice, and their relative success in enabling persons to live more ethical lives, suggest that they enjoy some degree of cognitive success as responses to the sacred. We are justified in believing that there exists a sacred, transcendent reality that makes some contribution to the social, cultural and experiential processes that produce religions. Byrne is a moderate realist about religion, but he is agnostic about the detailed doctrinal claims of specific religions.

8. Byrne, *Prolegomena to Religious Pluralism*, 100.
9. Byrne, *Prolegomena to Religious Pluralism*, 100–1.
10. Byrne, *Prolegomena to Religious Pluralism*, 102.
11. Byrne, *Prolegomena to Religious Pluralism*, 102.

Though it is plausible to believe in the possibility that religions may succeed to some degree in making cognitive contact with the transcendent, the diversity of religions and the lack of objective, neutral criteria for assessing religious beliefs, prevent us (at least at this point in the history of religious development) from assigning to any one religion more success than others in describing the transcendent or in characterizing the path to salvation. Byrne accepts the anthropological approach to the study of religion and sees it as establishing that the diverse religions of the world are, to a large extent, human cultural creations. The diverse cultural forms that religions take and the variety of religious experience enjoyed by religious adherents are evidence that religions are largely cultural artifacts. However, they are not entirely so. Byrne resists an entirely naturalistic, anthropological interpretation of religion because the ubiquity of belief in a mind-independent transcendent reality makes plausible the view that the transcendent exists and contributes causally to the formation of religions. Byrne attempts to strike a delicate balance between the realist and agnostic aspects of his theory. The diversity of religions and the intractable doctrinal disagreements between them leads to a severe agnosticism about the detailed descriptions of the sacred. If this tendency toward agnosticism were not restrained, Byrne's position would be forced to sheer religious skepticism and metaphysical naturalism. Byrne resists naturalism and religious skepticism because of the universality of belief in the existence of a transcendent reality among diverse religious traditions, and the obvious ethical and spiritual fruitfulness of religion. Hence pluralism is more plausible than either naturalism or adherence to a particular religion.

Byrne shares John Hick's view that the great religions of the world (with the possible exception of some forms of Buddhism) are united in their belief that there is an ultimate, sacred, transcendent reality and that the ultimate purpose of human existence is to attain a proper relation to that reality.[12] He also agrees that ethical criteria[13] are important for justifying the claim that the great world religions are more or less equally successful in fostering the main purpose of religion—the spiritual and moral transformation of human beings. Byrne agrees that the various names for this reality—YWWH, Allah, Brahman, Nirvana, The Tao, etc.—are authentic cultural references to, expressions of, and responses to that reality, which are associated with detailed accounts of how to reorient one's life, individually and corporately, to it. However, Byrne's theory rejects the Kantian epistemological framework that leads to some of the problems with Hick's

---

12. Byrne, *Prolegomena to Religious Pluralism*, 210–30.
13. Byrne, *Prolegomena to Religious Pluralism*, 316–42.

version of religious pluralism. The Kantian distinction that Hick draws between the unknowable Real-in-itself and the particular cultural expressions of the ultimate reality,[14] which are affirmed by the various religions, is what allows all religions to be equally true and in fundamental agreement, insofar as they are all equally valid responses to the ultimate reality, in spite of the obvious apparent differences in their various cultural interpretations and detailed descriptions of that reality. However, the extreme ineffability of the Real implied by Hick's version of pluralism leads to difficulties that Byrne's version of pluralism seeks to avoid. The equal success of the many religions as meaningful responses to the Real is attained in Hick's pluralism by denying that we have cognitive access to the Real. The Real-in-itself is beyond human conceptualization. For Byrne this view is too extreme and is tantamount to idealism. Byrne replaces Hick's Kantian epistemology with his carefully balanced combination of realism and agnosticism. Where Hick is able to ascribe equality to all the great religions by denying literal truth to any of their doctrinal claims, Byrne leaves open the possibility that religions may make literally true claims about the transcendent. The equality of religions demanded by pluralism consists in the fact that all religions lack certainty that they are more successful than others in describing the transcendent or in characterizing the means of attaining a saving relation to the transcendent. It is an equality that in principle could change if in the future one religion is able to justify its doctrines as more true than those of other religions.

Byrne situates religious pluralism between naturalism, which holds that all religions are false, and confessionalism, which holds that one religion is true and all others are false. Confessionalism can be divided into exclusivism and inclusivism, both of which insist that one religion is superior to the others in its cognitive and soteriological success. The exclusivist and inclusivist both claim, contrary to Byrne's third thesis, that one religion, namely one's own, is "certain enough in its particular dogmatic formulations to provide the norm for interpreting the others."[15] The exclusivist claims that salvation is only available to adherents of the one true religion. Inclusivism is essentially the same as exclusivism with respect to its position about the truth of its claims concerning the transcendent. It differs from exclusivism in allowing that salvation is available to adherents of other religions. Byrne finds pluralism more plausible than either form of confessionalism due to the fact of religious diversity and the lack of any means

---

14. Byrne, *Prolegomena to Religious Pluralism*, 241–51.
15. Byrne, *Prolegomena to Religious Pluralism*, 12.

of adjudicating between conflicting claims between different religions. Still, the ubiquity and ethical efficacy of religion make pluralism more plausible than naturalism.

In order to account for the possibility of successful reference to the transcendent while maintaining agnosticism about specific descriptions of it, Byrne rejects descriptive theories of reference, according to which successful reference of terms depends on at least some true descriptions of the object referred to. Byrne's agnosticism makes unavailable knowledge of true descriptions of the sacred, which the descriptive theory of reference would require for successful reference to it. He defends a causal theory of reference, which requires only that there be an appropriate causal connection between the object referred to and the referring term. In order for the words *God* and *Brahman* to refer to the sacred, transcendent reality, the descriptive theory of reference requires that we have true descriptions of that object, such as "God is an omnipotent, omniscient personal being" or "Brahman is without properties and identical with all that exists."

It is clear that the descriptive theory is not going to make it easy to see how "God" and "Brahman" could both equally well refer to the same sacred, transcendent reality, which is what Byrne's pluralism requires. The two descriptive statements of the transcendent reality just cited are clearly incompatible with each other. However, according to the causal theory, reference does not require true descriptions of the object referred to. For example, in order for the term *atom*, which etymologically means "indivisible particle," to refer to atoms it does not matter whether we know whether or not atoms are indivisible. Beliefs about the atom have evolved as science progressed, but despite disagreement about the nature of the atom, the persons who thought that it was a simple and indivisible particle of matter and those who think it is an energy wave packet are referring to the same thing, because whatever the atom is really like, there is an appropriate causal connection between atoms and the word. Similarly, the lack of agreement about descriptions of the sacred, transcendent reality, whether it is a personal being, whether it has properties or not, or whether it is really distinct from the physical universe, for example, does not prevent successful reference of religious terms to that reality. It is sufficient that there be the right sort of causal connection between the transcendent, sacred reality and the terms that diverse religions use to refer to it. If there is a transcendent, sacred reality that plays the right sort of role in causing persons to believe that it exists, to believe that they have experienced it, and to have various beliefs about it (whether true or false), then the persons who have those beliefs succeed in referring to that reality, even though they lack detailed true descriptions of it. The lack of true descriptions of the transcendent, sacred reality does not prevent reference to it, and so realism survives, but Byrne holds that the lack of true descriptions does support a moderate agnosticism about the nature of the transcendent.

Byrne supposes that his agnosticism is not so severe that it rules out the possibility of correction of error in religion. Religions are dynamic, self-critical, and engaged in dialogue with opponents. Byrne affirms not only the fallibility of religious belief, but also the possibility of critique and revision. Religious discourse and dialogue can over time result in progress toward more adequate religious understandings. Although religions are limited insofar as they are largely sociocultural artifacts and products of history, pluralism recognizes "a redeeming logic of discovery, anticipation and encounter behind some of their aspects. . . . As well as being cultural-linguistic systems making forms of life and experience possible, religions also exhibit the human ability over many centuries and cultures to reach out and achieve contact with transcendent reality. . . . [W]e should see the religions as connected, overlapping attempts on the part of human beings to understand, and orient themselves, toward the sacred . . . [and] stepping stones toward right relation to the transcendent."[16] In spite of this somewhat optimistic picture of the prospect for progress in religious understanding, Byrne's agnosticism does not recognize sufficient grounds for finally judging any one religion to be superior to the others. Hence his position remains pluralist, in the sense that it regards no one religion as superior to the others or able to provide the basis for the interpretation of other religions. Byrne does not hold that beliefs of different religions that contradict each other can be equally true. He is saying rather that we lack sufficient grounds for saying that the beliefs of one religion enjoy more cognitive or salvific success than beliefs of other religions. We are not justified in believing that some religions have a more accurate understanding of the sacred transcendent reality or that any are more successful than others in fostering success in the attainment of salvation. This latter point leads to Byrne's second thesis, that all major religions are equal with respect to their offering the means to attaining salvation. Given the equality of the cognitive and soteriological success of all major religions, we are led to the second half of Byrne's third thesis, that no one religion provides the basis for interpreting any of the other religions. The realist bent of Byrne's version of pluralism and the moderateness of his agnosticism supports the first part of the third thesis, that religious traditions contain revisable, limited accounts of the nature of the sacred.

---

16. Byrne, *Prolegomena to Religious Pluralism*, 195.

CRITIQUE OF BYRNE'S FIRST AND THIRD THESES

Byrne's theory goes some way toward articulating a version of pluralism that avoids some of the difficulties encountered by Hick. From Byrne's point of view, Hick's notion of the Real-in-itself does not permit a sufficiently realist understanding of religious truth. Byrne avoids the problems resulting from Hick's removal of all cognitive content from discourse about the Real and his characterization of the Real as radically ineffable.[17] Hick's position renders unintelligible how religions can be cognitively and ethically informed by their responses to the Real, such that some form could be given to the notion of transformation from self-centeredness to reality-centeredness. Without some cognitive grasp of the Real, how can we make sense of the relation between salvation construed as reality-centeredness and the concrete moral life recommended by the great religions? If our response to the Real is devoid of cognitive significance, how can we know what forms of life would exemplify reality-centeredness? For Hick the truth of the beliefs of particular religions is analyzed pragmatically, ethically, and soteriologically.[18] Religious beliefs are true insofar as they are authentic responses to the Real, which promote salvation (the transformation from self-centeredness to reality-centeredness), as measured by the tendency to produce moral saintliness in persons. The descriptive content of belief is interpreted as metaphor and myth.[19] Byrne allows for the possibility of religious belief rising beyond metaphor and myth, thus giving more significance than does Hick to the cognitive dimension of religious belief, even though his agnosticism prevents affirmation of one religion being more successful in this regard than others. It is a strength of Byrne's pluralism that it does not achieve the equality of all religions at the expense of giving up all cognitive significance of their truth claims. In contrast to what Hick's theory seems to do, Byrne's pluralism does not diminish the importance of the diverse specific doctrines of particular religions and the fruitfulness of interfaith dialogue. Byrne affirms the corrigibility of particular religious traditions, the value of interreligious dialogue, and the openness of religions to the possibility of critique and refinement over time.

Despite the considerable advantages of Byrne's religious pluralism over Hick's, it still faces some serious problems. One problem is that the first thesis seems at odds with the third, the first part of which says that religious traditions contain revisable accounts of the sacred, transcendent reality. On

17. Byrne, *Prolegomena to Religious Pluralism*, 236–40.
18. Byrne, *Prolegomena to Religious Pluralism*, 229–42.
19. Byrne, *Prolegomena to Religious Pluralism*, 349–59.

Byrne's view, there does not seem to be much need for progress in our ability to affirm the existence of a sacred, transcendent reality. If religious traditions are already equally successful in their ability to refer to the transcendent, it is only with respect to their detailed descriptions of the transcendent that there could be need for revision and further progress. However, it is hard to see how progress could be forthcoming, given religious pluralism's agnosticism at the level of specific descriptions of the sacred and its insistence on a lack of criteria for resolving disagreements between different descriptions.

Byrne says very little specifically about how he thinks religious beliefs are revisable. How can religious beliefs be revisable if there are no rational, objective means of adjudicating disagreements between different religions about the nature of the sacred? Byrne's agnosticism about the detailed descriptions of the transcendent reality militates against the prospects for successful revision of religious doctrine toward improved understanding of the sacred. According to Byrne, his case for pluralism uses "the very fact of religious diversity in respect of cognitive claims to tell against confessionalism."[20] If progress toward greater religious knowledge is possible, it would seem that at least some of it must occur at the level of first-order religious beliefs. It is in the detailed descriptions of the sacred that religions disagree, but Byrne claims that at that level of specificity there are no criteria for resolving the disagreements. So how is revision possible? How is progress possible? If revision is possible, doesn't it require that there be some means of adjudicating between disagreements between different religions? When Byrne is emphasizing his agnosticism about the specific detailed descriptions of the transcendent that are affirmed by different religions, his view seems very pessimistic about the prospects for progress beyond the deadlock between different religions. Yet the third thesis explicitly affirms as essential for this version of pluralism the proposition that the accounts of the sacred and of salvation offered by different religious traditions are revisable. This possibility would seem to entail that there must be some prospect for genuine revision in the sense of progress toward the truth of some of the competing religious claims.

Furthermore, if we take seriously the first part of Byrne's third thesis, and progress toward religious truth is indeed possible, we cannot be sure that the cognitive success of all religions will remain equal as religious traditions undergo continued revision. We should see Byrne's pluralism as a provisional position that we may expect will eventually give way as greater certainty at the level of first-order religious beliefs is attained. As it stands,

---

20. Byrne, *Prolegomena to Religious Pluralism*, 193.

pluralism's insistence on the equality of all religions seems in conflict with the thesis that religions are revisable.

The tension between Byrne's first and third theses exposes a tension between his realism and agnosticism. Byrne acknowledges that "there are points at which pluralism is vulnerable to refutation . . . [and] is under some internal strain, for its heavy agnosticism is combined with a form of realism and an acceptance of salvific success in the religions."[21] Pluralism acknowledges the indispensability of commitment to first-order religious beliefs in order to successfully make cognitive contact with the sacred. So the philosophy of religion and religious pluralism is no substitute for first-order religious beliefs and practice. At the same time, pluralism asserts that the doctrinal claims of religions are deeply flawed. The philosopher of religion reflecting on the diversity of religious traditions can have reasonable belief that particular religions are making contact with the transcendent sacred and that this contact results in salvation for their practitioners. However, none of the actual practitioners of those religions can know that their beliefs about the sacred are true. This might make it seem as though it is the philosopher of religion who has some religious knowledge, while religious believers, operating at the level of first-order beliefs and practice, lack religious knowledge. Byrne insists, however, that his "pluralism is modest enough not to offer itself as a philosophical replacement for religion. It holds out absolutely no promise that philosophical reflection is an alternative or better route to cognitive and salvific contact with sacred reality. . . . Reference to the sacred is based in forms of experience and practice which are traditionally and communally grounded."[22]

Here Byrne comments on the paradox:

> If pluralism is true, then rich, living, doctrinally loaded accounts of the nature of transcendent reality and of salvation are both necessary and inevitably flawed. They are necessary for the moulding [sic] of the practical and experiential complexes by means of which humankind can genuinely relate to the sacred. They are inevitably flawed, for from the nature of the case they cannot claim strict truth with any certainty. That is to say, taken literally and positively they cannot claim with any certainty to correspond in detail with the reality they refer to. The pluralist does not know which of these detailed, first-order beliefs is false. Some may be true. He or she considers that they are all radically uncertain. Therefore, they are no basis for any interpretation of

---

21. Byrne, *Prolegomena to Religious Pluralism*, 195.
22. Byrne, *Prolegomena to Religious Pluralism*, 199.

religion we can now offer. In particular, they are no basis for absolute claims about salvation, revelation, and the like.[23]

This is a very revealing passage. It acknowledges that the success of persons in making contact with the sacred requires that they participate experientially and practically within a specific religious tradition. Being religious, then, requires participation in a particular religious tradition. All such traditions have their "doctrinally loaded accounts of the nature of transcendent reality and of salvation." Byrne admits that some religious beliefs may be true and that the pluralist cannot know that any are false. He admits that the pluralist "can accept that it is logically possible for religious reality to be just as one of the traditions claims it to be."[24] However, the pluralist also holds that although all religions are successful in referring to the transcendent and in offering a path to salvation, they are still "deeply flawed and radically uncertain." None of the religious traditions "can claim strict truth with any certainty." Pluralism acknowledges the necessity of first-order religious belief, practice, and experience in order for religion to attain its cognitive and salvific success. Insofar as pluralism entails agnosticism about first-order religious beliefs that are foundational to religious practice, pluralism seems finally to cut itself off from the possibility of authentic participation in the religious life that is supposed to be capable of enjoying that success. Authentic participation in a religious tradition's rituals and practices would seem to require faithful affirmation that the foundational beliefs of that tradition are true. So not only does religious pluralism not provide a superior form of religious knowledge, it threatens to alienate persons from the possibility of religious belief and practice. Pluralism seems to simultaneously affirm the cognitive success of religious traditions and undermine the possibility of authentic participation in them.

Byrne's struggle with the tension between his realism and his agnosticism is due to the implications he draws about religious truth from the uncertainty of religious belief. The uncertainty of religious doctrinal claims seems consistent with their being true in the sense of corresponding to reality, which is what realism would entail. What does Byrne mean by the presumption that religious doctrines cannot claim "strict truth"? If he means to deny that religious doctrines can claim truth in the sense of corresponding to reality, then he is backing off from the realism that was advertised as a component of pluralism. Byrne admits that "it is logically possible for religious reality to be just as one of the traditions claims it to be," and that the Christian who believes that Jesus is the son of God might

23. Byrne, *Prolegomena to Religious Pluralism*, 200–1.
24. Byrne, *Prolegomena to Religious Pluralism*, 202.

be right. At least "pluralism does not affirm that an affirmation such as 'Jesus is the son of God' is proved false."[25] This sounds very straightforwardly realist. However, pluralism also asserts that one cannot say "Jesus is the son of God" and reasonably believe it to be true, in the sense of corresponding to reality. Doctrinal statements may refer to religious reality, but they are presumed by pluralism not to describe that reality truly, in detail, and with any certainty, since no one can do that. So someone who affirms doctrinal statements after going through the reflective process which leads to embracing pluralism as a philosophical thesis cannot affirm doctrinal statements to be unequivocally, categorically true. "I believe" cannot mean the same for a person in "I believe Jesus is the son of God" as it means in "I believe that grass is green."[26]

The paradoxical position to which pluralism has led seems in part due to confusion between the lack of certainty and the lack of "strict truth." Byrne says that no one can describe religious "reality truly, in detail, and with certainty," and for this reason, pluralism presumes that doctrinal statements do not do this. For descriptions of reality to get all three—detail, truth, and certainty—is a tall order, and would be hard to achieve in any field, not just religion. The inevitable uncertainty in religion should not be thought to undermine the possibility of attaining some approximation of truth, realistically construed. Many theistic believers are quite willing to admit that they cannot describe God truly, in detail, and with certainty, but they nevertheless believe that the doctrines they affirm are true in a realist sense. In the last sentence of the quoted passage, Byrne seems to be saying that the deep and inevitable flaw in religious claims is not merely the lack of certainty but also the impossibility of their corresponding to reality. Byrne says that "I believe" means something different when the belief is about Jesus than when the belief is about grass. No doubt there are big differences between believing in Jesus and believing that grass is green, but at least part of what the Christian who believes that Jesus is the son of God might mean is that the statement "Jesus is the son of God" corresponds to reality. Again, Byrne admits that the pluralist "can accept that it is logically possible for religious reality to be just as one of the traditions claims it to be,"[27] but then in the next paragraph he says that pluralism presumes doctrinal statements not to describe religious reality truly. Does this mean merely that no one can be certain that religious beliefs correspond to reality, or does it mean that they do not correspond to reality? The latter interpretation

---

25. Byrne, *Prolegomena to Religious Pluralism*, 202.
26. Byrne, *Prolegomena to Religious Pluralism*, 202.
27. Byrne, *Prolegomena to Religious Pluralism*, 202.

contradicts the statement that "it is logically possible for religious reality to be just as one of the traditions claims it to be." Additionally, it seems to seriously undermine pluralism's thesis about the revisability of religions. It also seems to undermine Byrne's first thesis. So it seems we must accept the first interpretation—that no one can know with certainty that his or her religious beliefs correspond to reality, but that it is possible for some of them to be true in that sense. This is consistent with the idea that religious doctrines are finally matters of faith, not rational proof, but that they can correspond to reality.

The uncertainty of religious belief alone does not support the pluralist's presumption that religious doctrinal statements do not describe reality truly. Many religious believers acknowledge the lack of objective certainty about religious doctrinal claims, but as they regard the truth of those doctrinal claims as essential to religious faith and practice, they insist that the doctrinal claims correspond to reality despite their uncertainty. However, it is not just uncertainty that leads Byrne to the pluralist presumption against affirming religious truth claims, but also "the very fact of religious diversity in respect of cognitive claims," and the high degree to which religions are the product of sociocultural factors.[28] To the contrary, diversity of belief does not entail the pluralist's presumption, nor does the lack of criteria for resolving disagreement, unless it is taken to be in principle incurable. In that case, if the lack of criteria is permanent and incurable, then the revisability thesis is undermined. Byrne also thinks that the pluralist's presumption is supported by "the socio-cultural basis of thought" that "ties in with the cultural-linguistic view of religious discourse," which "entails a modest constructivism in the interpretation of religious experience."[29] Byrne does not work out these ideas in detail. The sociocultural basis of thought would pertain to all thought, including scientific thought, which is obviously also a cultural artifact, but is also generally regarded as trafficking in objective truth. Byrne does not explain in detail the modesty of the constructivism in religion, but to the extent that it is a consequence of the sociocultural basis of all human thought, it is not the source of a flaw in religious doctrinal claims that is any more severe than that of other forms of thought. The cultural-linguistic view of religious discourse entails that religion is to a large degree a cultural artifact, and thus supports a modest constructivism, but again, the constructivism is apparently modest enough for pluralism to allow that "it is logically possible for religious reality to be just as one of the traditions claims it to be." Unless the uncertainty of religious doctrinal

28. Byrne, *Prolegomena to Religious Pluralism*, 193, 199.
29. Byrne, *Prolegomena to Religious Pluralism*, 199.

claims and the modest constructivism implied by the "cultural-linguistic view of religious discourse" entail a flaw serious enough to undermine Byrne's commitment to religious realism, the presumption of his pluralism that religious doctrinal statements do not describe reality truly is unwarranted. In order to maintain the realist component of pluralism, the agnostic component must be less severe than Byrne has characterized it to be.

If we take seriously the revisability thesis and hold that it is in principle possible for some doctrinal statements to be true, then the lack of certainty about them should not be taken as permanent, insurmountable, or as a barrier to religious faith and practice. Nor should it be taken as support for religious pluralism rather than confessionalism, some forms of which freely admit and even seem to relish the rational uncertainty of religious belief and insist that faith is quite consistent with uncertainty. Since Byrne admits the possibility of progress in religion, we should hope that that progress could include getting truer descriptions of the transcendent. We should be open to the possibility that eventually one or more religions may emerge as superior to others. If it is an *a priori* assumption that we must at all costs avoid religious exclusivism and make sure all religions enjoy equal cognitive and soteriological success, then we cannot expect movement toward one religion ever emerging as superior to the others. Of course Byrne is concerned to articulate a plausible version of pluralism, but he should not, given his insistence on the revisability of religious belief, rule out the possibility that rational ways of adjudicating disagreements among religions may emerge, or even that one religion might eventually immerge as ultimately superior to others. So at most, pluralism should be a tentative, provisional thesis, and Byrne should be open to the possibility that the religious dialogue, which he acknowledges to be valuable, could lead to progress toward the emergence of the plausibility of not just the general thesis of the reality of the sacred transcendent, but also of the superiority of one religion's detailed descriptions of and beliefs about it. If this possibility is not acknowledged, given the depth of the differences between the claims of diverse religions, Byrne's agnosticism seems to become terminal and devastating to religious realism.

CRITIQUE OF BYRNE'S SECOND THESIS

If Byrne's second thesis means merely that all religions are equal insofar as they all have some notion of salvation, then it is relatively unproblematic but trivially true, insofar as it is arguably part of the definition of religion that it involves a notion of salvation. In order for the second thesis to be philosophically interesting, it must involve a substantive claim about what different religions teach about salvation and the success of religions in fostering salvation. A problem with this pluralist account of salvation is that it implies more than a second-order philosophical reflection on religious diversity should claim. Byrne's agnosticism about the details of the doctrines of particular religions should cause reluctance to make any claims about the truth of what really constitutes salvation. He admits the possibility that one religion might be true, or closer to the truth than the others. Suppose for the sake of argument that the Christian idea of salvation is true (an analogous argument could be made for the assumption of the conception of salvation of other religions). Suppose it is true that all human beings are, prior to salvation, estranged from a personal God. Suppose that prior to the kind of ethical transformation with which Hick is concerned, human beings need to be redeemed by God. Suppose it is true that all human moral virtue falls short of God's moral standards. I am not assuming that this Christian view of salvation is correct. However, Byrne claims that he is not ruling out the possibility that it is correct, and if it is correct, then the kind of moral transformation that Byrne says constitutes salvation would not be attainable except through Christ. The kind of moral virtue that Byrne identifies as an end in itself and a mark of a kind of transcendence of self-centeredness would fall short of the redemption that Christianity says constitutes salvation in the fullest sense. A central teaching of Christianity is that all have sinned and fallen short of God's absolute standard of righteousness. It seems that Byrne's pluralist view of salvation entails that this Christian view is not merely uncertain, but false. More than agnosticism is required in order to justify the claim that this Christian view of salvation is false. Byrne would need more certainty about a particular claim of a specific religion than his official pluralistic position allows.

As is widely noted in discussions of religious diversity, and as Byrne himself admits, despite the fact that specific religions offer similar descriptions of the personal qualities and virtues that indicate salvation, they differ widely in their conceptions of the nature of the transcendent reality and the way to attain the kind of relation to it that constitutes salvation. Byrne rightly notes that there is a great deal of agreement among religions about the importance of love and compassion for attaining salvation. It is also true, as T. J. Mawson notes, that some forms of Christianity emphasize the impossibility of attaining salvation through ethical behavior or good works.[30] Keith Yandell emphasizes the fact that not only do religions disagree strongly on the way of attaining salvation, but one point on which

---

30. Mawson, "'Byrne's' Religious Pluralism."

most religions agree is that salvation is only attainable by following the path laid out by one specific religion, with each religion, of course, insisting that its own teaching concerning the path to salvation is the correct one.[31] If the fact of agreement between religions about the reality of the transcendent is support for religious realism, then it would seem that the virtually universal agreement among religions in thinking that there is one preferred path to salvation would be a good reason to take that belief seriously. Although religions differ in their accounts of salvation, with few exceptions each religion holds that there is one true (or preferred, or best) path to salvation, and each thinks that its way is that one true way. So it would seem that Byrne's emphasis on the fact that all religions agree about the existence of the transcendent as support for his religious realism would also demand appreciation of a feature that is perhaps nearly as ubiquitous among religions—that they hold that salvation is a difficult thing to attain and requires utmost adherence to the right way of attaining it, with each religion holding that its way is the only correct one. God is in the details, as they say. Of course, the religions that claim this might be wrong, and it might be that salvation is readily available to devotees of any religion. In order to know the truth about this issue, it would seem that we would need more than Byrne's agnosticism concerning specific religious doctrines permits.

In the absence of knowledge of the truth or falsity of specific claims that different religions make about salvation, the nature of the sacred, transcendent reality, the kind of relation to it that constitutes salvation, and the way to attain that kind of relation, we cannot know whether they are all equally successful in their prescriptions for the attainment of salvation. Of course, the pluralist may say that those disagreements about details don't matter; what matters is the broad agreement about the moral and spiritual transformation of human persons from self-centeredness to a life of love and compassion. On the contrary, most specific religions do not agree that such a broad description captures the essence of salvation, and they do not agree that their disagreements with the accounts of salvation offered by other religions do not matter. If the lack of neutral, objective, rational criteria for adjudicating disagreement between religions about salvation entailed that none of them can be true, then we might have some reason to say that they are all equal in their salvific success. Again, Byrne admits that it might be the case that one religion is truer than others about the nature of the sacred, transcendent reality, and about salvation. Therefore, the lack of knowledge of the truth of specific claims that diverse religions make about salvation, and Byrne's acknowledgment of the possibility in principle

---

31. Yandell, "How to Sink in Cognitive Quicksand" and "Reply to Byrne."

of future religious progress, should lead us to leave open the question of the parity of all religions on the issue of salvation.

Byrne has not proposed a version of religious pluralism that is rationally defensible and that serves as a stimulant to fruitful religious dialogue. The agnosticism is too severe and tends to undermine the realism, and the realism is too weak to provide a basis for fruitful religious dialogue and progress in religious understanding. Perhaps the severity of Byrne's agnosticism should be moderated. Byrne emphasizes the disagreements between religions in their detailed descriptions about the nature of the transcendent, sacred reality. However, religions generally agree on the point that all descriptions of the ultimate religious reality fall short of absolute, literal truth. As David Bentley Hart points out, most of the great religions agree that the ultimate reality is the transcendent source of all being and value and that it is beyond human comprehension. Hart emphasizes remarkable agreement between religions about the transcendence, incomprehensibility, and indescribability of the ultimate reality.[32]

If we take seriously Byrne's religious realism, then we have grounds for thinking it is possible for religious dialog to result in progress toward greater religious knowledge. It does seem that there has been progress in religious understanding in the past. Advanced cultures no longer believe in the finite, polytheistic deities of ancient religions. As Hart contends, virtually all the great world religions affirm the reality of the transcendent, sacred ground of being and they agree on several key propositions about it.[33] The transcendent is more aptly spoken of as Being itself, rather than as a particular being, which seems to imply finitude and a status on the same ontological level as things in the material world. The transcendent is commonly regarded as infinite in greatness and goodness, and absolutely perfect. It is the ground and source of all that exists and of all value. It is that in relation to which the ultimate goal and purpose of human life is conceived and attained (insofar as particular religions regard it as attainable). Virtually all religions regard the transcendent as beyond human comprehension. Some religions regard the transcendent as absolutely ineffable and beyond human concepts. This seems to be Hick's view, which we have already seen to be problematic. If the Real is absolutely ineffable, then it cannot be the ultimate object of religious consciousness. However, although most religions regard the transcendent as beyond human understanding, they have various ways of talking about this ultimate reality, how human beings can relate to it, and in some sense and to some degree, how to know it.

32. Hart, *The Experience of God*, 30.
33. Hart, *The Experience of God*, 32.

In the Christian tradition there are various views about how religious language refers to God. Thomas Aquinas's view of analogical predication is a way of forging a middle way between views like those of Pseudo Dionysius and Moses Maimonides, which deny the possibility of predicating positive attributes of God and allow only negative predication, and other views that permit literal, univocal predication of positive attributes of God. For Aquinas God is beyond human comprehension and we cannot predicate positive attributes of God literally, but we can predicate attributes like goodness, wisdom, and love to God in a sense that is analogical to, but infinitely greater than the sense in which we predicate such attributes to human beings. God's goodness is infinitely greater than any goodness that we experience in our finite world, but insofar as human goodness is dependent on divine goodness, our knowledge of goodness is sufficient for us to have a glimmer of insight into what it means for God to be good. The sense in which God is ineffable is consistent with the possibility of analogical knowledge of divine attributes. According to Aquinas, our limited knowledge of God also makes possible metaphorical statements about God and statements about God's actions.

Aquinas is willing to say many things about God that are very different than what a Hindu would say about Brahman or a Taoist would say about the Tao. The Tao de jing has a different way of struggling with the tension between the ineffability of the transcendent absolute and the need to in some meager way make sense of it and talk about it. Nonetheless, there is a great deal of common ground between theism, Hinduism, and Taoism in how they use language to talk about a reality that is in some sense and to some degree beyond human understanding or description. For this reason, I think Byrne's agnostic strain makes too much of the disagreement between the great religions in "their detailed descriptions of the transcendent, sacred reality." Although these descriptions sometimes look very different, there is in many religious traditions a strong awareness that all descriptions of God are woefully inadequate and fall far short of literal accuracy. Many descriptions of God that look very different when interpreted literally, are nonetheless equally appropriate ways of using language to express our awareness of the transcendent, sacred, infinite, supremely unified reality. I think Byrne goes too far in emphasizing the ineffability of the Real and in making all religions equally true by totally depriving them of descriptive truth. It is appropriate, however, to recognize that most religions admit that their descriptions of the transcendent fall short of perfectly accurate literal truth.

The agnostic strain of Byrne's pluralism is too severe. If it is possible that religions are revisable then it is false that we are totally lacking means of assessing religious claims. Even though the sacred, transcendent reality is to a large degree beyond human comprehension, we can to some degree rationally evaluate competing claims about the transcendent by using the same canons of rationality that we deploy in any intellectual enterprise. We can look for internal coherence, explanatory power, and consistency with what we know from other fields, such as science, common sense, and ethics. Is the transcendent, sacred reality an impersonal, absolutely ineffable reality of Asian religions such as Buddhism and Hinduism, or is it the personal God of monotheistic religion?

One way to begin to address this question is to see whether there are clues in modern science. Does a theistic worldview or a worldview based on an impersonal conception of the transcendent resonate more harmoniously with what science teaches us about the universe? Which worldview, given what we can learn from modern science, enjoys the greater degree of logical coherence and better unifies what we know from the widest range of sources of knowledge?

We shall address these questions in chapter 9 by looking at religious and worldview implications of modern cosmology. We have seen that Big Bang cosmology and cosmic fine-tuning are consistent with the existence of God and a theistic worldview. In chapter 9 we will consider Buddhism as a prime example of a religion that is based on a conception of reality that views the ultimate religious reality as impersonal. We will consider the question whether Buddhism is more compatible with modern scientific cosmology than theism. I will argue that, contrary to the opinion of many who argue that modern science would favor Buddhism over theism, the notion of an omnipotent, supremely intelligent creator is easier to harmonize with contemporary scientific cosmology than is the metaphysical framework of Buddhism. This supports the claim that an examination of the relation between science and religion can help somewhat in adjudicating between conflicting truth claims of different religions.

9
Buddhism, Theism, and Science

The book of Genesis opens with the statement, "In the beginning God created the heavens and the earth," and although there is some disagreement among biblical scholars on the issue whether creation *ex nihilo* is the explicit teaching of the biblical creation story, there is no doubt that the eventual explicit formulation of the doctrine was based on interpretation of the biblical text. There are creations myths in many religious traditions, but the Abrahamic traditions are unique in arriving fairly early at a doctrine of explicit monotheism and a doctrine of creation that entails an absolute beginning of the universe. The tendency in Asian religion is to regard the cosmos as eternally existing and subject to a cyclical pattern of transformation into different particular worlds. That the Abrahamic traditions regard both monotheism and the doctrine of creation as foundational to their faith places these religions much closer to modern Big Bang cosmology than are other religious traditions.

BUDDHIST METAPHYSICS AND MODERN SCIENCE

It is a widely held view today that Buddhism is more compatible with modern science than other religions, especially theistic religions. This perception dates back at least to the nineteenth century, and enjoyed increased credibility in the twentieth century with the development of the theory of relativity and quantum physics, which certain ideas in Buddhism seem to anticipate. Paul O. Ingram reports that "some Buddhist writers point to parallels between Buddhism's 'nontheistic' worldview and current scientific cosmology as evidence that Buddhism is more in harmony with the sciences than Christian theism."[1] As Buddhist scholarship developed in Europe in the nineteenth century, European and American thinkers welcomed the prospect of a viable religious alternative to Christianity. Buddhism offered a religion compatible with science and without the baggage of dogmas and demanding rituals and requirements. Thomas Henry Huxley wrote in 1894 that Buddhism is

> A system which knows no God in the western sense; which denies a soul to man; which counts the belief in immortality a blunder and the hope of it a sin; which refuses any efficacy to prayer and sacrifice; which bids men to look to nothing but their own efforts for salvation; which, in its original purity knew nothing of vows of obedience, abhorred intolerance, and never sought the aid of the secular arm; yet spread over a considerable moiety of the Old World with marvelous rapidity, and is still, with whatever base admixture of foreign superstitions, the dominant creed of a large fraction of mankind.[2]

For many thinkers of the late nineteenth century Buddhism was a religion, unlike Christianity, that recognized that the universe is entirely governed by natural laws, without the need for a cosmic designer or intervener. They saw Buddhism as the religion "most suited to serious dialogue with science, because both postulated the existence of immutable laws that governed the universe."[3]

Early in the twentieth century Buddhist intellectuals countered Christian missionaries with the argument that Buddhism was superior to Christianity because it was more compatible with modern science. In 1925 the Sinhalese Buddhist activist Anagarika Dharmapala delivered a lecture in New York in which he proclaimed the following:

> The Message of the Buddha that I have to bring to you is free from theology, priestcraft, rituals, ceremonies, dogmas, heavens, hells and other theological shibboleths. The Buddha taught to the civilized Aryans of India 25 centuries ago a scientific religion containing the highest individualistic altruistic ethics, a philosophy of life built on psychological mysticism and a cosmogony which is in harmony with geology, astronomy, radioactivity, and relativity. No creator god can create an ever-changing, ever-existing cosmos. Countless billions of aeons ago the earth

---

1. Ingram, *Buddhist-Christian Dialogue in an Age of Science*, 50.
2. Quoted in Lopez, "Buddhism," 216.
3. Lopez, *Buddhism and Science*, 7.

was existing but undergoing change, and there are billions of solar systems that had existed and exist and shall exist.[4]

Buddhism affirms neither the existence of an omnipotent personal God nor a doctrine of creation that implies a universe that began to exist at some point in the finite past. There are several schools of thought within Buddhism, and some affirm the existence of various finite deities, but it is crucial to the central themes of Buddhist thought that there is no omnipotent creator. As a religion Buddhism offers a diagnosis of the human condition and the spiritual disease that infects all human beings, and offers a detailed prescription of the remedy for that disease. The remedy entails a very elaborate, worked-out metaphysical framework, which is incompatible with theism.

In contrast to Christianity, which sees the fundamental problem confronting human beings as sin against a holy God, for Buddhism the fundamental predicament is that human beings are ignorant of ultimate reality, and their ignorance leads them to ways of living that inevitably produce suffering. The First Noble Truth taught by the Buddha is that suffering, or unsatisfactoriness, pervades all of human life. Of course, Buddhism acknowledges the obvious fact that life is a mix of pleasant and unpleasant experiences, but it emphasizes the fact that even in the happiest of circumstances life includes elements of incompleteness, dissatisfaction, frustration, and disappointment. Many of our deepest desires go unfulfilled, and none of our desires are ever completely satisfied. Hence unsatisfied desire, or unsatisfactoriness, pervades all of life, prior to the attainment of the enlightenment that liberates one from the human predicament. Even when desires are satisfied, the possibility of losing what is desired looms. The happiest moments are fleeting. We are subject to sickness, the inexorable march of time toward the gradual diminishing of our faculties and powers, and ultimately the complete disintegration of our existence in death. We are never able to completely brush aside the awareness of these deficiencies. Indeed, the negative aspects of the human condition are the constant subject of our arts, entertainments, and humor, as we strive to manage the pain of our existence.

The Second Noble Truth teaches us that the cause of suffering is desire. Desire is the longing for what we do not have, and the disparity between this longing and the lack of satisfaction of our desires causes suffering, which is experiencing unsatisfactory mental states. Sometimes the failure to satisfy the desire is prolonged, and suffering increases. Sometimes desires are momentarily satisfied, and boredom and the desire for something new arise.

4. Quoted in Lopez, "Buddhism," 218.

What is the solution to this predicament? There are basically two conceivable solutions. One would be the complete and permanent satisfaction of desire. This is what some religions promise, but such complete satisfaction of desire is metaphysically impossible according to Buddhism. The Third Noble Truth offers the other logically conceivable solution, which is the only one that is possible in reality. The cessation of suffering is possible only by the elimination of its cause, which is desire—the selfish craving and attachment to what is wrongly thought will bring lasting satisfaction. The cessation of suffering requires getting at the root cause of desire, which is ignorance of the way things ultimately are. Ignorance of the impermanence of all things, including our bodies and minds, leads us to cling to things and to the self, in a desperate and futile attempt to find and hold on to the permanence of our existence. Our suffering can end only when we escape the delusion that permanent existence is possible and let go of our vain efforts at finding permanence.

The escape from suffering requires enlightenment, which involves seeing the ultimate truth—seeing reality as it truly is. The Fourth Noble Truth is that of the Noble Eightfold Path, which is the way to attain the enlightenment that allows reality to be seen as it is and the cessation of suffering to be attained. The Eightfold Path includes constituents that fall into three categories—moral self-discipline that leads to right action, meditation that leads to mental discipline and permits steadfast concentration on the truth that liberates, and wisdom, which is ultimate knowledge of reality as it truly is. The various ethical prescriptions—right speech, right action, and right livelihood—are expressions of love and the elimination of hatred, which is a principal cause of desire that leads to suffering. Meditation produces blissful mental states in the present and subsequent lives, but does not bring about liberation from rebirth. The complete cessation of suffering requires liberation from rebirth, which in turn requires enlightenment and wisdom—consciousness of ultimate reality as it truly is.

Buddhism first arose and developed in India in the context of a religious culture that affirmed the doctrines of karma and rebirth. Karma is a kind of principle of moral causality and cosmic justice, and rebirth allows karma to operate across many lifetimes. Every good and bad deed has its moral consequences, which must inexorably play out, even if not within the span of one lifetime. The deeds one does in this life will have consequences when one is reborn into another life after death. The normal Hindu way of interpreting rebirth involves the self or soul being reincarnated in a different body after death to live another life in that new body. While the Buddha accepted karma and rebirth, he did not accept the existence of an enduring soul or self, which could be reincarnated and retain its identity as the same soul throughout subsequent lives. There are no permanent substances or natures at all for Buddhism, not even a permanent soul that persists through several lives or even one life. There are a wide variety of different views within various Buddhist traditions about the details of how liberation from suffering is attained, but a common theme that unites all of them is the idea that liberation from suffering requires first and foremost liberation from the desire to attain permanence for oneself.

One of the most important truths that must be realized in order for liberation to take place is that there is no enduring, permanent soul or self. The desire to be a permanent self is the source of many other desires that result in various misguided attempts to establish permanence by attempting to attach to oneself other objects—such as wealth, material possessions, prestige, power over others—which are falsely believed to provide stability and security for oneself. Part of the delusion that must be overcome, somewhat paradoxically, is the illusion that there is a self that can be or not be liberated. Liberation involves being liberated from the illusion of a permanent self that can be liberated. Desire for liberation is itself an attachment to self that must be overcome. It is the failure to see the truth of impermanence and that there is no permanent self, that perpetuates the deluded craving and clinging that is the cause of suffering. Liberation from suffering requires liberation from rebirth. This is nirvana, the extinction of the deluded, clinging self, which allows liberation from karma and the cycle of rebirth with its perpetual suffering.

This "no-self" view is connected with the general view that everything that exists lacks its "own existence," or any permanent, substantial, intrinsic existence. This lack of "own existence" is not only the human condition, but the condition of everything, and knowledge of the way things really are, lacking inherent existence, is of paramount importance for the attainment of the ultimate religious end. The basic cause of the desires that produce suffering is ignorance of the way things really are—their impermanence and lack of substantial, self-owned existence. Nothing owns its existence because everything depends for its existence on causes and conditions other than itself. This is the doctrine of dependent origination, which was realized by the Buddha in his initial enlightenment.

According to this doctrine, all things are dependent on causes and conditions, which are other things or states, which in turn depend on other causes and conditions, and so on, *ad infinitum*. All things are co-dependent on their causes and conditions and also on all other things of which they are causes and conditions. All causes are affected in turn by their effects. Therefore all things and states are interdependent. This is one reason that Buddhism rejects the idea of an omnipotent, transcendent creator. It is thought to be impossible for a God to be both a cause of events in the universe and at the same time radically transcendent and independent of the universe.

A traditional Buddhist assumption is that because all things are dependent on causes and conditions other than themselves, they are therefore impermanent. Impermanence is a consequence of dependence. Everything that exists enjoys, at most, fleeting existence. Composite things that seem to be relatively permanent, such as automobiles, houses, and human beings, are made up of component parts that continually come into existence and pass away. There is within Buddhist tradition difference of opinion concerning whether composite things are composed ultimately of non-composite components, but there is general agreement that composite things are nothing more than the sum of their component parts, which enjoy only momentary existence. This point is important for the Buddhist idea that there is no enduring self or soul that is the subject of all a person's mental states.

That which is said to be the soul is really nothing more than the combination of various mental states that are temporarily clustered together in what is believed to be a self or person. There is no one mental state that is the subject of consciousness, nor does the totality of one cluster of mental states constitute a unified subject or self that has an identity over and above the various specific, fleeting mental states. The belief that one is a unified self that is the subject of a cluster of mental states is itself just one mental state (or complex of mental states) that is part of the mix of mental states combined in what is mistakenly thought to be a permanent, unified person. The belief that one is a unified person with a unified consciousness is one of the most unsatisfactory of mental states and the source of much suffering.

All composite things lack independent, self-existence. Everything is what it is due to its relations, especially causal relations, to all other things. Everything is empty of independent self-existence, or "own existence." This is the doctrine of śūnyatā, or emptiness. Everything that exists is empty of own-being. There are no substances, in the classic Western sense of something that exists in itself. There are no essences or natures of things. The tree seems to be a robust, substantial entity that has its own substantial being. On the contrary, whatever existence the tree has depends on the soil, water, the ecosystem, the planet, the sun, the universe. Apart from the whole, the tree is nothing, and the whole is nothing but the sum of its parts. The doctrines of dependent origination, the interconnectedness of all things, impermanence, and emptiness, are all interrelated. Everything that exists comes into existence as the result of causes and conditions that are causally connected ultimately with everything in the universe. All things are interrelated, so everything is empty of its own independent existence. Things enjoy only momentary existence. At the most elemental level, the components of the universe continually arise and then cease to exist.

When there is attainment of a mental state that is fully conscious of the impermanence, interrelatedness, and emptiness of all things, including self, then there is liberation from the ignorance that prevents the cessation of desire and the suffering that results from desire. Buddhism's religious diagnosis of the human condition and its prescribed cure for the disease that afflicts human beings is highly dependent on the metaphysical framework that it teaches. Again, the root problem in the human predicament is ignorance, so the cure requires knowledge and wisdom concerning the way things really are.

Some aspects of the Buddhist view of reality may be subject to assessment in light of modern science. For well over a century many Western scholars sympathetic with Buddhism have argued that the Buddhist metaphysical framework is more compatible with modern science than those associated with other religions. An assessment of this claim, along with an assessment of the Buddhist metaphysical framework itself, should be helpful in adjudicating conflicting truth claims between Buddhism and Christian theism.

BUDDHISM AND BIG BANG COSMOLOGY

Those who think that Buddhism is the religion that is most compatible with modern science point to a number of specific Buddhist ideas that seem to anticipate developments in modern science. The notion of virtual particles spontaneously coming into existence in empty space and passing away in an instant suggests the Buddhist ideas of emptiness and impermanence. The unstable "Nothing" from which Lawrence Krauss says that the universe came into existence suggests the Buddhist notions of emptiness and dependent origination. The entanglement of particles according to quantum mechanics suggests the Buddhist idea that everything is interconnected. Science is now telling us that what were once thought to be particles of solid matter that eternally exist and remain exactly as they are at every moment of their existence are actually energy waves. The critical role of the observer in quantum physics seems to support the Buddhist idea of the interdependence of matter and consciousness. The idea that our universe is just one of an infinite number of worlds in a vast, perhaps infinite, multiverse seems to resonate with the Buddhist belief in countless, interrelated worlds that are parts of an eternally existing whole.

In his recent book, *The Universe in a Single Atom*, the Fourteenth Dalai Lama of Tibet expresses his own personal and lifelong interest in natural science and his conviction that Buddhist teaching must continually be adjusted and reinterpreted in light of scientific discoveries.[5] The Dalai Lama discusses the relation between modern science and Buddhism. He recognizes the affinity between the Big Bang beginning of the universe and the Christian doctrine of creation and its inconsistency with the Buddhist teaching that the universe is eternal and cyclical. He also notes, however, that not all scientific cosmologists accept the inference from the Big Bang theory to an absolute beginning of the universe. He notes that there are a number of alternative Big Bang scenarios that do not entail that the Big Bang is an absolute beginning. One in particular, the cyclical or oscillating universe model, is noted by the Dalai Lama as one that is particularly attractive from a Buddhist perspective. In a chapter dealing with the Big Bang theory, he writes,

> At the heart of Buddhist cosmology is, therefore, not only the idea that there are multiple world systems—infinitely more than the grains of sand in the river Ganges, according to some texts—but also the idea that they are in a constant state of coming into being and passing away. This means that the universe has no absolute beginning. The questions this poses for science are fundamental. Was there one Big Bang or were there many? Is there one universe or are there many, or even an infinite number? Is the universe finite or infinite, as the Buddhists assert? Will our universe expand infinitely, or will its expansion slow down, even reverse, so that it ultimately ends in a big crunch? Is our universe part of an eternally reproducing cosmos? Scientists are debating these issues intensely. From the Buddhist point of view, there is this further question. Even if we grant that there was only one big cosmic bang, we can still ask, Is this the origin of the entire universe or does this mark only the origin of our particular universe system? So a key question is whether the Big Bang—which, according to modern cosmology, is the beginning of our current world system—is really the beginning of everything. From the Buddhist perspective, the idea that there is a single definite beginning is highly problematic. If there were such an absolute beginning, logically speaking, this leaves only two options. One is theism, which presupposes that the universe is created by an intelligence that is totally transcendent, and therefore outside the laws of cause and effect. The second is that

---

5. Dalai Lama, *The Universe in a Single Atom*.

the universe came into being from no cause at all. Buddhism rejects both of these options. If the universe is created by a prior intelligence, the questions of the ontological status of such an intelligence and what kind of reality it is remain.[6]

It is interesting to note that, according to the Dalai Lama, interpretations of the Big Bang theory that entail that the universe began to exist are incompatible with Buddhist metaphysics. While Christian theism favors, and is supported by, the view that the universe began to exist, it is compatible with interpretations of the doctrine of creation that imply a beginningless universe. So on the question of whether the universe began to exist, theism is somewhat more flexible than Buddhism.

The Dalai Lama cites Dharmakirti, the great seventh-century Buddhist logician and epistemologist, as having "cogently presented the standard Buddhist critique of theism"[7] in his classic *Exposition of Valid Cognition*. In this work Dharmakirti presents and refutes a version of the argument from design for the existence of a supreme designer of the universe.

> The crux of Dharmakirti's critique involves demonstrating a fundamental inconsistency he perceives in the theistic standpoint. He shows that the very endeavor of accounting for the origin of the universe in theistic terms is motivated by the principle of causality, yet—in the final analysis—theism is forced to reject this principle. By positing an absolute beginning to the chain of causation, theists are implying that there can be something, at least one cause, which is itself outside the law of causality. This beginning, which is effectively the first cause, will itself be uncaused. This first cause will have to be an eternal and absolute principle. If so, how can one account for its capacity to produce things and events that are transient? Dharmakirti argues that no causal efficacy can be accorded to such a permanent principle. In essence, he is saying that the postulation of a first cause will have to be an arbitrary metaphysical hypothesis. It cannot be proven.[8]

So the notion of a first cause violates the fundamental Buddhist idea of dependent origination, according to which everything that exists is dependent for its existence on the totality of other existing things. According to this view, the absoluteness and necessity of God's existence prevents God from being causally related to anything else. Matthew Ricard, a Buddhist monk,

---

6. Dalai Lama, *The Universe in a Single Atom*, 81–82.
7. Dalai Lama, *The Universe in a Single Atom*, 81–82.
8. Dalai Lama, *The Universe in a Single Atom*, 83.

the official French translator of the Dalai Lama, who also writes on science and Buddhism, argues that a God who is the First Cause would have to be immutable. "Change would imply the intervention of another cause that wasn't part of the prime cause."[9] He also argues that an immutable being could not create anything. "Any creator must in turn be modified by its creation, because each action implies interaction. No cause can be one-way. Causality is necessarily reciprocal. Any creator is acted upon by its creation."[10] Of course, this contradicts the immutability of the creator. Thus, according to Buddhism, the idea of an omnipotent, immutable, creator God who can create and interact with the world is incoherent.

For Buddhism there is no need for a creator because Buddhism denies that the universe had a beginning. Ricard writes,

> One of Buddhism's essential ideas states that because things have no independent reality, they can't really "begin," or "end" as distinct entities. . . . All religions and philosophies have come unstuck on the problem of creation. Science has gotten rid of it by removing God the Creator, who had become unnecessary. Buddhism has done so by eliminating the very idea of a beginning. . . . If reality were permanent, and its properties too, then nothing would change. Phenomena could not appear. But because things have no intrinsic reality, they can have infinite manifestations.[11]

The notion of a creator of the universe seems absurd to Ricard. He agrees with his coauthor, Trinh Xuan Thuan, who writes that,

> the very notion of cause and effect loses its meaning when applied to the universe. . . . According to the Big Bang, time and space appeared simultaneously with the universe. If time didn't exist before this, then what does "and God created the universe" mean? The act of creating the universe is meaningful only in time. . . . A God contained in time would no longer be all-powerful, because he would be subject to the laws of time. A God outside time would be omnipotent, but unable to help us, since our actions happen in time. If God transcended time, then he would already know the future. If he knew everything in advance, why would he bother to become involved in the struggle of humankind against evil?[12]

9. Ricard and Thuan, *The Quantum and the Lotus*, 55.
10. Ricard and Thuan, *The Quantum and the Lotus*, 55.
11. Ricard and Thuan, *The Quantum and the Lotus*, 31–32.
12. Ricard and Thuan, *The Quantum and the Lotus*, 52.

Ricard adds,

> God must be either, immutable and unable to create, or else inside of time and thus not immutable. This is one of the contradictions that the notion of a prime cause leads to. . . . Second, how could an immutable entity create something? If there is an act of creation, is the creator involved or not? If he is not, why call him a "creator"? If he is involved, then because creation inevitably occurs in stages, the something or someone involved in these stages is not immutable.[13]

It is clear from this passage that Ricard is thinking of causality as efficient or event causation, according to which a cause of an event must be some prior event in time. There cannot be a time before the beginning of time, and there cannot be a moving cause of an event outside of time. As already noted, theists such as Augustine argue that God's bringing the universe into being from nothing is not an event in time, and it did not take place at a time temporally before the beginning of time or the beginning of the universe. Furthermore, God's being absolutely transcendent, and thus outside the temporal dimension of time of our universe, does not prevent him either from acting in the world or being omnipotent. If the whole universe is causally dependent on God, not in the sense that God acted as a craftsman in mechanically constructing it by a stage-by-stage process, but rather in the sense that God brings the universe into existence instantaneously and sustains it at every moment of its existence, then God may exercise whatever degree of sovereignty he chooses over every event in the history of the universe. It is consistent with God's omnipotence for him to choose to grant to creatures, especially human beings, whatever degree of freedom of choice and autonomy that he wills. From the standpoint of theism, neither God's transcendence nor omnipotence are incompatible with his acting in the world or allowing human freedom.

In response to the Buddhist critique of the Christian notion of creation and the claim that in order for God to be a creator, he must be affected by the creation, I would simply state that theism does not accept the Buddhist assumptions about causality and dependent origination. The Buddhist notions of emptiness, dependent origination, and the co-dependence of causes and conditions are fundamental assumptions that are not provable independently of the overall Buddhist metaphysical framework. Christian theism makes different metaphysical assumptions about causality, in the context of which the agency of God as an omnipotent creator makes sense.

---

13. Ricard and Thuan, *The Quantum and the Lotus*, 52.

Buddhism also has its own difficulties in making sense of human freedom. The law of karma seems to imply a rather rigid determinism, which is hard to reconcile with human freedom. Even if karma and the doctrine of dependent origination are interpreted in such a way that allows a degree of indeterminacy in the course of events in the phenomenal world, it is difficult to make sense of how persons are responsible for their free choices if there is no unified, enduring self that is the agent who performs morally significant actions and maintains its identity across multiple lifetimes.

Ricard quotes approvingly the famous dictum of the great second-century Mahayana Buddhist metaphysician and dialectician, Nagarjuna, "Since all is empty, all is possible."[14] Ricard also quotes the famous Perfection of Wisdom scripture, "Though phenomena appear, they are empty; though empty, they appear."[15] He goes on to say, "In Buddhism, emptiness isn't just the true nature of phenomena, it's also the potential that allows the propagation of an infinite variety of phenomena. . . . [I]f reality were permanent, and its properties too, then nothing would change. Phenomena could not appear. But because things have no intrinsic reality, they can have infinite manifestations."[16] Emptiness seems to be a kind of metaphysical ground that "allows for the propagation of an infinite variety of phenomena."[17] It seems from this passage to be a kind of transcendent cause of the totality of empirical phenomena. It is certainly not a physical or moving cause that somehow mechanically produces empirical phenomena. So it would seem that Buddhism could allow the possibility of a transcendent ground of the material world that accounts for its existence without being a moving cause that operates like a craftsman in time. The objection to God, then, should not be to the idea that God is transcendent or outside of time, but rather simply to the idea that God is immutable. It is admittedly difficult to understand how an immutable being can bring into existence from nothing a universe of changing phenomena. However, God does have the advantage of being pure actuality. The Buddhist notion of emptiness that "allows for the propagation of an infinite variety of phenomena" seems to be a kind of pure potentiality rather than pure actuality as is the Christian God. The Buddhist notion of emptiness may seem to have the advantage of being easier to think of as the source of change, but the changing world that it propagates lacks actuality, or its "own being." According to Ricard, "the true nature of interdependent phenomena can't be called either existent or nonexistent.

---

14. Ricard and Thuan, *The Quantum and the Lotus*, 31.
15. Ricard and Thuan, *The Quantum and the Lotus*, 31.
16. Ricard and Thuan, *The Quantum and the Lotus*, 32.
17. Ricard and Thuan, *The Quantum and the Lotus*, 32.

The intellect has its limitations, and we can't grasp the true nature of reality just by means of ordinary conceptual processes."[18] So the phenomenal world that emptiness propagates is not fully existent or intelligible. The world God creates, by contrast, is both fully real and fully intelligible. If emptiness is not actual and rationally intelligible, what reason is there to think that the infinite phenomena that arise from it are necessarily going to be intelligible and open to scientific investigation?

The fact that contemporary physics supports the proposition that the universe did in fact begin to exist in the finite past, and the fact that theism provides a plausible metaphysical explanation of how the universe could have begun to exist, while avoiding the absurdity of an event temporally prior to the existence of time, would seem to be points in favor of theism over both Buddhism and naturalism. The Dalai Lama reports that he is told by the scientists with whom he consults that the "jury is still out as to whether the Big Bang is the absolute beginning of everything."[19] This is true, but according to the BGV theorem, even if the Big Bang that started our universe is not the absolute beginning, there is still an absolute beginning of any expanding multiverse at some moment in the finite past. If this is true, it would seem to favor theism over the Buddhist view of an eternal, cyclical universe.

The Dalai Lama writes approvingly of the oscillating universe model, but that does not work so well for a Buddhist worldview for at least two reasons. First, it conflicts with the Buddhist idea of the interdependence of all things, since the discrete universes in the series are completely separate. It is hard to see how the law of karma could work across separate cycles of the multiverse. Second, although the oscillating universe theory does not specify how long the cycles take, they seem much longer than the cycles indicated in Buddhist Scriptures. However, this may not be too problematic because the Buddhist can interpret scriptural texts in light of scientific discoveries that conflict with a literal reading of Scripture, just as Christians do. More importantly, the Buddhist understanding of scientific truth allows some flexibility in resolving apparent conflicts between science and Buddhist Scriptures.

According to Ricard, the idea of "the universe beginning or ending belongs to relative truth. In terms of truth, it's meaningless. When you consider a castle seen in a dream, you don't need to worry about who actually built it."[20] Given this view of the status of scientific truth, the Buddhist

18. Ricard and Thuan, *The Quantum and the Lotus*, 32.
19. Dalai Lama, *The Universe in a Single Atom*, 85.
20. Ricard and Thuan, *The Quantum and the Lotus*, 31.

conception of reality would be consistent with whatever science says about the multiverse. This is accomplished by stripping science of any claim to objective truth.

This brings us to a very important idea in Buddhist thought—the distinction between relative or conventional truth, and ultimate or absolute truth. Conventional truth is the truth of how things seem through the prism of ordinary phenomenal experience. Propositions have conventional truth if they accurately describe how things seem to the unenlightened as they normally perceive the world. Ultimate truth is the truth of how things really are, as known by the enlightened consciousness. Ultimate truth is not available to ordinary empirical or rational consciousness. To the unenlightened it seems that there is a world consisting of a large number of different things that are substances with various attributes or properties. The properties of things can and do change, but the commonsense belief of the unenlightened is that when there is a change in the properties of a thing, there is an underlying substance that is constant. A dog may grow, but it is still a dog, and still the same dog. A thing can undergo change, and still be the same thing with the same basic nature. Aristotle's view captures the commonsense view of the unenlightened—all change involves something that changes and something that remains the same. However, according to Buddhism, Aristotle was not enlightened, so his genius grasped only conventional truth.

What are the implications of this distinction between ultimate and conventional truth for the Big Bang and the existence of the universe? According to the Buddhist view of truth, science deals with the commonsense world of unenlightened consciousness—the realm of conventional truth. Science deals with the way things appear to be, not how they really are. The world of things, properties, and persons who perceive and have knowledge of them is ultimately not real. It is what in modern Western philosophy would be called a "construct." In Western philosophy to say that the world of things and properties is a construct is to say that the fact that we perceive it as we do is to some degree a product of our mode of perceiving and conceptualizing. The world as known by us is to some degree a human creation—the result of our way of perceiving, conceptualizing, interpreting, and integrating the objects of our experience into a coherent framework. Sometimes philosophers who regard empirical reality as a human construction acknowledge that reality is to some degree independent of the human mind, but how reality is in itself is beyond human knowledge. So reality as we know it is to some degree a human construct and to some degree the product of what exists independently of the human mind. A more extreme form of constructionism is idealism, which holds that reality is entirely dependent on mind and consciousness. According to Ricard,

> For Buddhism, the reality of our universe is seen from a quite different perspective. Buddhism considers that phenomena aren't really "born," in the sense that they pass from nonexistence into existence. They exist only in terms of what we call "relative truth" and have no actual reality. Relative, or conventional, truth comes from our experience of the world, from the usual way we perceive it—that is, by supposing that things exist objectively. Buddhism says that such perceptions are deceptive. Ultimately, phenomena have no intrinsic existence. This is the "absolute truth." The idea of creation becomes necessary only if we believe in an objective world.[21]

So it seems that an implication of what Ricard is saying is that Buddhism avoids inconsistency with the proposition that the universe began to exist by denying the objectively real existence of the universe. If the universe ultimately has no more reality than the phenomena experienced in a dream, then it does not need an omnipotent creator. However, most scientists are realists, in the sense that they believe that science gives us knowledge of a world that objectively exists. To the extent that scientists are committed to scientific realism they should find theism a more satisfactory metaphysical framework than Buddhism, even if some parts of the latter's description of the realm of conventional truth bears some similarity to some ideas in contemporary science.

For Buddhism, ultimate truth is known only by the enlightened, although putting it this way can be misleading, because it suggests that when enlightenment happens, there is a person who becomes enlightened, who was the same person who was unenlightened before becoming enlightened. Of course, this way of speaking indicates a failure to get beyond conventional truth. Enlightenment entails no longer clinging to the belief in a permanent self, so there cannot be a self-same unenlightened self who becomes an enlightened self, but is still the same self who was formerly unenlightened. The ultimate truth is realized when enlightenment happens, but this is not a matter of some continuously existing person being transformed from an unenlightened state to a state of enlightenment. It is precisely the extinction of the belief in the continuously existing self who seeks and attains enlightenment that is required in order for enlightenment to happen.

Radical forms of idealism are prominent in Buddhist traditions. The Dalai Lama points out that "in the earliest scriptures attributed to the Buddha, we find similar statements on how, ultimately, mind is the creator of the entire universe. There have been Buddhist schools that took such statements

---

21. Ricard and Thuan, *The Quantum and the Lotus*, 29.

literally and adopted a radical form of idealism whereby the reality of the external material world is rejected."[22] Buddhism, according to Ricard, "considers that the universe is not independent from consciousness. We should say that subject and object mold each other."[23] The consciousness-dependence of reality is a little more difficult to make sense of in Buddhism than it is in Western forms of idealism because Buddhism denies the existence of a mental substance that can be the subject of consciousness and the ground of the reality that depends on consciousness. There is no absolute mind or self that can be the constructor of the constructed reality. Consciousness is analyzed by Buddhism in terms of five kinds of mental states. There is no self that is the subject of these mental states, over and above the cluster of mental states themselves. Enlightenment, which sees reality as it is rather than as it appears to unenlightened consciousness, is an unowned mental state. There is no individual personal being who is originally unenlightened and takes the constructed world of conventional truth as real, and who later becomes an enlightened individual person who sees reality as it is. Enlightenment is, as it were, an unowned mental state that is free of attachment to unsatisfactory mental states and is thus conscious of reality as it is. If you are disappointed that you won't be there to enjoy the bliss of enlightenment, then you are still attached to self.

It is hard to see how mind can be the creator of the entire universe if there are no intrinsically existing minds or mental substances. Radical idealism is not very plausible to most thinkers in the contemporary Western world, but a case can be made for the mind-dependence of reality if you have a metaphysical framework that affirms the reality of mind, in the sense of robust mental substance, not merely unowned, fleeting mental states. It is even easier to make the case if the mind is an absolute, omnipotent, transcendent God. Without either God or finite minds it is rather difficult to see how Buddhism can provide a comprehensive and coherent account of a consciousness-dependent reality.

Of course, the Buddhist can take refuge in the claim that ultimate reality is not understandable by rational means, and the best that science and reason can get us is conventional truth—a description of how things appear to us, but not how they really are. I think that science has more of a purchase on reality than that. I also think that theism provides a framework that acknowledges that science gives us more genuine truth than Buddhism allows.

---

22. Dalai Lama, *The Universe in a Single Atom*, 9.
23. Ricard and Thuan, *The Quantum and the Lotus*, 33.

BUDDHISM AND FINE-TUNING

As we have seen, cosmic fine-tuning arguably provides evidence for the existence of a designer of the universe. The fine-tuning design argument does not constitute a proof of God's existence, but it increases the plausibility of theism to some degree. A designer of the universe would explain the remarkable anthropic coincidences that must obtain in order for life to exist in our universe and the fact that the universe permits the existence of intelligent life. Buddhist thinkers admit the existence of the anthropic coincidences, but they do not believe that theism offers a better explanation of them than Buddhism. According to Ricard,

> The apparently amazing fine-tuning is explained simply by the fact that the physical constants and consciousness have always coexisted in a universe that has no beginning and no end. . . . The universe and consciousness have always coexisted and so cannot exclude each other. To coexist, phenomena must be mutually suitable. . . . The anthropic principle comes down to picking up two halves of a walnut and saying, "It's incredible, it looks like these two pieces have been designed to fit perfectly together."[24]

We have already seen Ricard's view that mind and the universe are interdependent in his statement that "subject and object mold each other." If consciousness cannot exist without a physical universe and the universe cannot exist without consciousness, then it would seem to be necessarily the case that the universe is ordered in such a way as to permit consciousness-supporting life. It seems plausible to many philosophers and scientists (but not to theists) that consciousness depends on the material world. It seems less plausible (except to theists and idealists) that the existence of the material universe depends on the existence of consciousness.

One fact that seems to count against the interdependence of the universe and consciousness is that apart from the consciousness possessed by God, if God exists, and whatever conscious beings God might have created beyond our experience, consciousness seems to be very rare in the universe. Consciousness seems not to have existed for most of the history of the universe, and it seems now to exist only in a small portion of the whole universe. So why should we think that the universe cannot exist without consciousness? Of course, this question assumes that the universe consists of real things with real properties, which would be there even if no conscious being was aware of them. This assumption, from the Buddhist perspective,

---

24. Ricard and Thuan, *The Quantum and the Lotus*, 42.

has at best only conventional truth. The phenomenal world, which appears to have existed for several billion years before life came on the scene, is not really as it seems to be for phenomenal consciousness. What seems to be true, at least in the conventional sense, is that consciousness exists only in very complex life-forms that have very complex brains. On the other hand, if consciousness and the material universe are interdependent, then perhaps at all times that the universe has existed, even before complex life forms existed, there were unowned mental states, just as there are various nonmental states, scattered throughout the universe. If these mental states are not thoughts belonging to minds, what reason is there for thinking that their existence depends on matter? And if the propositions that such mental states exist and depend for their existence on the material universe enjoy only conventional truth, how much of an explanation of cosmic fine-tuning can they provide? As we saw in the case of the Big Bang theory and the issue whether the universe had a beginning, the Buddhist notion that propositions about phenomenal reality have only conventional truth seems to diminish the status of science and undermine the power of Buddhist ideas for explaining certain facts about the universe that are discovered by science.

From the point of view of modern science, the fine-tuning of the universe is necessary for consciousness to exist because it seems that the existence of consciousness requires the existence of complex organisms with complex brains, sense organs, and nervous systems, and these organisms can exist only on planets with stable orbits around stars in galaxies that take billions of years to form. The way things seem to science is that the universe was evolving for several billion years before organisms capable of consciousness could be formed. The naturalistic story of this evolution says that it was entirely undirected by consciousness or mind, and it was an accident that minds were eventually produced. This story is, of course, rejected by both theism and Buddhism. To both of those traditions it seems more reasonable to think that the evolution of the universe to a condition that supports the existence of life, consciousness, and intelligent life requires a causal role for consciousness. For Buddhism, if consciousness was involved in the evolution of the universe during the period before there was life on earth or other similar planets, it would seem that there would have to be unowned mental states that are codependent on various physical phenomena involved in the unfolding of the universe. I know of no theory explaining how unowned mental states might be causally involved in directing the course of the universe toward the formation of suitable life sites for complex intelligent organisms. The only instances of mental states having causal powers and the capacity for purposive action that we are aware of (in our conventional mode of thinking) are those that involve what Buddhism considers to be combinations of mental states, which the unenlightened call persons with minds. The interdependence of consciousness and complex physical objects, such as brains, is intelligible from the standpoint of natural science. It makes sense for us that the kind of consciousness that we know about is dependent on matter. If we are not idealists, it is harder to believe that matter depends on consciousness, so it is difficult to believe that consciousness must exist even when there are no complex physical life forms. Even if unowned mental states have always existed, if they were not organized into what the unenlightened call minds, it is hard to see how they explain the anthropic coincidences and cosmic fine-tuning. A difficulty for the theist, which the Buddhist finds devastating, is making sense of the possibility of an omnipotent, immutable God creating a world and acting in it. A difficulty for Buddhism is explaining how consciousness can be causally interdependent with the universe if consciousness is not grounded and unified in minds that really exist and have causal powers. The latter difficulty seems more severe.

I may be assuming here more truth in the scientific account of the evolution of the universe than Buddhist thinkers would allow. Perhaps it only appears to us that life and consciousness did not exist in the universe for the first several billion years of the history of this universe. Perhaps our scientific opinion here is really just false and should be entirely rejected from the point of view of ultimate truth. If so, Ricard is not really giving us an alternative Buddhist explanation of fine-tuning. If the Buddhist does not admit that consciousness did not exist for billions of years before there was conscious life on planets like earth, he cannot explain the conditions required for the universe to produce conscious organisms. Buddhism does not explain why billions of years before the existence of conscious organisms the conditions required for the universe to produce such organisms billions of years later were already set in place. If we reject naturalism and admit that fine-tuning is better explained by an appeal to causal factors beyond purely naturalistic ones, and if we are open to the possibility of a transcendent reality to account for the fact that the universe is ordered for the possibility of life, consciousness, and intelligence, and if the existence of an omnipotent, supremely intelligent God is possible, then theism is a plausible position and provides an intelligible explanation of fine-tuning. Unless there is a strong reason to prefer the Buddhist conception of ultimate reality over theism, it would seem that Buddhism's explanation of fine-tuning is not preferable to that of theism.

Conclusion

Commitment to the methods of science does not preclude religious belief. It is possible for a scientist to be satisfied with a purely scientific approach to the formation of beliefs about important issues, and on the other hand it is also possible for a scientist to find the practice of science psychologically compatible and logically consistent with commitment to religious belief. It is possible for religious believers to respect and value science or even to be scientists. It is also possible for either scientists or religious believers to behave either rationally or irrationally in the formation of their beliefs about matters they care deeply about, and in their treatment of persons with whom they differ about fundamental issues. Religious belief is not proof of the irrationality of blind faith.

Since science deals with the natural world, it is silent on the question whether a transcendent ground of the cosmos exists. It seems that by its very nature, natural science cannot attain a complete understanding of reality. Science has not yet produced a complete, comprehensive, logically consistent construction of the rational order of the cosmos. Whether human intelligence is capable of such an attainment is an open question, but even if such a complete scientific theory were attainable, it would not answer the fundamental philosophical question of why anything at all exists—why there is something rather than nothing, and it would not answer the religious questions concerning whether there is any ultimate meaning and purpose of human existence. Science might reveal facts about the world that present serious intellectual and psychological challenges to the credibility of religious belief, but science cannot prove that those challenges cannot be met, and cannot prove that God does not exist.

Some of the most notable recent scientific discoveries reveal things about the cosmos that many have regarded as supportive of theistic belief—notably that the universe is not past eternal and that it is fine-tuned for the possibility of embodied intelligent life. That the existence of the universe does not extend infinitely into the past suggests that it began to exist at a point in the finite past. That the laws of physics break down, or at least our physics breaks down at the Big Bang singularity, suggests that there is no time before the singularity and hence no prior event that could be the cause of the Big Bang. Some have taken this to entail that the Big Bang must be uncaused and thus to refute the proposition that God could be the cause of the Big Bang. On this view, the universe just exists and requires no cause beyond itself. Even on the view that the universe exists eternally, the claim that it exists as a brute fact seems a less intellectually satisfying position than the view that it has a transcendental ground of its existence, unless the idea of such a ground is incoherent or implausible for other reasons. However, with the discovery that it is likely that the universe has a finite past, the claim that it somehow just exists as a brute fact seems manifestly less plausible than the view that its existence is caused. The Augustinian, theistic idea that God is outside of time provides a way of conceiving of the universe as having a cause of its existence without the absurdity of a time before the beginning of time in which the event of creating the universe occurred. This seems preferable to thinking that the existence of the universe is a brute, uncaused, inexplicable fact. It is often said that the theist is in no better shape, since she is left with the brute fact of God's existence. The difference for the theist is that God is plausibly conceived as a necessary being, while the universe is manifestly contingent. Furthermore, although Sean Carroll and others insist that the finitude of the past does not imply that the universe "popped into existence," but only that if we roll the timeline back into the past we get to a boundary beyond which we cannot go, the far more natural interpretation of the implications of the universe having a finite past would be that the universe did indeed come into existence. It seems natural to think that if something has existed for a finite length of time, then its existence had a beginning. The idea that the universe is all there is, and so we cannot go beyond the universe to get a perspective from which to conceive of it coming into existence does not, I think, prevent us from inferring from the non-eternal past of the universe that the universe began to exist. There is no good reason to deny that the coming into existence of the universe would need a cause, and that the cause would have to be a nontemporal, nonspatial being. At the very least, the Big Bang theory provides some support for the premises of the *kalam* cosmological argument.

The fine-tuning of the universe is better explained by theism than naturalism. The vastly improbable highly ordered initial conditions of the beginning of the universe seem especially difficult to explain apart from the idea of an intelligent cause of the beginning of the universe. Fine-tuning constitutes evidence for the existence of an intelligent cause of the universe, countering the often heard charge that religious faith is based on no evidence.

The proposition that the universe began to exist and that it is fine-tuned for embodied intelligent life seems more harmonious with Christian theism than Buddhism. In general Buddhist thinkers have been very receptive to science, and they have found much support for Buddhist beliefs in many areas of science, especially biology, psychology, neuroscience, and cognitive science.[1] Buddhists have found support for their doctrine of dependent origination in quantum physics and cosmology. Cyclical cosmologies seem harmonious with Buddhist metaphysics. The Big Bang theory would perhaps be reconcilable with Buddhism if one can get around the implication of a beginning of the universe. The universe having a beginning is difficult to reconcile with the Buddhist affirmation of an eternal, cyclical universe. Furthermore, the fine-tuning of the cosmos seems to favor theism over Buddhism.

In summary, theism seems more in harmony with some recent scientific developments than Buddhism, especially those developments that seem to favor the proposition that the universe began to exist and that the universe is fine-tuned for the existence of embodied intelligent life. Theism also seems more supportive than Buddhism of scientific realism and a robust affirmation of the rational intelligibility of the universe. Of course all these conclusions can be contested, and debate will continue on these issues among Christians, Buddhists, adherents of other faiths, and metaphysical naturalists. That scientific discoveries can help in the assessment of conflicting claims of Buddhism, Christian theism, and other religious traditions as well, supports the claim that disagreements between science and religion and between different religions can be rationally addressed. The religious pluralist claim that there are no rational ways to adjudicate doctrinal disagreements between different religious traditions seems to underestimate the possibilities for rational dialogue. Such dialogue can be conducted in ways that respect both truth and the integrity of other perspectives.

---

1. Ingram, *Buddhist-Christian Dialogue in an Age of Science*, ch. 5.

Bibliography

Adams, Fred. *Origins of Existence: How Life Emerged in the Universe*. New York: Free Press, 2002.

Adler, Mortimer. *How to Think About God: A Guide for the 20th Century Pagan*. New York: Bantam, 1980.

Aquinas, Thomas. *Summa Theologica*. Translated by Fathers of the English Dominican Province. New York: Benziger Bros., 1946.

Augustine. *Confessions*. Translated by Henry Chadwick. New York: Oxford University Press, 2009.

Balthasar, Hans Urs von. "On the Concept of Person." *Communio: International Catholic Review* 13 (1986) 18–26.

Barr, Stephen M. *Modern Physics and Ancient Faith*. Notre Dame, IN: University of Notre Dame Press, 2003.

Biologos. "How Have Christians Responded to Darwin's *Origin of the Species*?" http://biologos.org/common-questions/christianity-and-science/christian-response-to-darwin.

Bostrom, Nick. "Are You Living in a Computer Simulation?" *Philosophical Quarterly* 53, no. 11 (2003) 433–55.

Byrne, Peter. *Prolegomena to Religious Pluralism: Reference and Realism in Religion*. New York: St Martin's, 1995.

Carlson, Richard F., ed. *Science and Christianity: Four Views*. Downers Grove, IL: InterVarsity, 2000.

Carr, B. J., and M. J. Rees. "The Anthropic Cosmological Principle and the Structure of the Physical World." *Nature* 278, no. 12 (1979) 605–12.

Carroll, Sean. "Big Picture Part One: Cosmos." *Preposterous Universe*. May 8, 2016. www.preposterousuniverse.com/blog/.../big-picture-part-one-cosmos/.

———. "Does the Universe Need God?" In *The Blackwell Companion to Science and Christianity*, edited by J. B. Stump and Alan G. Padgett, 185–97. Oxford: Blackwell, 2012.

———. *From Eternity to Here: The Quest for the Ultimate Theory of Time*. New York: Dutton, 2010.

Carter, Brandon. *Confrontation of Cosmological Theories with Observation*. Reidel: Dordrecht, 1974.

Churchland, Paul. *Matter and Consciousness*. Cambridge, MA: MIT Press, 1984.

BIBLIOGRAPHY

Cobb Jr., John B. "Some Whiteheadian Assumptions about Religious Pluralism." In *Deep Religious Pluralism*, edited by David Ray Griffin, 243–62. Louisville: Westminster John Knox, 2005.

Collins, Francis. *Language of God: A Scientist Presents Evidence for Belief*. New York: Free, 2006.

Collins, Robin. "The Fine-Tuning of the Cosmos: A Fresh Look at Its Implications." In *The Blackwell Companion to Science and Christianity*, edited by J. B. Stump and Alan G. Padgett, 207–19. Malden, MA: Blackwell, 2012.

———. "The Fine-Tuning Evidence is Convincing." In *Debating Christian Theism*, edited by J. P. Moreland and Khaldoun A. Sweis, 35–46. Oxford: Oxford University Press, 2013.

———. "A Scientific Argument for the Existence of God: The Fine-Tuning Design Argument." In *Reason for the Hope Within*, edited by Michael Murray, 47–75. Grand Rapids: Eerdmans, 1999.

———. "Stenger's Fallacies." http://home.messiah.edu/~rcollins/Fine-tuning/Stenger-fallacy.pdf.

———. "The Teleological Argument: An Exploration of the Fine-Tuning of the Universe." In *The Blackwell Companion to Natural Theology*, edited by William Lane and J. P. Moreland, 202–81. Malden, MA: Blackwell, 2009.

Craig, William Lane. *The Kalam Cosmological Argument*. Eugene, OR: Wipf and Stock, 2000.

———. *Reasonable Faith: Christian Truth and Apologetics*. 2nd ed. Wheaton, IL: Crossway, 1994.

Craig, William Lane, and Moreland, J. P., eds. *The Blackwell Companion to Natural Theology*. Malden, MA: Blackwell, 2009.

Craig, William Lane, and James D. Sinclair. "The Kalam Cosmological Argument." In *The Blackwell Companion to Natural Theology*, edited by William Lane Craig and J. P. Moreland, 101–201. Malden, MA: Blackwell, 2009.

Craig, William Lane, and Sean Carroll. "God and Cosmology: The Existence of God in Light of Contemporary Cosmology." http://www.reasonablefaith.org/god-and-cosmology-the-existence-of-god-in-light-of-contemporary-cosmology.

Crick, Francis. *The Astonishing Hypothesis: The Scientific Search for the Soul*. New York: Touchstone, 1994.

Dalai Lama. *The Universe in a Single Atom: the Convergence of Science and Spirituality*. New York: Morgan Road, 2005.

Davies, Paul. *The Accidental Universe*. Cambridge: Cambridge University Press, 1982.

———. *The Cosmic Blueprint*. West Conshohocken, PA: Templeton Foundation, 2004.

———. *Cosmic Jackpot: Why Our Universe is Just Right for Life*. New York: Houghton Mifflin, 2007.

———. *Superforce: The Search for a Grand Unified Theory of Nature*. New York: Touchstone, 1984.

Dawkins, Richard. *The God Delusion*. New York: Houghton Mifflin, 2008.

———. *River Out of Eden: A Darwinian View of Life*. New York: Basic, 1995.

———. Untitled Lecture at Edinburgh Science Festival, April 15, 1992.

Dennett, Daniel. *Breaking the Spell: Religion as a Natural Phenomenon*. New York: Viking, 2006.

———. Interview of Daniel Dennett. *Der Spiegel*. December 26, 2005. http://www.spiegel.de/international/spiegel/spiegel-interview-with-evolution-philosopher-daniel-dennett-darwinism-completely-refutes-intelligent-deisign-a-392319.html.
Dennett, Daniel, and Alvin Plantinga. *Science and Religion: Are They Compatible?* Oxford: Oxford University Press, 2011.
D'Costa, Gavin. "The Impossibility of Pluralist View of Religions." *Religious Studies*, 32 no. 2 (1996) 223–32.
Evans, C. S. *Natural Signs and Knowledge of God: A New Look at Theistic Arguments*. Oxford: Oxford University Press, 2010.
Forrest, Barbara. "Methodological Naturalism and Philosophical Naturalism." *Philo* 3 no. 2 (2000) 7–29.
Goetz, Stewart, and Charles Taliaferro. *Naturalism*. Grand Rapids: Eerdmans, 2008.
Grieg, J. Y. T., ed. *The Letters of David Hume*. 2 vols. Oxford: Clarendon, 1932.
Griffin, David Ray, ed. *Deep Religious Pluralism*. Louisville: Westminster John Knox, 2005.
Griffin, David Ray. "John Cobb's Whiteheadian Complementary Pluralism. In *Salvations: Truth and Difference in Religion*, edited by S. Mark Heim, 243–62. New York: Orbis, 2000.
———. "Religious Pluralism: Generic, Identist, Deep." In *Deep Religious Pluralism*, edited by David Ray Griffin, 10–21. Louisville: Westminster John Knox, 2005.
Grunbaum, Adolf. "Creation as a Pseudo-Explanation in Current Physical Cosmology." *Erkenntnis* 35 (1991) 238–239.
Guth, Alan. "Inflation and the New Era of High-Precision Cosmology." web.mit.edu/physics/news/physicsatmit/physicsatmit_02_cosmology.pdf.
Hackett, Stuart. *The Resurrection of Theism*. 2nd ed. Eugene, OR: Wipf and Stock, 2009.
Harris, Sam. *The End of Faith: Religion, Terror, and the Future of Reason*. New York: Norton, 2005.
———. *The Moral Landscape: How Science Can Determine Human Values*. New York: Free Press, 2011.
Harrison, Peter. *Territories of Science and Religion*. Chicago: University of Chicago Press, 2015.
Hart, David Bentley. *The Experience of God: Being, Consciousness, and Bliss*. New Haven, CT: Yale University Press, 2013.
Hawking, Stephen. *A Brief History of Time*. New York: Bantam, 1988.
Hawking, Stephen, and Leonard Mlodinow. *The Grand Design*. New York: Bantam, 2010.
Heim, S. Mark. *Salvations: Truth and Difference in Religion*. New York: Orbis, 2000.
Hick, John. *An Interpretation of Religion: Human Responses to the Transcendent*. 2nd ed. New Haven, CT: Yale University Press, 2004.
Hitchens, Christopher. *God is Not Great: How Religion Poisons Everything*. New York: Hachette, 2007.
Holt, Jim. *Why Does the World Exist: An Existential Detective Story*. New York: Houghton Mifflin Harcourt, 2012.
Hook, Sidney. *The Quest for Being*. New York: Greenwood, 1963.
Hume, David. *Enquiry Concerning Human Understanding*. Indianapolis: Hackett, 1977.
———. *The Letters of David Hume*. 2 vols. Edited by J. Y. T. Creig. Oxford: Clarendon, 1932.
———. *A Treatise of Human Nature*. Oxford: Oxford University Press, 1958.

Ingram, Paul O. *Buddhist-Christian Dialogue in an Age of Science*. Lanham, MD: Rowman & Littlefield, 2008.
Jackson, Frank. "What Mary Didn't Know." *Journal of Philosophy* 83 (1982) 291–95.
Jaspers, Karl. *The Origin and Goal of History*. New Haven, CT: Yale University Press, 1953.
Krauss, Lawrence M. *A Universe from Nothing: Why There is Something Rather Than Nothing*. New York: Free Press, 2012.
Kuhn, Thomas S. *The Structure of Scientific Revolution*. Chicago: University of Chicago Press, 1962.
Kurtz, Paul. "Darwin Re-Crucified: Why Are So Many Afraid of Naturalism?" *Free Inquiry* 18 no. 2 (1998) 15–17.
Lehe, Robert T. "A Critique of Byrne's Religious Pluralism." *Religious Studies* 50 no. 4 (2014) 505–20.
Lennox, John C. *God's Undertaker: Has Science Buried God?* Oxford: Lion Hudson, 2007.
Leslie, John. *Universes*. London: Routledge, 1989.
Lewis, C. S. *Mere Christianity*. London: Collins, 1952.
Lewontin, Richard. "Billions and Billions of Demons." Review of *The Demon-Haunted World: Science as a Candle in the Dark*, by Carl Sagan. *The New York Review of Books*, January 9, 1997. http://www.nybooks.com/articles/1997/01/09/billions-and-billions-of-demons/.
Lopez, Donald S. *Buddhism and Science: A Guide for the Perplexed*. Chicago: University of Chicago Press, 2008.
———. "Buddhism." In *Science and Religion Around the World*, edited by John Hedley Brooke and Ronald L. Numbers, 210–28. New York: Oxford University Press, 2011.
Mackie, J. L. *The Miracle of Theism*. Oxford: Clarendon, 1982.
Mavrodes, George. "A Response to John Hick." *Faith and Philosophy* 14 no. 3 (1997) 289–94.
Mawson, T. J. "'Byrne's' Religious Pluralism." *International Journal for Philosophy of Religion* 58 (2005) 37–54.
McCabe, Herbert. "God and Creation." *New Blackfriars* 61 no. 724 (1980) 408–15.
McCool, Gerald A, ed. *A Rahner Reader*. New York: Seabury, 1981.
McGinnis, Jon. "The Eternity of the World: Proofs and Problems in Aristotle, Avicenna, and Aquinas." *American Catholic Philosophical Quarterly* 88 no. 2 (2014) 271–88.
McGrath, Alister E. *Science and Religion: An Introduction*. Oxford: Blackwell, 2009.
Moreland, J. P. "Intelligent Design and the Nature of Science." In *Intelligent Design 101: Leading Experts Explain the Key Issues*, edited by H. Wayne House, 41–66. Grand Rapids: Kregel, 2008.
Murray, Michael ed. *Reason for the Hope Within*. Grand Rapids: Eerdmans, 1999.
Nagel, Thomas. *The Last Word*. Oxford: Oxford University Press, 1997.
———. *Mind and Cosmos: Why the Materialist Neo-Darwinian Conception of Nature is Almost Certainly False*. New York: Oxford University Press, 2012.
———. "What Is It Like to Be a Bat?" *The Philosophical Review* 83 no. 4 (1974) 435–50.
National Academy of Sciences. *Teaching About Evolution and the Nature of Science*. Washington, DC: The National Academies Press, 1998. https://doi.org/10.17226/5787.

Page, Don. "On God and Cosmology." http://www.preposterousuniverse.com/blog/2015/03/20/guest-post-don-page-on-god-and-cosmology/.

Pearce, Jonathan M. S. *Did God Create the Universe from Nothing? Countering William Lane Craig's Kalam Cosmological Argument.* N.p.: Onus, 2016.

Penrose, Roger. *The Emperor's New Mind.* Oxford: Oxford University Press, 1989.

———. *The Road to Reality.* New York: Alfred A. Knopf, 2005.

Peterson, Michael. "The Encounter Between Naturalistic Atheism and Christian Theism." In *Philosophy of Religion: Selected Readings,* 5th ed., edited by Michael Peterson et al., 438–49. New York: Oxford University Press, 2014.

———. Peterson, Michael, et al., eds. *Philosophy of Religion: Selected Readings.* 5th ed. New York: Oxford University Press, 2014.

Peterson, Michael, and Raymond J. Vanarragon, eds. *Contemporary Debates in Philosophy of Religion.* Malden, MA: Blackwell, 2004.

Plantinga, Alvin. "The Reformed Objection to Natural Theology." *Christian Scholars Review* 11 no. 3 (1982) 187–98.

———. *Where the Conflict Really Lies: Science, Religion, and Naturalism.* New York: Oxford University Press, 2011.

Polkinghorne, John. *Science and Theology: An Introduction.* Minneapolis: Fortress, 1998.

Race, Alan. *Christians and Religious Pluralism: Patterns in the Christian Theology of Religions.* Maryknoll, NY: Orbis, 1982.

Rahner, Karl. "Faith, Hope, and Charity." In *A Rahner Reader,* edited by Gerald A. McCool, 206–44. New York: Seabury, 1975.

Ratzsche, Del. "The Demise of Religion: Greatly Exaggerated Reports from the Science/Religion 'Wars.'" In *Contemporary Debates in Philosophy of Religion,* edited by Michael Peterson and Raymond J. Vanarragon, 72–87. Malden, MA: Blackwell, 2004.

Reppert, Victor. "The Argument from Reason." In *The Blackwell Companion to Natural Theology,* edited by William Lane Craig and J. P. Moreland, 344–90. Malden, MA: Blackwell, 2009.

———. *C. S. Lewis's Dangerous Idea: In Defense of the Argument from Reason.* Downers Grove, IL: InterVarsity, 2003.

Ricard, Matthieu, and Trinh Xuan Thuan. *The Quantum and the Lotus: A Journey to the Frontiers where Science and Buddhism Meet.* New York: Three Rivers, 2001.

Ross, Hugh. *The Creator and the Cosmos: How the Greatest Scientific Discoveries of the Century Reveal God.* Colorado Springs, CO: NavPress, 2001.

Ross, Hugh, writer and executive producer. *Journey toward Creation: Travel Back to When Light First Sprang from Darkness.* Directed by Michael Lienau. Chicago: Questar, 2005. DVD.

Ruse, Michael. *Science and Spirituality: Making Room for Faith in the Age of Science.* Cambridge: Cambridge University Press, 2010.

———. "The Naturalist Challenge to Religion." In *Philosophy of Religion: Selected Readings,* 5th ed., edited by Michael Peterson et al., 431–32. Oxford: Oxford University Press, 2014.

Smith, Quentin. "The Uncaused Beginning of the Universe." *Philosophy of Science* 55 (1988) 39–57.

Spitzer, Robert. *New Proofs for the Existence of God: Contributions of Contemporary Physics and Philosophy.* Grand Rapids: Eerdmans, 2010.

Stump, J. B., and Alan G. Padgett, eds. *The Blackwell Companion to Science and Christianity*. West Sussex, UK: Blackwell, 2012.
Swinburne, Richard, *The Existence of God*. Oxford: Oxford University Press, 1979.
Tipler, Frank J. *The Physics of Immortality*. New York: Anchor, 1994.
Tolman, Richard C. *Relativity, Thermodynamics, and Cosmology*. New York: Dover, 1987.
Van Till, Howard J. "Partnership: Science and Christian Theology as Partners in Theorizing." In *Science and Christianity: Four Views*, edited by Richard F. Carlson, 195–294. Downers Grove, IL: InterVarsity, 2000.
Vilenkin, Alexander. *Many Worlds in One: The Search for Other Universes*. New York: Hill and Wang, 2006.
Vilenkin, Alexander, and Audrey Mithani. "Did the universe have a beginning?" arXiv: 1204.4658v1.
Yandell, Keith. "How to Sink in Cognitive Quicksand: Nuancing Religious Pluralism." In *Contemporary Debates in Philosophy of Religion*, edited by Michael L. Peterson and Raymond J. VanArragon, 191–200. Malden, MA: Blackwell, 2004.
———. "Reply to Byrne." In *Contemporary Debates in Philosophy of Religion*, edited by Michael L. Peterson and Raymond J. VanArragon, 215–17. Malden, MA: Blackwell, 2004.

Index

Adler, Mortimer., 69
agnosticism, 6, 137, 139, 141–54
al Ghazali, 69, 72
al-Kindi, 69
anthropic coincidences, 106, 173, 175
anthropic principle, 113–15, 173
Aquinas, Thomas, see Thomas Aquinas
antirealism, 131
argument from reason, 56
Aristotle, 9, 27, 67, 170
atheism, 31, 38, 47, 60, 65–68
Augustine, Saint, 4, 25–26, 29, 96, 167

Balthasar, Hans Urs von, 26–27
Barr, Stephen M., 65, 76, 78, 87n2
BGV theorem, 82, 88, 101, 117, 169
Big Bang, x, 4–6, 14, 20, 44, 47, 67–83, 86–88, 93–102, 106, 108, 120, 156, 157, 163–66, 169–70, 174–78
Borstrom, Nick, 118
Brahman, 27, 126, 129, 132, 141, 143, 155
Buddhism, x, 2, 6–7, 20, 121, 124, 127–29, 141, 156–78
Byrne, Peter, 6, 17, 137–56

Calvin, John, 26, 29
Carr, B. J., 109
Carroll, Sean, 39–40, 83– 84, 97– 101, 116, 177
Carter, Brandon, 105, 113
causality, 36, 39–40, 70–71, 92, 97, 132, 160, 165–67

cause, primary and secondary, 36–37
Christian theism, see theism
Christianity, 3, 6, 8, 11, 12, 18, 20, 24, 28–29, 56, 62, 67, 101, 121–26, 128, 136, 152, 158–59
Churchland, Paul, 48, 54
Cobb Jr., John B., 135–36
Collins, Francis, 43
Collins, Robin, 105–9, 120
complexity, 31, 94, 109–10
consciousness, 7, 12, 17, 21, 46, 48–51, 60, 64–65, 94, 119, 125, 127, 154, 160, 162–63, 170–75
constants of nature, 5, 44, 103–104, 109, 111, 113, 115–16, 120, 173
cosmological argument, 69, 71, 78, 83, 100
cosmological constant, 5, 76, 87, 103, 105
cosmos, 22–24, 29–30, 33, 39, 45–47, 64–66, 68, 98, 105–06, 157–58, 164, 176, 178
contingency, 139–40
Craig, William Lane, 68–74, 83–84, 95, 96, 112
creation, x, 3–4, 12, 20, 25–39, 68, 73, 90–97, 104, 112–13, 141, 157–59, 164–67, 170–71
creation *ex nihilo*, x, 93, 157
Crick, Francis, 18

Dalai Lama, 164–69, 171
Darwin, Charles, 24, 31, 43–44, 47, 52–57
Davies, Paul, 68, 109-12, 116–19

INDEX

Dawkins, Richard, 13, 15–16, 29–34, 60–62, 66
D'Costa, Gavin, 123, 134
dependent origination, 7, 161–63, 165, 167–68, 178
deism, 30–31
Dennett, Daniel, 13, 31–33, 54, 62,
diversity, religious, 1–3, 6, 8, 18–20, 121–22, 134, 137, 141–42, 146–52
dualism, 51

Einstein, Albert, 76
eliminative materialism, 48
emptiness, 126, 162–63, 167–69
entropy, 15, 77–80, 83–84, 92, 101, 104–5, 108, 117
ethics, 156, 158
evolution, ix, 4, 15, 18, 24, 43, 46–47, 51–60, 174–75
evolution of the universe, 86, 98–99, 174–75
Evolutionary Argument Against Naturalism, 52–58
exclusivism, 122–26, 134–35, 142, 151

first cause, 73–74, 90–94, 100, 110, 165–166
free will, 11, 18, 30, 37–38, 60, 119
fine-tuning, x, 5–7, 94, 104–20, 156, 173–78
fine tuning argument, 104–20
Forrest, Barbara, 45–47, 52, 57

Galileo, 23–24
genetic fallacy, 46
God of the gaps argument, 108
gravity, 76, 80, 86, 88, 104–5
Griffin, David Ray, 125, 135
Grunbaum, Adolf, 95–97
Guth, Alan H., 78, 80, 82

Hackett, Stuart, 95
Harris Sam, 13, 59, 62
Harrison, Peter, 23
Hart, David Bentley, 26, 154
Hawking, Stephen, 84–85, 98, 101
Heim, S. Mark, 135,

Hick, John, 6, 19–20, 26–30, 127–38, 141–45, 152, 154
Hinduism, 27, 121, 127, 129, 155–156
Holt, Jim, 93–94
Hook, Sidney, 42–43
Hume, David, 59, 61, 63, 68, 70–71, 92, 97

identity theory, 49–50
incarnation, 11–12
inclusivism, 122–24, 142
inference to the best explanation, 120
inflation theory, 78–80, 86–88, 113, 117
Ingram, Paul O., 157
Intelligent Design, 43–45
intelligent designer, 5, 43, 120
Islam, 8, 24, 28–29, 69, 121, 128

Jackson, Frank, 50
Jaspers, Karl, 129n15
Jesus, 1, 11, 24, 121, 124, 129, 148–49
Judaism, 7, 28, 121, 128

Kalam cosmological argument, 68–75, 78, 101
knowledge argument, 50n15
Krauss, Lawrence M. 14, 32–33, 88–95, 99–100, 163
Kuhn, Thomas S., 61
Kurtz, Paul, 43

law, 12, 48
  beyond nature, 97
  causal, 3, 90, 97, 164–65
  fundamental, 111
  governing creation, 90
  of God, 11
  Hubble's, 76–77
  of karma, 168–69
  of logic, 63
  mathematical, 109–10
  of nature, of physics, physical, 3, 13– 15, 18, 25, 33–40, 44, 46, 55–57, 59, 64–65, 68, 74, 77, 94, 97, 103, 109, 111–13, 116, 120, 158, 177
  of quantum physics, 86

of thermodynamics, 15, 67, 77–78, 80–84, 92, 101
of time, 166
Lennox, John C., 108
Leslie, John, 114–15
Lewis, C. S., 56, 95
Lewontin, Richard, 66
life, explanation of, 5, 31, 43–44, 46, 65, 94, 103–17, 174–78
after death, 160
origin of, 44, 46, 64
Lopez, Donald S., 158n 2, 159n4

McCabe, Herbert, 28n11, 36
McGinnis, Jon, 27n10
McGrath, Alister E., 26n5
Mackie, J. L., 70n10
materialism, 13, 39, 48–49, 55–57, 62–66
Mavrodes, George, 133
Mawson, T. J., 152
metaphysics, 39, 45– 46, 49, 98–99, 165, 178
mind, 17, 23, 46–52, 57, 60–66, 80, 110–11, 139, 141, 170–75
morality, 12, 18, 58–60, 63, 95
Moreland, J. P., 44–45
multiverse, 6, 82, 86–89, 91, 93, 101, 113–19, 163, 169–170

Nagarjuna, 168
Nagel, Thomas, 47, 64–66
naturalism, 1–4, 7–18, 21–22, 34, 37, 45–66, 95, 99, 119, 125, 127, 141–43, 169, 175, 177
broad, 50–51
methodological, 13, 41–47
strict, 14, 48
natural selection, 4, 51–54, 56
necessary being, 11, 90–94, 109–12, 177
Newton, Isaac, 30, 44, 103
neuroscience, 14, 178
nirvana, 123, 126, 132, 141, 161
no-self, 161, 172
nothing, 14, 27–34, 69–74, 77, 85, 87–97, 101, 163, 167, 176

Page, Don, 92n11
Pearce, Jonathan M. S., 70–71
Penrose, Roger, 80, 104–105
personhood, 17, 26–27, 38, 46, 58, 60, 129
Peterson, Michael, 47, 60
Plantinga, Alvin, 35, 52–58
pluralism, religious, x, 2–6, 17–20, 122–56
Plato, 39, 56
Polkinghorne, John, 36–37
possible world, 118–19

quantum physics, 14, 27, 36–37, 69, 74–78, 83–84, 86–90, 117, 157, 163, 178

Race, Alan, 122
Rahner, Karl, 123–24
random variation, 4, 52, 56
Ratzsche, Del, 28, 62
The Real, 26–27, 128–34, 142, 145, 155
realism, modal, 118–119
religious, 6, 62, 131–33, 137, 142–54
scientific, 62, 171, 178
reductive materialism, see identity theory
Reppert, Victor, 56n21
Ricard, Matthieu, 165–75
Ross, Hugh, 67–68, 105–6
Ruse, Michael, 18, 43–44, 46, 57–60

Saadia, 69
salvation, 10, 19–20, 33, 39, 122–27, 131,35, 138–42, 144–48, 151–54, 158
scientism, 13, 38–39, 42, 45, 58,
Smith, Quentin, 97
Spitzer, Robert, 80n21, 81n26, 82n27, 28, 105
Śūnyatā, 126, 162
supernaturalism, 45–47, 51–52, 57, 125,
Swinburne, Richard, 94

188 INDEX

Tao, Taoism, 27, 74, 126–27, 129, 132, 141, 155
teleological, 64, 66, 113
theism, and big bang cosmology, 5, 20, 68–76, 93–99
  and Buddhism, x, 20, 157–175
  Christian theism, 1–3, 8, 12, 20, 24, 26–27, 32–33, 120, 158, 163–67, 178
  compatibility with science, x, 6, 24–40, 60, 64–67, 120, 156
  and cosmic fine-tuning, 107–8, 112, 117, 177–78
  explanatory power of, 4, 17, 45– 47, 52, 57–58, 60, 64–68, 94–95, 98, 110
  and morality, 58–60
  and a multiverse, 118–20
  and naturalism, 1, 46–58, 64–66
  and problem of religious diversity, 155–56
  as a worldview, 1–6, 8, 11–12, 15–17, 20–21
Thomas Aquinas, 26, 36, 62, 69, 100, 155
Thuan, Trinh Xuan, 166
Tolman, Richard C., 82
transcendent, x, 3–6, 9, 11–13, 17, 26–29, 32–38, 43, 46–47, 64–65, 67–68, 73–75, 85, 91–92, 97–100, 108–12, 125–29, 131, 135, 138–48, 151–56, 161–64, 167–68, 172, 175–77
Trinity, 26–27
truth, 1–7, 9, 13–14, 18–20, 25–26, 33, 38, 42, 45–46, 52–61, 63, 92, 121–24, 126, 130–36, 138, 145–56, 169
  conventional truth, 170–74
  scientific truth, 169
  religious truth, 3, 6–7, 26, 123, 131, 133–34, 138, 145–46, 148, 150
  ultimate truth, 1, 3, 7, 160, 170–71, 175

ultimate reality, 9–10, 19, 27, 121, 125, 127–28, 130, 134–36, 142, 154, 159–60, 172, 175
universes, computer simulated, fake, 118–19
  cyclical, x, 6, 80–82, 169, 178
  many, 5, 113, 115 (see also multiverse)

Van Till, Howard J., 43
Vilenkin, Alexander, 82–83, 86

worldview, ix, 2–4, 6–7
  Buddhist, 2, 169
  Christian, 10–12, 23
  naturalistic, 2–3, 12–18, 22
Yandell, Keith, 152

www.ingramcontent.com/pod-product-compliance
Lightning Source LLC
Chambersburg PA
CBHW031431150426
43191CB00006B/472